Science Fiction, Fantasy and Horror Reference

Science Fiction, Fantasy and Horror Reference

An Annotated Bibliography of Works about Literature and Film

compiled by
Keith L. Justice

McFarland & Company, Inc., Publishers
Jefferson, North Carolina, and London

British Library Cataloguing-in-Publication data available

Library of Congress Cataloguing-in-Publication Data

Justice, Keith L.
  *Science fiction, fantasy and horror reference : an annotated
bibliography of works about literature and film* / by Keith L.
Justice.
      p.   cm.
   Includes indexes.
   ISBN 0-89950-406-X (lib. bdg. : 50# alk. paper) ⊗
   1. Science fiction—History and criticism—Bibliography.
2. Fantastic fiction—History and criticism—Bibliography.
3. Horror tales—History and criticism—Bibliography. 4. Science
fiction films—History and criticism—Bibliography. 5. Fantastic
films—History and criticism—Bibliography. 6. Horror films—
History and criticism—Bibliography. I. Title.
   Z5917.S36J86 1989
   016.8093′876—dc19   89-2841
                                                               CIP

Manufactured in the United States of America.

McFarland & Company, Inc., Publishers
  Box 611, Jefferson, North Carolina 28640

For Peter Shillingsburg,
who taught, listened, advised,
helped, and believed.

Contents

Introduction

Science fiction and fantasy literature are likely to remain in "literary limbo" for some time to come; across-the-board acceptance of a genre with a hundred *Godzillas* for every *Space Odyssey* will be a slow process, taking, perhaps, longer than it would take a multi-generation starship to reach the galactic hub. Yet despite the self-mutilation of the "lowbrow" forms of the genre, despite the continued popularity of the western-turned-childish-futuristic-adventure form called "space opera," despite the filmic sagas of men in rubber dinosaur suits who stomp on balsa and plastic models of buildings, despite the icky/slimy green aliens oozing assorted unsavory colloids who inexplicably find earth women so attractive, despite everything, SF is a viable form, a reality that cannot be ignored—however much the majority of it deserves to be ignored.

SF is now too *popular* to ignore. Science fiction, fantasy and horror films and novels are the box-office and bestseller's list success stories of the modern film and publishing age. Many young people who read SF may read little else. There must be some sound reasons for these phenomena, though exploring the complete range of cause-and-effect relationships between genre film/literature and popular culture is far beyond the scope of this book—and, quite possibly, beyond the scope of any book. However, one thing is clear; SF speaks directly to a cultural need, an imaginative and extrapolative prerequisite in human communication that probably stretches in a direct and unbroken line from campfire storytelling hundreds of thousands of years ago to the gaudy-covered mass market paperbacks and comic books today.

SF (and the allied literatures of fantasy, horror and the supernatural) have changed and matured over the past few decades, and they are no longer ignored by the academic establishment. There was a time when the publication dates of nonfiction and reference books on science fiction and fantasy were few and far between, and any library (or even any individual) with a need to keep abreast of secondary sources could do so with little effort. Those days disappeared in the late 1970s and early 1980s. Now it requires a concentrated effort, not to mention an alarming amount of money, to keep up with SF reference publishing.

This bibliography was compiled to help librarians, collectors, researchers, and others with an interest in SF/fantasy/horror reference materials determine what books might be of use or interest to them or their library's patrons. The book is not comprehensive; however, it is the first book ever published which is devoted exclusively to listing and evaluating secondary materials (books) for the SF, fantasy and horror genres. There are several SF/fantasy/horror bibliographies that cover some of the same ground as this volume, but they are general wide-spectrum bibliographies which attempt to list articles, dissertations, theses and other materials, as well as books. The present study is intended to list and evaluate only books, monographs, booklets, pamphlets, and other "book-like" items published separately.

Other bibliographies have abbreviated entries; their purpose is simply to indicate the existence of a book or other item. The purpose of *Science Fiction, Fantasy and Horror Reference: An Annotated Bibliography of Works about Literature and Film* is to provide not only bibliographical data, but, where necessary or appropriate, critical or evaluative information as well. Where the accuracy or usefulness of a volume is not in question, the annotation provides more description than evaluation. Depending upon the type of book, the description may contain a list or partial list of contributors; a list or partial list of essay/article titles; a list or partial list of subject matter emphases; information about the original publication date of the book; or such information as whether the book should be considered a standard reference, a supplementary acquisition, or an outdated/superseded reference source. In other cases, annotations may contain critical evaluation—an indication of "usability," warnings about structural defects (lack of an index, omissions, other problems) and so forth. Many of the annotations have specific recommendations as to the suitability of the book for library acquisition.

The main listing is divided into nine sections. Two of the sections, representing comics/art/illustration and anthologies/collections/annotated editions, were added to give the bibliography a somewhat broader and more helpful perspective. There was no effort made to locate books which would fit into Section Eight or Section Nine; books covered by these categories were added only when they were encountered. The SF illustration sub-genre has taken on a life of its own in the past decade, and a collector specializing in such volumes can expect a small but persistent flood of these books to continue pouring from the publishing houses. While most of these books are not strictly reference materials in any substantial sense, one-artist or one-subject SF/fantasy art compilations can provide unique and useful perspectives on some subject areas.

The heart of the bibliography is the main listing in sections One through Seven. Over 200 of the books annotated in this volume are represented in the personal reference collection of the compiler. The other 100 books were found on the shelves of public and university libraries. No book is listed or annotated which was not personally examined by the compiler; inclusion of items known to exist but not personally examined by the compiler would have defeated the purpose of the bibliography. There are SF/fantasy/ reference books in existence which were not listed (indeed, if a great deal more time had been set aside for research, this listing might have contained 500 entries rather than 300), but the books included provide a broad and representative sampling of the secondary sources which are on library shelves and available for use by students and researchers.

Many of the books listed are officially out of print. These were listed for two reasons; because there are SF/fantasy specialist booksellers who can provide many of the out of print titles (and there are reprint programs which periodically bring older reference volumes back into print), and to provide librarians or other interested individuals access to information about older reference items, making it possible to evaluate the older books in a reference collection and compare them to newer volumes which may supersede previously published books. All SF/fantasy/horror-related materials encountered during the research phase of this project were added to the listing, including books intended (or suitable for) use at elementary school levels.

The structure of the listings was designed to be as simple and easy to use as possible. Entries are numbered "straight through" to avoid the awkward and confusing "III-B-xcvi-4" coding systems often used in bibliographies. The listing is alphabetical by author within the nine subject groupings. Each entry has the standard bibliographical data and an annotation/evaluation of variable length, depending upon the book. Extremely important reference materials generally receive more attention than obscure items likely to be unavailable or of little use to the average researcher. Only one "non-standard" item is included in the bibliographical citation; after the author/ title/publishing information, many entries have one or more groups of letters. Each group of three letters is a code which refers to one of the bibliographies or indexes listed in this volume. The compiler of this book has been interested in SF/fantasy for more than 25 years, and has been an SF reference book collector for more than 10 years, but it is not possible for any one person to be an authority on every aspect of SF/fantasy; for this reason, the three-letter codes indicate volumes which contain annotations or other information that can provide a cross-check or "second opinion" on a book. Some of the evaluations in this bibliography may not agree completely with the evaluations in other bibliographical volumes, so checking alternate sources for additional information before acquisition decisions are made is suggested. The MIN code refers to the book *Science Fiction Master Index of Names*, a book which provides index access to SF/fantasy reference materials (some of which have no integral indexes).

Code List

AOW   *Anatomy of Wonder*, ed. Neil Barron. Item 220.
MIN   *Science Fiction Index of Names*, comp. Keith Justice. Item 229.
RSF   *A Research Guide to Science Fiction Studies*, comp. Marshall B.
       Tymn, Roger C. Schlobin, L.W. Currey. Item 167.
SRB   *The Science Fiction Reference Book*, comp. Marshall B. Tymn.
       Item 241.
TYS   *The Year's Scholarship in Science Fiction and Fantasy 1972-1975*,
       comp. Marshall B. Tymn & Roger Schlobin. Item 166.

For the purposes of compiling this bibliography, the phrase "secondary materials" was interpreted to mean reference, nonfiction, and other secondary materials, including biography, autobiography, interviews, and even volumes of collected letters. The three appendices and three indices represent an effort to provide the very broadest possible access to every aspect of the information in the main listing. There is an appendix which evaluates entire critical and bibliographical book series, one which lists the series volumes that appear in the main listings of this bibliography, and a very general list of suggested reference core collection titles. The indices include a listing by subject intended primarily to provide access to single-author studies not cross-referenced within the index (the lack of cross-reference occurs when a particular author is the subject of only one book in the bibliography); a full alphabetical listing by title; and a full alphabetical listing by author.

The complete author and title indices also may provide quick-reference access to books known to a reader or researcher but which may not be found in the "expected" section. In order to assign the books to certain sections, judgments had to be made about the contents. Many books about SF/fantasy/horror authors are large compendiums that may include both biographical and bibliographical data, and perhaps other types of information as well (letters, autobiographical essays, etc.). To classify a book and place it in a particular section, it was necessary to examine each volume and decide what was the *primary* intent of the author, editor or compiler. It is possible that a book might as easily have been classified a bibliographical volume as a critical or biographical book. The extensive appendices and indices should make information access as easy as possible despite the occasionally arbitrary nature of bibliographical listings.

SF/fantasy/horror film and fiction, and the academic recognition of these genres as rich and rewarding fields of study, have grown at a rate that is little short of astonishing to readers who still remember when SF film was a monster-dominated genre and SF literature was recognized more for what it isn't than for what it is. Many SF fans view academic interest in SF with suspicion, but by and large the academics who have expended their energies in attempting to understand and explain the genre have not treated it too badly. The work of the academics, critics, and researchers will become more and more important in the future, especially if the SF/fantasy/horror genres continue to expand as they have for the past quarter-century. With popularity comes acceptance, and acceptance often is followed by serious study; 30 years ago the number of college-level courses in SF literature could be counted on the fingers of one hand, but today there are hundreds of such courses. The fantastic genres, it appears, are coming into their own, though full acceptance of genre literatures or "paraliteratures" as being on a par with "mainstream" literature is not likely to occur soon. Secondary sources will continue to provide the access needed by the scholars, the researchers, and the students, and someone must be responsible for choosing which secondary sources should be made available to those who will be engaged in literary research. It is the compiler's hope that the information in this volume may be of some use to librarians and others charged with the responsibility for making those difficult decisions.

Section 1
General History
&
Criticism

1. **Aldiss, Brian W.** *Billion Year Spree: The True History of Science Fiction.* Garden City, NY: Doubleday, 1973. 339p. AOW, MIN, RSF, SRB, TYS.

When it was first published in 1973, *Billion Year Spree* carried the subtitle "The True History of Science Fiction". It is difficult to believe that subtitle (or at least the word "true" in the subtitle) was not used at least with some degree of tongue-in-cheek, but the book does have a reasonable premise—that "true" science fiction began with Shelley's *Frankenstein*. Acceptance of the premise would save SF historians from making the trip back through everyone from More to Lucian to Plato for every book or article on SF when the intent of "proto-SF" hundreds or thousands of years ago clearly docs not have the same intent as SF today. Aldiss titles his first chapter "The Origin of the Species: Mary Shelley", and from there he moves on to provide what he calls "a contour map of the whole science fiction landscape". The field is covered thoroughly, from the gothics onward, and though Aldiss may be somewhat lacking in patience with historians who rope everyone from Swift to Shakespeare into the SF genre, he argues his case convincingly. Aldiss is a major contemporary author and SF author, SF critic, anthologist and SF historian. His views on the genesis and evolution of science fiction are not universally accepted, but have gained wider acceptance in the years since the first publication of BYS. Aldiss' history of SF is a milestone work which should be available to any reader who wants

1

to find out something about the background and history of SF, but because Aldiss and David Wingrove have expanded the original work, *Trillion Year Spree* is now the recommended acquisition. For other Aldiss-related materials see items 2, 3, 195 and 282.

2. Aldiss, Brian W. *The Shape of Further Things.* London: Faber & Faber, 1970; Garden City, NY: Doubleday, 1971; London: Corgi Books, 1974. 206p. AOW.

Like its Wellsian namesake, *The Shape of Further Things* is a broad-based book-length essay (or series of interconnected essays) which touches on a wide range of subjects. As Aldiss himself writes in Chapter Nine, "This is not only a book but a book about becoming-a-book." It is written in a diary-like style and at first imparts little SF-related information. Topics mentioned or discussed include dream research, theories about the evolution of the human brain, and psychology, as well as less scientifically oriented literary matters, opinions on SF, some small Aldiss-related tidbits of SF history, astute observations on the use of SF-specific themes and motifs, and other miscellaneous matters. The entire exercise is described by Aldiss as "speculative layer-cake or whatever you like to call this recipe," and that is as good a description as any for what seems to be a dry run for an idea that ran away with itself, eventually metamorphosing into *Billion Year Spree* and, finally, *Trillion Year Spree*; given another 20 years to add further things to his "speculative layer cake," Aldiss might yet guide the book's evolution into *Zillion Year Spree*. There is a fair amount of useful and interesting SF-related material in *The Shape of Further Things*, but the book has no index and, therefore, no ready access to the information. Some of Aldiss' speculations are now dated, and the book itself is more a curiosity than a research tool. For other Aldiss-related materials see items 1, 3, 195 and 282.

3. Aldiss, Brian W. and David Wingrove. *Trillion Year Spree: The History of Science Fiction.* London: Victor Gollancz, 1986. 511p.

The metamorphosis of *Billion Year Spree* into *Trillion Year Spree* involves both minor and major changes. For example, Aldiss' definition of science fiction undergoes only two minor word substitutions in the changeover from one book to the other—the word "man" is changed to "mankind" and "mould" becomes "mode." But in other areas of the book entire paragraphs have been rewritten or added to the existing text. The additions do not change any major premises but, instead, add examples, clarify statements and provide more specific references. Rather than a true "collaboration," the revised book seems to be more a case of expert copyediting. Two groups of plates have been added for a total of 29 black and white photos of SF personalities and SF magazines. An index and select critical bibliography are included, and the voluminous notes almost comprise a separate and parallel but more "contemporary" survey of SF. In every respect, TYS is a landmark critical and historical document, and should be included in any basic collection of SF-related nonfiction. Of the several general SF histories that have been published, the three best are Gunn (item 32), Aldiss and del Rey (item 26); they are recommended for acquisition in that order of priority. For other Aldiss-related materials, see items 1, 2, 195 and 282.

4. Appel, Benjamin. *The Fantastic Mirror: Science Fiction Across the Ages.* New York: Pantheon Books, 1969. 139p.

The Fantastic Mirror is a brief "tour" through the evolution of SF from the "voyage extraordinaire" with social, political, economic or religious parallels to recognizably genre-specific and formulaic technological fantasy. Appel provides connective sequences which explain SF "prophecies" (for example, Lucian's "shallow well" and "vast mirror" become, with proper interpretation, a bugging device and a spy satellite) and bridge the gaps between selected fiction excerpts. The survey begins with an excerpt from Lucian's *True History* and proceeds through Kepler's *Somnium,* Godwin's *The Man in the Moone,* Poe's *The Balloon Hoax,* Swift's *Gulliver's Travels,* and novels or short fiction by Nathaniel Hawthorne, Fitz-James O'Brien, Mark Twain, Jules Verne, Frank R. Stockton, H.G. Wells, Valentina Zhuraleva, and Murray Leinster. Shelley's *Frankenstein* is notable for its absence, and the book perpetuates the myth of SF-as-prophecy, but several works which cannot be easily located are synopsized or excerpted along with more familiar works, so the book makes a good if brief and simplified one-volume introduction and overview for junior high or perhaps high school students. There are numerous illustrations, but no index.

5. Ash, Brian. *Faces of the Future: The Lessons of Science Fiction.* New York: Taplinger, 1975. 213p. AOW, RSF, SRB, TYS.

As the subtitle implies, *Faces of the Future* is a general survey of SF with some emphasis on the "lessons" it has taught at various stages of its metamorphosis from mythology to social and technological speculation. Predictably, the survey begins with Lucian and proceeds through Bacon, More, Kepler, Godwin, de Bergerac, Shelley, Walpole, Poe, Verne, Chesney, Wells, Butler, Huxley, Orwell, Gernsback, Stapledon, and on to the modern SF writers—Asimov, Heinlein, etc. *Faces* is a competent survey, but it covers no ground that has not been covered before. Aldiss' *Billion Year Spree* (item 1) was published two years prior to *Faces,* and is by far the better survey. *Spree* is an in-depth literary study and is much more comprehensive than *Faces*; the latter book is more a social and technological study, but even so, the two overlap considerably. Of the numerous SF histories that have been published, the three best are Gunn (item 32), Aldiss and del Rey (item 26). *Faces* may be slightly better for use at the high school level, or as a supplement to the three recommended histories, but if acquisition is limited to one volume of general SF history, *Faces* is not the recommended acquisition.

6. Asimov, Isaac. *Asimov on Science Fiction.* Garden City, NY: Doubleday, 1981. 318p. New York: Discus/Avon, 1982. 300p. MIN.

Virtually everything Asimov writes eventually finds its way into one of his books—including forewords, afterwords, introductions and other miscellaneous pieces. This collection of articles and other miscellanea does include a great deal of information about science fiction, but much of the information falls into the category of trivia. Asimov writes eloquently on every imaginable subject from definitions of SF to hints on writing SF to comparisons between SF as film and SF as written word, but this compendium is not an organized body of information and, therefore, is likely to be of more use for browsing than research. Asimov is a major writer and anthologist, so anything he writes—especially a collection of miscellaneous articles which deal, even tangentially, with SF or SF-related topics—is likely to contain information of historical value, but access to the information is limited because there is no index. The articles are grouped into categories: "Science Fiction in General," "The Writing of Science Fiction," "The Predictions of Science Fiction" and so on. For purposes of historical research, the most useful section is likely to be "Science Fiction Writers," a group of short profiles/essays on Mary Shelley, Jules Verne, H.G. Wells, John Campbell, Peg Campbell (Mrs. John Campbell), Horace Gold and others. The book is not a high priority acquisition, but if budget and storage space permit, it would make a reasonably useful addition to a collection of SF general history and criticism volumes. For other Asimov-related materials, see item 121.

7. Atheling, William, Jr. (James Blish). *The Issue at Hand: Studies in Contemporary Magazine Science Fiction.* Chicago: Advent, 1964. 158p. AOW, MIN, RSF.

The publication of the first Atheling/Blish book in 1956, and Knight's *In Search of Wonder* in 1964, marked the beginnings of serious literary criticism in the SF field. (The distinction of beginning a serious critical tradition for SF is sometimes awarded to Kingsley Amis, but *New Maps of Hell* was not published until 1960; Clareson's *Extrapolation* was launched in 1959, and Blish's first book of SF criticism predates Clareson's journal.) Blish brought into his review and critical work a refreshing wit and sense of humor, as well as a recognized writing talent and a formidable familiarity with literary matters outside the SF genre. Much of the criticism in *The Issue at Hand* concerns magazine fiction in the 1950s, and in that respect the book is somewhat dated. But the first chapter, "Some Propositions," still serves as the best explanation of, and rationale for, criticism in the SF field that has ever appeared in print. Many of the authors whose works are discussed in the book still are actively writing or their works still are very popular—Heinlein, Sturgeon (both now deceased), Asimov, Anderson, etc.—and Blish's essay on *Stranger in a Strange Land* is one of the best short pieces ever written about that novel. The book is indexed, and is recommended as a basic text in SF criticism for two reasons—for the pure dynamic excellence of Blish's criticism, and for the practical application of intelligent criticism in an attempt to establish a supporting foundation of common sense, good humor and informed perspective to evaluate a genre fiction that suffered in the 1950s (and in some ways still suffers today) from a lack of reasonable critical standards for analysis. The Atheling/Blish book is part of the very foundation of modern SF criticism; the need for acquisition may be determined accordingly. For other Blish-related materials see items 8, 103 and 138.

8. Atheling, William, Jr. (James Blish). *More Issues at Hand: Critical Studies in Contemporary Science Fiction.* Chicago: Advent, 1970. 154p. AOW, MIN, RSF.

The second volume of SF criticism by Blish is one of the four or five volumes which form the very foundation of criticism of modern science fiction. Published originally in book form in 1970 by Advent, and constantly in print ever since, *More Issues At Hand* (and the first volume of Atheling/ Blish criticism, *The Issue At Hand*) belongs in every library where there is any intention to provide at least the most basic critical access to science fiction. The book is indexed, and includes chapters which deal with "definitions" of SF; basic critical materials for the genre; gadgetry and prediction in SF; Robert Heinlein; Algis Budrys; Theodore Sturgeon; A. Merritt; magazine SF; science-fantasy; and the last chapter returns to the idea of what SF is and how it might be defined. Blish writes clearly, concisely, and elegantly, and his criticism should be useful at all levels of study. Any basic collection of SF reference or critical works will need a copy of this book. For other Blish-related materials see items 7, 103 and 138.

9. Bailey, James Osler. *Pilgrims Through Space and Time: Trends and Patterns in Scientific and Utopian Fiction.* New York: Argus Books, 1947; Westport, CT: Greenwood Press, 1972. 341p. AOW, MIN, RSF, SRB, TYS.

Thomas Clareson, in his introduction to the Greenwood Press edition of Bailey's seminal study, calls the work "...*the* intellectual and literary history of the development of science fiction from its origins in seventeenth and eighteenth century literature" and "...the first full-scale academic study devoted to the genre as a whole." These two statements fairly well summarize the importance of the book. Bailey's study is one of the few SF reference books to deserve, fully and without reservation, the accolades it still receives. The book is divided into two sections: "Through Time" and "And Space Anatomized"; the first section has six chapters and the second has four. The sub-chapters survey general subject areas (the "wonderful machine," "the wonderful journey," underground, utopias, etc.) but range widely and represent thorough and detailed historical studies. The section "To Other Planets," for example, is a survey of "interplanetary travel" fiction beginning with Lucian and moving forward through Ariosto, Kepler, Godwin, etc. Because there is yet no comprehensive theme/motif indexing in SF, some of the important contributions made by Bailey's book are only beginning to be realized—such as his breakdown of works in Chapter 10 by "type" or "subject," including such categories as "inventions based on new principles," "inventions concerned with electricity," "inventions concerned with transportation," psychological weapons, airplanes, explosives, guns, battleships, tanks, balloons, and so on. Included are a bibliography and index. Though slightly dated, the book is one of the most important SF references, and must be considered a basic core title for any SF nonfiction/reference collection.

10. Barr, Marlene S. *Future Females: A Critical Anthology.* Bowling Green, OH: Bowling Green University Popular Press, 1981. 191p.

Though feminist concerns have had a major impact on the study of mainstream literature for more than 25 years, this volume is the first book-length collection of specifically feminist articles on science fiction. As might be expected, Ursula K. Le Guin's fiction receives a disproportionate amount of coverage, but in spite of too much attention paid to UKL, the articles address a fairly wide range of topics and literary concerns. There are six groups of articles which consider topics as diverse as "Woman as Nature in Science Fiction" and "The Form of Marge Piercy's Novels." Some articles are specific single-work analyses ("Alexei Panshin's Almost Non-Sexist *Rite of Passage*"), and others are broad-based surveys ("The Role and Position of Women in the English Eutopia"). The six sections are not necessarily titled so as to be descriptive of the materials they contain, e.g. Section I is "Beyond BEMs and Boobs"; Section II is "Paradise Lost"; Section III is "Paradise Regained," etc. Of more importance is the quality of the criticism, which is uniformly high; contributions were accepted from male as well as female critics, scholars and authors, including Eric S. Rabkin, Joanna Russ, Robert Scholes, Lyman Tower Sargent and Suzy McKee Charnas, among others. Included are several short "response" articles intended as supplements to, or rebuttal of, major entries; these prove a particular point of view is not being emphasized at the expense of another view, a circumstance which adds a great deal of balance to the anthology. Roger Schlobin contributed to the volume a lengthy select checklist of SF by women writers. The book is an important source of informed critical opinion on the changes (or lack of change) in female image and character in SF, and is recommended for libraries maintaining general SF history and criticism collections at the undergraduate or graduate level. The book has one glaring fault—the lack of an index.

11. Berger, Harold L. *Science Fiction and the New Dark Age.* Bowling Green, OH: Bowling Green University Popular Press, 1976. 231p. MIN, RSF, SRB.

Several aspects of the "new dark age," as reflected in SF novels and stories, are examined in Berger's study. Subject areas include three broad categories: "The Threat of Science," "The New Tyrannies" and "Catastrophe." Within the major categories are sub-groupings such as "The Hostility to Science," "Man Versus Machine" and "The Synthetic Experience." Although the book is primarily concerned with the change from a positive to a negative view of science and technology that occurred near the turn of the century, the survey of SF as a body of literature is thorough. Hundreds of novels and short stories are mentioned, many are synopsized and examined at great length, and support for the critical approaches is drawn from an impressive variety of research sources in several disciplines, including philosophy and psychology. A particular strength is the integration both of classic "mainstream SF" (*We, Nineteen Eighty-Four, Brave New World*) and classic popular SF (fiction by Pohl, Silverberg, Asimov, Dick, Simak, Lafferty, Blish) into the discussions, providing a generous cross-reference of perspective often lacking in scholarly works. Some of the sub-sections, such as "Race War in America," deal with topics not often considered in SF history and criticism. The book is indexed, and is recommended as a useful acquisition for libraries maintaining SF research collections for use at the undergraduate and graduate levels.

12. Bleiler, E.F., ed. *Science Fiction Writers: Critical Studies of the Major Authors from the Early Nineteenth Century to the Present Day.* New York: Charles Scribner's Sons, 1982. 623p. MIN.

In some ways, Bleiler's two monumental surveys of authors—one on supernatural, fantasy and horror writers (item 13) and one on SF authors—could be considered supplementary volumes. The format employed is the same in both volumes, and many of the same critics and academics were contributors to both books. But there is some duplication; Edgar Allan Poe is included in both volumes, as are H. Rider Haggard and H.P. Lovecraft, yet authors such as Franz Kafka are represented in neither. The seven "periods" into which SF is divided are: Early Science Fiction; Primitive Science Fiction, the American Dime Novel and Pulp Magazines; Mainstream Georgian Authors; American Science Fiction—The Formative Period; The Circumbellum Period; The Moderns; and Continental Science Fiction. The "continental" category includes only Jules Verne, Karel Capek and Stanislaw Lem. The book has a total of 75 essays of four to ten pages each with supplementary bibliographical material. As with the supernatural authors volume, there is too much attention paid to dividing the authors into unhelpful and artificial categories and not quite enough to making the book as simple and easy as possible to use. There is no question why some authors were chosen for inclusion in the book—Verne and Wells, for example, are the foundation upon which modern SF was built. But other choices are not quite so clear. Huxley and Orwell are included, though a library-full of material already exists on these two authors, while deserving SF authors who have received little critical treatment (Kris Neville, Barry N. Malzberg, Doris Piserchia, Mirian Allen de Ford, Edgar Pangborn, and dozens more) were left out. Even so, the book is one of the most authoritative and most important of the new bio-critical reference works on SF authors, and is highly recommended as a necessary acquisition for collections needing useful, basic biographical, bibliographical and critical reference materials to support SF author research on virtually any level of inquiry from secondary to post-graduate.

13. Bleiler, E.F., ed. *Supernatural Fiction Writers: Fantasy and Horror* (2 vols.) New York: Charles Scribner's Sons, 1985. 1,169p.

Bleiler's two-volume survey of "supernatural fiction" writers shows clearly the problems of genre definition: the subtitle is "fantasy and horror," and some sections of the book (notably "British and American Modern Writers") includes authors as likely to be called SF writers as writers of fantasy or horror. More than 145 authors are covered in 15 separate sections. The authors are not listed chronologically or alphabetically within the sections—in fact, they seem to be tossed in more or less at random. Groupings include: Early Writers; French Writers; German Writers; British Gothic and Romantic Writers; British Victorian Writers; British Fin-de-Siecle Writers; British Early-Twentieth-Century Writers; British Writers of the Interbellum Period; British Postwar Writers; American Early-Nineteenth Century and Victorian Writers; American Fin-de-Siecle Writers; American Mainstream Writers of the Early to Middle Twentieth Century; Early American Pulp Writers; American Pulp Writers of the Circumbellum Period; and British and American Modern Writers. The groupings are imaginative, some are puzzling (are there really enough "interbellum" or "circumbellum" writers, of any nationality, to require a separate section?), and, realistically, the division scheme is more a hindrance than a help. It would have been simpler, and much more useful to the average researcher, if the book had been arranged alphabetically with a chronology or one-page diagram of this cumbersome and ultimately not-very-helpful division scheme. Despite serious structural problems, the contributors to this reference set form a long and distinguished list of critics and academics. Each essay ranges from four to ten pages and includes some biographical information and extensive critical evaluation of major works (some of the authors have been so prolific that it would have been impossible to evaluate everything they have written). Following each essay is a multi-part bibliography, generally including lists of the author's fiction and nonfiction, plus lists of critical, biographical, and bibliographical sources for each writer. The average modern fan/reader is likely to be most interested in Volume II which presents, in the "British and American Modern Writers" section, essays on popular writers from Poul Anderson and Piers Anthony to Tanith Lee, Ursula K. Le Guin, Peter S. Beagle, Michael Moorcock, Andre Norton, Stephen King, R.A. Lafferty and others. The work covers the fantasy/supernatural/horror spectrum completely, including subject areas such as The Arthurian Romances and supernatural authors as diverse as Maupassant, Hoffmann, Walpole, Radcliffe, Dickens, Le Fanu, Haggard and James. The set is a major reference, highly recommended for any library supporting research into supernatural, fantasy and horror authors at any level of inquiry.

14. Bretnor, Reginald, ed. *Modern Science Fiction—Its Meaning and Its Future.* New York: Coward-McCann, 1953. Chicago: Advent, 1979. 327p. AOW, MIN, RSF, SRB.

Modern Science Fiction was an early attempt to establish context, history, tradition and value for SF as a form of popular literature. The book was rescued from oblivion by Advent in 1979, 26 years after its first appearance; some corrections were made in the Advent edition, and an index added. The articles are grouped into three major divisions: Science Fiction Today; Science Fiction as Literature; and Science Fiction, Science and Modern Man. Contributors to the volume are John W. Campbell, Jr., Anthony Boucher, Don Fabun, Fletcher Pratt, Rosalie Moore, L. Sprague de Camp, Isaac Asimov, Philip Wylie and Gerald Heard, as well as the editor, Reginald Bretnor. Separate articles deal with wide-ranging topics: SF publishing, SF and film/TV, social science SF, SF and morals/religion, and others. Most of the articles have worn well over the years. Fabun's comments on SF television and film, for example, might have been written today rather than 35 years ago, and Pratt's survey of credible, non-credible and incredible plot devices used in SF novels is as applicable and common-sensical now as it was when first published. *Modern SF* is not an indispensible volume in SF research, but the stature of some of the contributors and the continued relevance of their comments—as well as the range of topics they explore—makes this a useful book for SF research on almost any level. Any collection that is strong on general SF research, or SF research from the historical perspective of the beginnings of organized criticism of the genre, will need a copy.

15.   Bretnor, Reginald, ed. *Science Fiction: Today and Tomorrow.* New York: Harper & Row, 1974. Baltimore, MD: Penguin Books, 1975. 342p. AOW, RSF, SRB, TYS.

Ostensibly a book about science fiction, *Today and Tomorrow* is a broad-spectrum evaluation which uses mankind and his problems with science as the starting point for 15 different explorations. The essays are divided into three groups: "Science Fiction Today"; "Science Fiction, Science and Modern Man"; and "The Art and Science of Science Fiction." The group titles make the book sound like a volume of criticism, but it is only marginally criticism. In the last category some criticism (or, more accurately, some critical surveys) appear, but for the most part the essays are not concerned with SF *per se*. Rather, they are concerned with the relationship between SF and other important aspects of life, such as change, technology and religion. Contributors include Ben Bova, Frederik Pohl, George Zebrowski, Frank Herbert, Theodore Sturgeon, Alan E. Nourse, Thomas N. Scortia, Reginald Bretnor, James Gunn, Poul Anderson, Hal Clement, and other knowledgeable SF writers; a sampling of the subject areas for a few of the essays includes SF and the mainstream, romance and glamor in SF, teaching and criticism of SF, SF in the "age of space," and SF as an "imaginary experiment." The positions taken by the contributors are as valid today as they were when the book was first published—if not more so. A brief biography and bibliography for each contributor is included, and the book is indexed. Recommended as a secondary or supplemental acquisition for collections with strong core-title holdings in general SF history and criticism.

16. Budrys, Algis. *Non-Literary Influences on Science Fiction: An Essay.* Polk City, IA: Chris Drumm, 1983. 24p.

Chris Drumm's booklets occupy a unique publishing niche—they are checklists, memoirs and other assorted nonfiction items by (or produced with the active assistance of) major SF/fantasy authors. The booklet format is not the best for libraries because storage, retrieval, and use pose problems, but the booklets are extremely useful in spite of the problems. Living authors can be particularly difficult for the scholar, fan or bibliographer to follow closely, especially if the author contributes regularly to a number of different genres or periodicals. This booklet contains the text of an essay originally published in edited form in *Science Fiction Dialogue*, ed. by Gary K. Wolfe. Budrys is a pivotal figure in SF, an author who has published recognized classics such as *Rogue Moon* and *Who?* and an editor, critic and reviewer who is intimately familiar with the world of commercial publishing. Textual criticism has never received much attention within the SF field, but in his essay Budrys points out the many ways SF from the "magazine years" often was altered to fit house-styling or the commercial requirements of magazine publishing, and in many cases the changes have been preserved in subsequent editions of a work. As SF grows in scholarly acceptance as a legitimate area for study, the question of textual criticism (or establishing an authoritative text) will become more important, and Budry's essay could become the basis for an entire sub-discipline within the SF field. For other Budrys-related materials see item 176; see Appendix I for an evaluation of the Drumm booklet series.

17.   Clareson, Thomas D. *Some Kind of Paradise: The Emergence of American Science Fiction.* Westport, CT: Greenwood Press, 1985. 248p.

The "world literature" origin and development of SF/fantasy has been explored in several literary histories, but *Some Kind of Paradise* is the first thorough, in-depth scholarly literary history of the emergence of American SF. In the first chapter, Clareson provides a capsule history of world literature and the traditions (scientific romances, the Gothic novel, supernaturalism, etc.) that contributed to the use of themes, motifs, ideas and attitudes which came to be identified with the SF genre. Coverage is extremely broad and yet complete, and is not limited to novels—a great deal of short fiction and numerous essays are surveyed in the same context as the novels. The work almost serves as an index of plot synopses for hundreds of books and stories long out of print and unavailable, but it is also a well-integrated history of American SF and the intellectual, political, social and scientific concerns that shaped the development of the genre. A brief chronology of industrial, scientific and other achievements in the U.S. (1868-1909) provides a useful index of accomplishments which may have spurred extrapolation in fiction. Several of the chapters concentrate on the history and development of specific motifs that evolved into recognizably distinct categories within the genre—journeys to other lands, war, utopia/dystopia, journeys to other worlds, and so on. The book is indexed, notes are presented at the end of each chapter, and a select but substantial bibliography of secondary materials is provided. This book is an extremely valuable contribution to historical and developmental studies of American SF, though it is technical enough to be recommended for acquisition primarily as an addition to collections supporting research at the graduate or post-graduate level.

18.   Clareson, Thomas D., ed. *Extrapolation: A Science Fiction Newsletter, Vols. 1-10.* Boston: Gregg Press, 1978. (Each volume is separately paginated, but the book contains a total of approximately 564 pages.) MIN, SRB.

Though fanzines, and even "sercon" (serious contribution) fanzines, have existed for decades, the first regularly published academic journal of SF criticism with uniformly high scholarly standards was *Extrapolation*. Volume 1 Number 1 was issued in December 1959, and this G.K. Hall outsize hardcover compilation, published in 1978, includes the first ten volumes. Articles range widely across the SF spectrum, but criticism in the early volumes tended to concentrate less on the "popular" contemporary SF authors and more on the academically recognized or acceptable authors, e.g., Wells, Verne, Huxley, etc. Material in *Extrapolation* includes notes, annotated bibliographies, a symposium transcript, essays, and other scholarly contributions, many of which were the first attempts to assemble accurate information on specialized topic areas. Author, title and topic indexes are appended, and *Extrapolation* is indexed in the MLA bibliography. Though in its first years it was titled a "newsletter," *Extrapolation* has since become a true journal, and probably is the more useful and accessible of the two American academic SF journals. The range of information contained in this book is so broad it cannot be recommended as a primary acquisition to represent any particular area of study, but where budgets permit the purchase of useful general supplementary material, *Extrapolation* can be an important volume in a collection of basic SF reference sources.

19.   Clareson, Thomas D., ed. *SF: The Other Side of Realism.* Bowling Green OH: Bowling Green University Popular Press, 1971. 356p. AOW, MIN, RSF, SRB.

The Other Side of Realism serves a dual purpose—it is a wide-ranging collection of scholarly essays and articles which provide a rich source of research material, and it is a "barometer" of critical opinion regarding SF in the decade of the 1960s. The oldest article was originally published in 1959, and the most recent was accepted by a journal that had not yet published the article when *The Other Side of Realism* appeared in 1971. One of the strengths of the collection is diversity. Previously published articles were taken from sources as diverse as *Extrapolation, The Virginia Quarterly Review, SF Horizons, The Partisan Review, Riverside Quarterly, Southern Humanities Review, Review of English Studies* and *History Today.* Subject matter ranges from the general, such as definitions of SF, realism and fantasy, and SF criticism, to the specific, such as articles on *That Hideous Strength, Slaughterhouse-Five, Stand on Zanzibar* and Shelley's *Frankenstein.* Most of the articles are useful or entertaining, and sometimes both, on their own merits, yet some—such as Butor's somewhat muddled criticism of SF, Blish's incisive criticism of SF criticism, and Hodgens' prophetic evaluation of the SF film—provide valuable overviews, both negative and positive, of SF literature and film. Many of these articles have retained their validity despite the two or three decades that have passed since original publication and the rapidly changing nature of popular fiction. *The Other Side of Realism* is not an irreplaceable volume, but it is an extremely useful one, and is recommended for libraries with budgets ample enough to allow acquisition of most general critical surveys of SF.

20. Clareson, Thomas D., ed. *Voices for the Future.* Bowling Green, OH: Bowling Green University Popular Press, 1976. 283p. AOW, MIN, RSF, SRB.

The fiction of SF writers has not been methodically examined and criticised until fairly recently. Thomas Clareson, one of the most knowledgeable critics and researchers working in the SF field, was one of the first to recognize the need for collections of articles examining different facets of the works of major authors contributing to the body of SF literature, and the Clareson-edited *Extrapolation* and *Voices for the Future* series are two of the most important sources for articles on SF and SF authors. Volume One of *Voices* contains 12 articles, one on the emergence of SF in the 1930s and 11 single-author examinations of Jack Williamson, Olaf Stapledon, Clifford D. Simak, Isaac Asimov, Robert Heinlein, Theodore Sturgeon, Ray Bradbury, Henry Kuttner, C.L. Moore, Arthur Clarke, and Kurt Vonnegut. The intent of the collection was to provide critical commentary on the fiction of writers who came to prominence in the 1930s and 1940s (with the obvious exception of Vonnegut). The authors represented in this collection of studies are well-known SF authors—indeed, virtually all of them are considered twentieth century masters of the form—so in that respect, the anthology provides critical commentary on writers already well represented by a substantial body of critical appraisal, but *Voices* maintains the highest standards of criticism and scholarship, and the books represent a basic literary research source. The volumes are recommended for collections requiring a strong core collection of general studies of major authors.

21. Clareson, Thomas D., ed. *Voices for the Future, Vol. 2.* Bowling Green, OH: Bowling Green University Popular Press, 1979. 207p. MIN, SRB.

Volume One of *Voices* dealt primarily with authors whose careers began in the 1930s and 1940s; Volume Two continues the series with eight articles on important SF authors who began writing in the 1950s. Authors represented are Robert Silverberg, Philip Jose Farmer, Walter M. Miller, Jr., J.G. Ballard, John Brunner, Mack Reynolds, Ursula K. Le Guin, and Roger Zelazny. The book lacks an index, so access to the information in the book is severely limited. Even so, the collection is important for several reasons, not the least of which is the fact that with the exception of Le Guin, none of the authors represented here—despite their widely recognized stature as important and popular SF authors—have been studied at length either in collections of critical articles or unified book-length studies (though this statement obviously does not apply to the "booklet" form of abbreviated critical survey, a form that appears to be growing quite rapidly in popularity). The *Voices* volumes feature articles by some of the most astute and articulate contemporary SF critics (Clareson, Thomas Wymer, David Samuelson, H. Bruce Franklin, Joe De Bolt, Patricia Warrick, Susan Wood, Joe Sanders), and the books are recommended as primary acquisitions for building a core collection of general SF literary studies.

22. Clareson, Thomas D., and Thomas Wymer, eds. *Voices for the Future, Vol. 3: Essays on Major Science Fiction Writers.* Bowling Green, OH: Bowling Green University Popular Press, 1984. 220p.

The third in this series of critical essay collections includes, for the first time, both authors considered to be primarily science fiction writers and those identified as authors of fantasy rather than SF. As with the two previous volumes, the critics contributing to this collection are some of the best-known and most knowledgeable SF and fantasy critics and academics in the field. Authors discussed in Volume Three include Gene Wolfe, Damon Knight, Cordwainer Smith (Paul Linebarger), Mervyn Peake, Frederik Pohl, C.S. Lewis, Samuel Delany, and Thomas M. Disch. Though Vol. 1 concentrates on writers who began their careers in the 1930s and 1940s, and Vol. 2 examines writers who came to prominence in the 1950s, the editors for Vol. 3 did not impose any chronological restrictions on which authors the contributors could elect to survey. Articles in the *Voices* volumes are particularly helpful for general research because they do not concentrate on one or two works by an author; they are, instead, broad-based examinations of the fiction of an author, often including short stories. This "general survey" feature makes the articles in these collections excellent research sources for students in SF classes who need general introductions to a body of fiction by an author and not detailed analyses of single works. As with the previous two *Voices* volumes, Vol. 3 is a highly recommended acquisition for a collection requiring a strong selection of basic titles for general research into the fiction of major SF authors.

23. Clarke, I.F. *The Pattern of Expectation 1644-2001.* London: Jonathan Cape, 1979. 344p. MIN.

Central to the development of SF was the shift from a "static" mentality to the acceptance of change as a part of the social and scientific environment—and, perhaps even more importantly, the acceptance of the ideas of more and more change as well as an accelerated rate of change. Though the expectation of change is the basic element that makes SF possible, Clarke's seminal study *The Pattern of Expectation* was the first scholarly work to trace what he terms "the literature of expectation" from Cheynell in 1644 to the twentieth century. The book is divided into three sections. The first part follows futuristic and predictive fiction from 1644 to H.G. Wells and the beginnings of the twentieth century; the second part examines the utopian/dystopian literature which became a separate branch of futuristic literature; and the third section analyzes the change, after World War I, of the predominantly positive futuristic expectations to the socio-scientific negativism that would culminate in *R.U.R., Nineteen Eighty-Four, Brave New World* and *We.* The volume has a separate section for notes, an index, and several sections of black and white illustrations. Clarke's study is valuable both for the information it provides on pre-twentieth-century books and authors who have contributed to the SF tradition and for its detailed research into the conditions and attitudes which shaped the emergence and development of futuristic fiction. Though not likely to be consulted by undergraduates, *The Pattern of Expectation* is a considerable contribution to the history and evolution of SF, and belongs in any reasonably comprehensive SF reference and research collection.

24. Davenport, Basil, Robert Heinlein, C.M. Kornbluth, Alfred Bester, Robert Bloch. *The Science Fiction Novel: Imagination and Social Criticism.* Chicago: Advent, 1969. 128p. AOW, MIN, RSF.

In 1959 when *The Science Fiction Novel* was published, SF criticism as an accepted, organized and recognized activity was only ten years old; SF criticism was still in its infancy and non-fiction about SF/fantasy was limited to less than a half-dozen titles per year. *The Science Fiction Novel* was an influential book at the time it was published, and still reads well today. The essays in this volume originally were delivered as lectures at the University of Chicago. Heinlein, in his essay, defines the genre, in very persuasive terms if not in absolute terms, and draws distinctions between SF, fantasy, and other literary traditions. Kornbluth's essay deals with the future of the SF novel as a form of social criticism; Bester advances the theory that SF should be fun but not necessarily "relevant" (he calls Heinlein's extrapolations "ingenious, imaginative and worthless"); and Bloch defends SF as the last type of fiction which offers genuine social criticism but decries the pulp-adventure aspects of the genre. The issues discussed in the book still are issues today, and the authors' views are important because they are well-expressed and because the authors themselves are major contributors to the genre. The book is a recommended addition to extensive holdings in general history and criticism of the genre. For other Bester-related material see item 145; for Bloch-related material see item 185; for Heinlein-related material see items 97, 118, 120, 129, 132 and 136.

25. de la Ree, Gerry, ed. *Fantasy Collector's Annual 1975.* Saddle River, NJ: Gerry de la Ree, 1974. 80p.

Essentially a fantasy "sampler," this 80-page (8½ x11) magazine contains several things of potential interest to collectors and researchers. The first 37 pages are a group of letters from Seabury Quinn (a pulp writer who created the Jules de Grandin character) to Virgil Finlay (noted SF/fantasy artist who illustrated some of Quinn's magazine fiction). Also included are several Finlay drawings, a portfolio of drawings by J.J. Weguelin which were used to illustrate the magazine version of H. Rider Haggard's *Montezuma's Daughter*, numerous inscriptions from popular authors to friends, the entire contents of a rare and unusual booklet called "The Mars Gazette", and several informative historical notes by well-known pulp magazine collector and historian Gerry de la Ree. This limited first edition magazine (500 copies) is difficult to locate, but the letters alone contain a wealth of information about Seabury Quinn, and biographical information on many major contributors to the SF/fantasy genres is extremely rare. The magazine was produced primarily for collectors, but would not be out of place in a library collection which supports research on pulp magazines or maintains holdings of biographical material on SF/fantasy authors.

26. del Rey, Lester. *The World of Science Fiction 1926-1976: The History of a Subculture.* New York: Garland, 1976; New York: Ballantine, 1979. 416p. AOW, MIN, SRB.

Lester del Rey's SF survey is not exactly scholarly but it is not exactly a popular treatment. It represents a nicely balanced compromise between the two, and is a good general introduction to SF as a twentieth century popular fiction phenomenon. There is a brief background chapter on "beginnings" (the standard/obligatory *Gilgamesh* to *Frankenstein* survey), a short history of pre-SF publishing (dime novels, scientific romances, etc.), and a survey of magazine publishing. The main historical survey is divided into four 12-year segments: "The Age of Wonder (1926-1937)," "The Golden Age (1938-1949)," "The Age of Acceptance (1950-1961)" and "The Age of Rebellion (1962-1973)," plus a section of "Parallels and Perspectives." There is an occasional contradiction, such as del Rey's assertion on p. 80 that SF could not be generally accepted today if not for the "ghettoization" of the genre in the past, followed by his claim on p. 88 that the "ghettoization" theory of SF development is difficult to accept. In any case, del Rey's history is one of several good SF histories published to date. The Aldiss history, *Billion/Trillion Year Spree* (items 1 and 3), is primarily a literary history; del Rey's history is more popularly oriented, containing a much larger percentage of information on the most recent years in the development of the genre. The del Rey history is indexed, and is highly recommended as a good general history for use at virtually any educational level. Where only one history must serve, Gunn's history (item 32) is the logical choice for an illustrated full-field history; of the many SF histories published to date, the three best are Gunn, Aldiss and del Rey, and they are recommended for acquisition in that order of priority. There is some overlap among the three, of course, but the differences in perspective (two of the authors are American and one is British) are substantial enough that these three histories essentially supplement each other rather than duplicate, so the ideal situation is to acquire all three books. For other del Rey-related materials see item 284.

27. Dizer, John T., Jr. *Tom Swift & Company: "Boys' Books" by Strate-meyer and Others.* Jefferson, NC: McFarland & Co., 1982. 183p.

Tom Swift is the main character of a juvenile science fiction series familiar to several generations of readers. Because the series was one of a number of juvenile novel series produced by the Stratemeyer syndicate, and because Edward Stratemeyer and his juvenile fiction syndicate are not well-known outside the juvenile book collecting field, Dizer's book is a useful introduction and checklist for juvenile literature collectors, and not just for those collectors interested in Tom Swift. The volume includes chapters on W.O. Stoddard and the Saltillo Boys series, and Clair Hayes and the Boy Allies series. Additionally, there is a chapter on Stratemeyer and his treatment of blacks; complete checklists of the Tom Swift and Tom Swift, Jr.

series; bibliographical listings of series books by Stratemeyer originally published in "story papers" or magazines; a serial-to-book chronology; indices by series and pseudonym; and a general index. Dizer's book provides a wide range of information that will be helpful for research in several areas, e.g. juvenile literature in general, series books, juvenile SF and adventure fiction, and juvenile and syndicate book publishing in the early twentieth century. Any library with extensive research holdings in any of these fields will want to consider acquisition.

28. Dunn, Thomas P. and Richard D. Erlich. *The Mechanical God: Machines in Science Fiction.* Westport, CT: Greenwood Press, 1982. 284p.

Several monographs and essay collections, and numerous separate articles, have dealt with "the machine" in fact and in abstract in the SF field, but this volume is concerned with "stories about the technology that makes possible, or will make possible, the increasing mechanization of *life itself*, with computers that 'feel' or appear to, with robots that look and act like people, and with cybernetic organisms in which human and mechanical elements are so intimately combined that one cannot say where the mechanical begins and the human ends." Treatment of the subject matter, broad as it might be interpreted, is as expansive as the thesis statement. The four sections of the book examine Authors; Children's Science Fiction; Attributes; and Cyborgs. The children's SF section has only one essay. Subjects covered include single-author or single-work examinations (Delany's *Nova*, Crichton's *Andromeda Strain*, Asimov's *I, Robot*) and general multi-novel or multi-film surveys (machines and the meaning of "human" in Vonnegut's novels, the robot in children's SF/fantasy, sexual mechanisms and metaphors in SF film). Includes an extensive list of "works useful for the study of machines in SF" (reference works, anthologies and collections, fiction, literary criticism, stage/film/TV drama, stage/film/TV criticism, music, background studies) and an index. The introduction is by Brian W. Aldiss; contributors include Carl B. Yoke, Donald M. Hassler, Russell Letson, Donald Palumbo, Joe Sanders, Gary K. Wolfe, and others. The book is not definitive, but it is as definitive as a volume can be when it treats a subject that necessarily changes quite rapidly, both in real technology and in SF literature. It serves as a guidepost for literary inquiry into the human/machine interface, and is recommended for collections with emphasis in major SF themes in general or the man-machine theme/motif in particular.

29. Ellison, Harlan. *Sleepless Nights in the Procrustean Bed.* ed. Marty Clark. San Bernardino, CA: Borgo Press, 1984. 192p.

SF, like most commercial fiction genres, has become a "novel oriented" form of what Darko Suvin calls a "paraliterature," though the SF short story field is as strong as (or stronger than) the short story field for any other genre. Harlan Ellison is not primarily a novelist, but as short story writer, editor, anthologist and screenplay writer (both for film and television) he has been one of the most influential contemporary SF writers and fantasists. Because Ellison has been so influential in SF/fantasy, any volume of his nonfiction is important—especially if it contains, as this volume does, a section with six SF-related essays. The book has a total of three sections: "Harlan and Television", "The World of SF" and "Profiles". Essays in the second grouping, which deal with topics as diverse as the Science Fiction Writers' Association and the role of the SF writer in the modern world, will be of particular interest to Ellison fans and researchers who study SF film/television. The book is indexed, and belongs in any collection that includes many of Ellison's other fiction and nonfiction books; it is also recommended as a supplemental or secondary acquisition to collections emphasizing SF film/TV. For other Ellison-related materials see item 135.

30. Eshbach, Lloyd Arthur, ed. *Of Worlds Beyond: The Science of Science Fiction Writing, A Symposium.* Reading, PA: Fantasy Press, 1947; Chicago: Advent, 1964. 104p. AOW, MIN, RSF.

When it was first published in 1947 by Fantasy Press, *Of Worlds Beyond* was the first "how to" book for writers interested in working professionally in the SF/fantasy field. Teaching the actual craft of writing in a book probably is not possible in any case—as Marion Zimmer Bradley has said, the best writing teacher of all is an application of the seat of the pants to the seat of the chair and consistent serious attempts to write—but *Of Worlds Beyond* is more interesting for the opinions of the writers than for any specific writing advice. Contributors to the book include Robert Heinlein, John Taine, Jack Williamson, A.E. van Vogt, L. Sprague de Camp, E.E. "Doc" Smith and John W. Campbell, Jr. Eshbach provides brief but informative introductions for each essay, and the introductory material for the essays includes small photos of the individual authors. Several of the essays are now completely dated and forgettable—the Taine essay is pedantic in the extreme and has an air of scientific snobbery, and the van Vogt item is muddled and meandering, apparently written before his "fictional sentence" theory was formulated but just as useless as a teaching tool. The Heinlein and Williamson essays, and to a lesser extent the de Camp and Campbell articles, were in 1947 the building blocks that became the definition of what SF and fantasy are and how they operate. Some allowance must be made for minor outdatedness in statements made over 40 years ago, but much of the speculation is still valid today. The essays have shaped the way several generations of readers and writers view SF, and are an important source of information for that reason alone. Recommended for any collection in which the current SF reference material is regularly supplemented by additions of historically valuable reprints.

31. Eshbach, Lloyd Arthur. *Over My Shoulder: Reflections on a Science Fiction Era.* Philadelphia: Oswald Train, 1983. 417p.

Unlike most popular genres, the history of the SF/fantasy genre's book-publishing beginnings is a history of fan, semi-pro and small-press publishers. That history was available only in fragmentary form until Eshbach published *Over My Shoulder*. The volume is not a formal history with footnotes, but is instead an informal and anecdotal history/memoir as told by a man who was himself a key figure in the small-press SF publishing field. All major and many minor early small-press publishers are covered, and Eshbach's first-hand knowledge of early SF/fantasy publishing allows him to correct mistakes published elsewhere. *Over My Shoulder* is the only major resource for information on all the early small-press SF publishers (with the possible exception of books on Arkham House, which because of H.P. Lovecraft and his devotees is arguably the best-documented small-press publishing house in the world). Eshbach's volume includes 16 pages of black and white group photos with dozens of major and minor SF fan and pro personalities, a bibliography of small-press SF/fantasy books (listed by publisher), and an index. The volume must be highly recommended for collections emphasizing early book production in the SF/fantasy genres, small press book publishing history, fan history or SF/fantasy personality memoirs.

32. Gunn, James E. *Alternate Worlds: The Illustrated History of Science Fiction.* Englewood Cliffs, NJ: Prentice-Hall, 1975; New York: A&W Visual Library, 1976. AOW, MIN, RSF, SRB, TYS.

Gunn's SF history was a pioneering effort, in 1975, to provide a broad-based illustrated history of all facets of science fiction. The approach is chronological with a prefatory chapter dealing with generalities and definitions, followed by an historical overview which rounds up *The Iliad, The Odyssey*, Plato, Lucian, More, Bacon and others and cements them in place as the foundation of SF. Subsequent chapters are both chronological and author-oriented. Chapter Three is titled "Toward Verne: 1800-1885", and spends more wordage on nineteenth century technological development than on Verne. Gunn analyzes the development of SF in light of the development of technology and the flow of world history. The technologically-associated names invoked are the standard litany, from Alexander Graham Bell to Edison and Ford. Chapter Five details "The Birth of the Mass Magazines 1885-1911", dispelling numerous myths about the emergence of magazine

SF only within the pages of Gernsback's *Amazing* in 1926. There are literally hundreds of black and white photos and many pages of full-color reproductions of magazine covers. An appendix lists Nebula and Hugo award winners; there is a list of 14 basic SF themes which also provides story and novel titles for the major themes; and a chronology of dates, events, people, literary works and authors places a wide range of social, literary and technological progress into a manageable perspective. The book is indexed; it represents the single best one-volume illustrated SF history yet published, and therefore is recommended as a standard text for any SF collection intended to provide a minimum level of basic access to information about science fiction. Of the several SF histories that have been published, the three best are Gunn, Aldiss (items 1 and 3) and del Rey (item 26); they are recommended for acquisition in that order of priority. For other Gunn-related materials see item 178.

33. Herbert, Frank. *The Maker of Dune: Insights of a Master of Science Fiction,* ed. Tim O'Reilly. New York: Berkley, 1987. 279p.

Collections of articles, essays, introductions and other nonfiction pieces are always useful for researchers who need to gain an insight into aspects of a writer's life which are related to, but not necessarily an integral part of, his fiction writing. For a major SF author such as Frank Herbert, library holdings of fiction can be enhanced by a collection of nonfiction because the enormous popularity of his fiction creates almost a ready-made audience for his essays. Subject matter for the essays in this volume ranges from ocean exploration and air pollution to poetry and science fiction. O'Reilly, who is able completely to sidestep the role of editor as literary cheerleader, provides a helpful and well-done general introduction plus sub-introductions for the seven loosely-related groupings of material. A bibliography gives plot synopses of the Herbert novels and a listing of short fiction, though research accessibility for the entire volume is impaired somewhat by the lack of an index. A statement on the cover of the trade paper edition, which declares the book to be "The Definitive Guide to the Life Work of Science Fiction's Grandest Creator," is misleading in the extreme because it implies that the book is a concordance, encyclopedia or dictionary providing index and annotation for the names, dates, etc. to be found in Herbert's fiction. The book is not a concordance, or even a general guide, though some of the essays deal with the genesis of the *Dune* series. For other Herbert-related material see items 109 and 114.

34. Hillegas, Mark R. *The Future As Nightmare; H.G. Wells and the Anti-Utopians.* New York: Oxford University Press, 1967; Carbondale, IL: Southern Illinois University Press, 1974. 200p. AOW, MIN, RSF, SRB, TYS.

Wells has been one of the most influential SF writers in history. Mark Hillegas, one of the foremost SF critics, has studied Wells and his influence on the writers who later became anti-utopians, or anti-Wellsians, and presents his conclusions in *Future As Nightmare.* Hillegas traces the utopian tradition up to the end of the nineteenth century, when the dystopia or anti-utopia came into prominence. Authors discussed in their literary (and, where appropriate, personal) relationships include Forster, Capek, Zamyatin, Huxley, Orwell and Lewis. Hillegas differentiates between "quality" SF represented by the great anti-utopias, which "...always make a significant comment on human life," because it is a vehicle for social criticism and satire, and the pure satiric utopias, such as *Erewhon,* which are "not science fiction." More recent authors discussed in later chapters of the book include Anthony Burgess and L.P. Hartley, and even some SF writers from the "modern period" are placed in the anti-utopian tradition: Clarke, Pohl, Lasswitz, Kornbluth, Sheckley, Vonnegut, Bradbury, and others. Hillegas concludes that *Facial Justice* (Hartley) and *Player Piano* (Vonnegut) are "easily the most important anti-utopias written since *Nineteen Eighty-Four,*" and that these two works "might well be the last flowering of the anti-utopian tradition before its disintegration." The book is indexed, and includes a select bibliography of history and criticism. Because the study ranges so widely across the literary spectrum, comparing works and examining imitation, influence and reaction not only in the "literary" SF arena but in the popular arena as well, *The Future as Nightmare* is a useful and valuable study of SF which can be appreciated at most any level of study. For other Wells-related material see items 100, 108 and 139.

35. Hillegas, Mark R., ed. *Shadows of Imagination: The Fantasies of C.S. Lewis, J.R.R. Tolkien and Charles Williams.* Carbondale, IL: Southern Illinois University Press, 1969. Revised edition, 1976. 190p. AOW, MIN, RSF, SRB.

With 13 essays divided more or less equally among the three best-recognized twentieth century masters of "serious" fantasy, *Shadows of Imagination* is a solid contribution to scholarship dealing with the fiction of Williams, Lewis and Tolkien. Only two of the essays included in the volume were previously published; the other 11 are original contributions. For this revised edition of *Shadows,* the thirteenth essay, "The Wonder of the Silmarillion," was added. C.S. Lewis and his fiction are the subjects of four essays, four are devoted to Tolkien, four to Williams, and one to both Tolkien and Lewis. Approaches are widely divergent, but cover important aspects of the subject authors' fiction—from general overviews of Williams' novels to the structure of Lewis' *Out of the Silent Planet*. Contributors include Chad Walsh, J.B.S. Haldane, Robert Plank, Charles Moorman, Clyde S. Kilby and Daniel Hughes. The level of scholarship represented by this collection of essays makes the book more likely to be of use to readers or researchers working at least on the graduate level. The three authors examined in this literary study are generally considered to represent more than half the foundation for fantasy fiction as it exists today, so the book is recommended for any collection intended to support graduate or postgraduate literary research into fantasy fiction or any of the three subject authors. For other Tolkien-related materials see items 85, 95, 104, 105, 123, 140 and 199.

36. Hirsch, David, ed. *The Official Starlog Communications Handbook, Vol. 1*. New York: Starlog Press, 1979. 92p.

This digest-sized booklet is little more than a professionally printed fanzine, and offers no useful information for research purposes. A large percentage of the magazine's space is given over to letters sent in by fans quibbling over a statement, an attitude, an illustration, or some other minor matter. Other sections are devoted to TV and film company addresses (so fans can write letters in support of their favorite shows), fan club addresses, "pen pal" addresses, and advertisements for *Starlog* books, magazines, and other merchandise. The handbook is now quite dated and is of little value to a library.

37. Hokenson, Jan and Howard Pearce, eds. *Forms of the Fantastic: Selected Essays from the Third International Conference on the Fantastic in Literature and Film*. Westport CT: Greenwood Press, 1986. 262p.

The 26 essays in *Forms of the Fantastic* are grouped into eight divisions, though the articles in each group are not necessarily closely related. Selected from a field of approximately 300 papers presented at the third international conference on the fantastic in literature and film, the essays treat topics as diverse as cubism and expressionism in *The Cabinet of Dr. Caligari* and the dragon as a symbol of evil in Le Guin's *Earthsea* trilogy. The sections, containing two to four articles each, include Periods of the Fantastic; Theoretical Approaches to the Fantastic; Echoes of Myth and Epic; Linguistic Archaism and Invention; Freedoms in the Fantastic; Monstrous and Marvelous Beings; The Fantastic and Sexuality; and Genre and Fantastic Game Play. Among the contributors to the volume are Donald H. Crosby, Mike Budd, William Schuyler, Jules Zanger, Robert G. Wolf and Michael R. Collings. Less than half the articles deal directly with modern science fiction and fantasy, though several approach from different viewpoints certain basic themes or motifs upon which fantasy is based—for example, "The Ethical Status of Magic" and "The Disenchantment of Magic" explore specific uses of magic as a relatively recent phenomenon in fantasy literature. The volume overall is likely to be of greatest utility to students or researchers working at least on the graduate level. A bibliography and index are included, and the book is recommended as a supplementary acquisition for collections with a topic-area emphasis in fantasy and fantastic literature.

38. Jones, Robert Kenneth. *The Shudder Pulps.* West Linn, OR: Fax Collector's Editions, 1975. 238p. MIN, RSF, TYS.

Jones' book on the "shudder pulps" is a popular history of what he calls "totems of our thrill-fiction past," beginning with *Dime Mystery Magazine* and branching out through the entire weird/horror/mystery pulp magazine system that emerged from the decade of the Great Depression. Jones provides detailed descriptions of trends, conventions, and editorial changes, and synopsizes specific stories as examples of those trends and changes. Numerous black and white interior illustrations and magazine covers appear throughout the book. Besides being a fertile seed-bed for the study of horror, mystery and weird fiction, this pulp-era historical survey should be of interest to SF and fantasy readers and researchers because of references to writers, editors and other personalities closely identified with SF and fantasy: Don A. Stuart (John W. Campbell, Jr.), Hamilton, Schachner, Pratt, Lowndes, Hubbard, Robeson, Farmer, Cummings, Farley, and others. There are some minor omissions (the author fails to mention in the text or indicate in the index that Don A. Stuart is a pseudonym for John W. Campbell, Jr.), and the history is informally rendered—there are no footnotes or bibliography. But Jones is a well-known pulp collector, widely read and intimately familiar with pulp magazines and pulp magazine publishing. Of particular note is the fact that he went to the trouble of tracking down several pulp writers of the 1930s, some still active in the writing trade and some retired, and offers some interesting quoted material from the interviews. Recommended for any collection with a subject emphasis in pulp magazines or historical accounts of popular magazine publishing.

39. King, Stephen. *Danse Macabre.* New York: Everest House, 1981. New York: Berkley Books, 1982. 437p.

Rather than a delicate balance between the popular and the scholarly, *Danse Macabre* swings from one extreme to the other. It is not a wild, syncopated swing, however—it is a steady, measured pendulum-swing. King is the best-known and most successful horror writer in history, and in view of his success (he is almost a recognizably separate publishing and film genre by himself, turning out King-horror novels and King-horror films with metronomic regularity), his ideas about the roots, the history, the purpose and the mechanics of horror are particularly important. The survey of horror ranges across the dramatic spectrum from early literary works to radio, television and films, but the focus of the book is intended to be "an informal overview of where the horror genre has been over the last thirty years." The hardcover edition is more desirable for library use, of course, but the paperback contains numerous corrections and slight revisions. Although there is a wealth of information about (and insightful analysis of) the horror genre in *Danse Macabre*, much of which probably could be useful even at the high school level, the occasional dependence on gutter vernacular for emphasis could cause some problems with high school use of the book. At higher educational levels there should be no problems with the use of a "popular" horror survey that is surprisingly scholarly and entertaining in its own right. The autobiographical content makes acquisition important for libraries specializing in popular contemporary authors in general, or horror fiction authors or Stephen King in particular. The volume has an index and two appendices: one appendix for films and one for books. For other King-related material see items 87, 89, 90, 128, 142, 147.

40. Knight, Damon. *The Futurians.* New York: John Day, 1977. 205p.

The early fan-cum-professional SF club known as The Futurians was comprised of members now recognized as some of the most formidable SF writing and editing talents of the twentieth century. Damon Knight, himself an artist, editor, critic, anthologist and translator, was perfectly suited—by virtue of his recognized writing talent and his membership in the club—to the task of writing a history of The Futurians. This history will be of interest to future SF historians and biographers because it contains a large body of previously unavailable information, as well as an alternate point of view, on numerous SF figures, especially Isaac Asimov, James Blish, Cyril Kornbluth, Judith Merril, Frederik Pohl, Donald Wollheim, and, to a lesser extent, John B. Michel, Robert Lowndes, Hugo Gernsback, William Sykora, Harry Dockweiler, and others. Included are references to now-rare fan publications, excerpts from the writings of numerous authors, long quotes from interviews with still-surviving principals, and numerous photos and illustrations. The book is important as a pseudo-autobiography for Damon Knight (until such time as he decides to pen an actual autobiography), and as the history of an influential SF club and a source of miscellaneous biographical data. The book is indexed, and is recommended for collections with extensive holdings in biography, autobiography, or modern SF history.

41. Knight, Damon. *In Search of Wonder: Essays on Modern Science Fiction.* Chicago: Advent, 1956; revised and expanded 1967. 306p. AOW, MIN, RSF, SRB.

Some index and reference material on SF, and some scattered criticism, had been compiled and written by the 1950s, but modern SF criticism began with Clareson's *Extrapolation,* Amis' *New Maps of Hell,* Blish's two books, and Knight's *In Search of Wonder.* For that reason alone, this book is a basic source of critical commentary on SF; but it is also good reading on its own merits, and interesting in its own right even when some of the works it reviews are not. The 27 chapters deal with Campbell, van Vogt, Heinlein, Asimov, Bradbury, Sturgeon, Kuttner and Moore, Kornbluth, Blish, Pratt, Moskowitz, and numerous other subjects. Knight is one of the most multi-talented personalities in SF—he has worked as writer, critic, editor, anthologist, historian, translator, and even as artist. The criticism in this volume is incisive and insightful, and can form the basis for a better understanding of, and appreciation for, reasonable critical standards applied to SF. It is regrettable that Knight has never updated *In Search of Wonder* (it was first published in 1956 and expanded/revised in 1967) to include commentary on more recent fiction, but the book helped open the door for common-sense criticism for a genre that had been lacking informed critical appraisal for decades. The book has a bibliography and index, and still is a basic volume for any general SF criticism collection.

42. Knight, Damon, ed. *Turning Points: Essays on the Art of Science Fiction.* New York: Harper & Row, 1977. 303p. MIN, RSF, SRB.

Turning Points is one of the most important collections of essays and articles to be assembled and published in the 1970s. Knight is a lifelong contributor to the SF field in virtually every capacity, from artist and editor to translator and writer, and his book *In Search of Wonder* was one of the half-dozen volumes that provided the basis for the development of modern SF criticism. *Turning Points* is a historical collection containing articles with original copyrights ranging from 1948 to 1973. Isaac Asimov's "Social Science Fiction," which first appeared in *Modern Science Fiction: Its Meaning and Its Future* (1953), and Heinlein's "Science Fiction: Its Nature, Faults and Virtues," delivered as a lecture in 1957 at the University of Chicago and subsequently published in *The Science Fiction Novel: Imagination and Social Criticism* (1959), were themselves landmark essays in SF criticism, and both are included in this book. *Turning Points* is divided into seven general topic areas: A Walk Around the Topic; History Without Tears; Criticism, Destructive and Otherwise; SF and Science; How To, In Four Tricky Lessons; SF as Prophecy; and Confessions. Contributors range from James Blish, Theodore Sturgeon, Joanna Russ, C.S. Lewis and Isaac

Asimov to Robert Heinlein, Brian Aldiss, Arthur Clarke and Richard McKenna. Many of the essays are conventional critical analysis and many are simply literate and entertaining opinion pieces, but the book should be considered more an "interim report" on SF, assembled with an eye to SF faults, virtues, failures and accomplishments up through the mid-1970s and less a formal critical evaluation of anything. Descriptions of the apparent purposes of the separate articles would have to cast a net wide enough to encompass autobiographical essays, explanations of writing technique, brief surveys of early SF, and assorted oddments of perspective, evaluation, analysis, viewpoint and opinion. Many of the articles are difficult to find elsewhere, and together constitute a major SF nonfiction resource of interest to a wide variety of potential readers and researchers, from fans to SF critics and research specialists. The book is highly recommended as a valuable addition to collections emphasizing criticism of SF or general surveys of the genre.

43. Kyle, David. *A Pictorial History of Science Fiction.* London: Hamlyn, 1976. London: Tiger Books International, 1986. 173p. RSF, SRB.

Kyle's pictorial history of SF and related genres is an adequate visual history containing hundreds of black and white photos and not a few full color illustrations, some of which take up an entire page in this outsize (9½ x13) "coffee table" book. Photographic or illustrative attention is given to the full spectrum of materials, from pre-nineteenth-century book illustration to photographs, book and magazine covers, comic strips and TV and film stills. Kyle, an SF collector for many years, has a firm grasp of the changing modes of SF as a popular fiction, and has selected illustrations that convey those changes. Many of the illustrations are striking examples of their forms, and a large percentage of the illustrations that appear here have not been used in previous pictorial SF histories or encyclopedias. To keep the book from being just a huge collection of unrelated photos/illustrations, there is a large amount of text which is divided into chapters dealing with specific time periods. "The Golden Years 1926-1936", for example, somehow manages to define an "age" in the SF chronology which has been under dispute for decades. Novelists and illustrators are covered in as much detail as space allows—which is to say the brevity does not allow complete explanation in many cases, a circumstance which contributes to the formulation of an occasionally lopsided view. There are some factual blunders, such as the statement, "Ironically, just as *Argosy* became a slick and rejected SF, the champion of the permissive society, *Playboy*, in the late forties, was accepting Pohl and Clarke and dozens more." The first issues of *Playboy*, now scarce collectors' items, were published in the 1950s. Any volume with vast amounts of data is bound to have a mistake here and there, but Kyle's history is more useful for its illustrations than for its information, and is recommended as a good pictorial history of the genre.

44. Lafferty, R.A. *It's Down the Slippery Cellar Stairs*. Polk City, IA: Chris Drumm, 1984. 42p.

All the material in this booklet is previously published, but the 13 pieces were originally published in fanzines or the SFWA publications, so they are not likely to be familiar to a general audience. One was first presented as a speech. Lafferty has written SF novels, mainstream novels, and short stories, but this Drumm booklet is the first publication of a substantial amount of Lafferty's nonfiction (essays, book reviews, etc.). Lafferty is recognized as a major stylist in the SF field, a creator not just of fiction but of fiction rendered in prose-poetry form. The facility with language, and the ability to make the most mundane observations in the most extraordinary way, are displayed in Lafferty's nonfiction as well as his fiction. As the first compilation of Lafferty nonfiction pieces, this booklet is an important addition to the Lafferty canon, a useful "window" through which scholars can view his writing, and it has the potential to become a collector's item. The 4x7 paperbound booklet with card-stock cover presents special problems for handling in libraries; however, Lafferty is one of the best prose stylists in the SF field, and this booklet should be considered for acquisition for any collection specializing in supplemental, unusual or collectors' items relating to major SF writers. For other Lafferty-related materials see item 181. See Appendix I for an evaluation of the Drumm booklet series.

45. Le Guin, Ursula K. *The Language of the Night*, ed. by Susan Wood. New York: G.P. Putnam's Sons, 1979. 270p. New York: Berkley Books, 1985. MIN.

Le Guin, long recognized as an important twentieth century SF/fantasy author, speaks very well for herself and does not need to be endlessly introduced; this book contains six separate "introductions" by Susan Wood; one introduction, at the beginning of the book, would have been sufficient because the articles and other miscellaneous material presented here say most of what needs to be said. The Le Guin essays present humor, criticism, and commentary as smoothly as Le Guin's fiction handles comedy and drama. The book is a collection of articles, lectures and speeches, all of which express the author's hopes for the expansion of the SF/fantasy field. Le Guin is most in her element when she discusses her own approach to fiction and her personal feelings about SF/fantasy, what makes them work, and where they are going. *Language* is not a unified critical evaluation of anything—that would be almost impossible considering the number of sources from which the articles were drawn and the number of subjects they cover, but the importance of the book is the importance of any book of literate, intelligent, insightful criticism authored by a recognized master storyteller. The six introductions by Wood are more hindrance than help because they explain things the author explains much better in the text of the essays, but the book overall is valuable for its insights into fiction writing in general and SF/fantasy fiction writing in particular. The book is a recommended acquisition for collections emphasizing Le Guin, fantasy fiction, or the mechanics of writing popular fiction. For other Le Guin-related material see items 83, 119 and 134.

46. Lundwall, Sam J. *Science Fiction—An Illustrated History.* New York: Grosset & Dunlap, 1977. 208p. MIN, SRB.

Lundwall's "history" of SF is in reality an historical examination of numerous themes and motifs popular in the SF field over a long period of time. The separate examinations of pulp fiction, robots, monsters, nightmares, utopias and other popular devices and images found in SF are adequate, but the real strength of this book is in the breadth of the illustrations, many of which are cover art reproductions from the SF magazines of foreign countries. Illustrations also are taken from comic strips, film stills and book covers, and a number of the illustrations are full-page and four-color. A bibliography and index are included, although the index contains numerous bothersome errors. For example, the fictional character Frank Reade is indexed as if he were a real person, and the name is spelled "Reede." The volume is more useful for "period browsing" to see what old SF books and magazines looked like than for gaining a solid foundation in the history of the SF genre. As an SF history, Lundwall's book rates somewhat below average, though it is useful for its non-American viewpoint (Lundwall is Swedish). Of the several SF histories that have been published, the three best are Gunn (item 32), Aldiss (items 1 and 3) and del Rey (item 26). In cases where there are no budgetary restrictions and a copy of Lundwall's book became available, it would make a useful supplement to holdings with an emphasis in SF history and SF art.

47. Lundwall, Sam J. *Science Fiction: What It's All About.* New York: Ace Books, 1971. 256p. AOW, MIN, RSF, SRB.

International perspective is relatively rare in the American SF community. When *Science Fiction: What It's All About* was first published in 1971 it promised to offer some of that international perspective, but the book did not live up to the expectation. The first edition was written in Swedish by Lundwall, and at Donald Wollheim's invitation was revised, enlarged and translated into English. Lundwall covers all the familiar areas which had been covered by earlier surveys and would be covered again in later surveys and histories, such as Brian Aldiss' books (items 1 and 3), yet he is inconsistent in tone and treatment. On one hand he decries the standard SF-historian tactic of gathering everything from Homer to *Gilgamesh*, Bunyan, Campanella and Lucian into the SF fold; but on the other hand he goes out of his way to include a long passage from a Swedish utopian novel published in 1879 that was "more modern than any science fiction written in the U.S.A. before 1930." He points out the folly of accepting any fantastic or futuristic element as the common thread of SF novels throughout all literary history, then does exactly the same thread-tracing himself, and with a special axe to grind—the fact that Swedish writers were writing SF, and even calling it that (in Swedish), while Americans were stumbling about using the terms "scientifiction" and "scientific fiction." Some of Lundwall's remarks, as for example those concerning the treatment of women in SF, are not nearly as illuminating as they are condescending, and there are serious problems with the accuracy and utility of the index. Names in the text are not indexed, and numerous index entries reference the wrong page numbers. Names, too, are garbled—L. Frank Baum is referred to in the text as Frank L. Baum, a very minor error that should have been caught by a proofreader if not by the author. Lundwall's SF survey, a moderately useful volume at the time it was first published, has been superseded by much better surveys; the three best are Gunn (item 32), Aldiss and del Rey (item 26).

48. Magill, Frank N., ed. *Survey of Modern Fantasy Literature* (5 vols.). Englewood Cliffs, NJ: Salem Press, 1983. 2538p. MIN.

Magill's fantasy survey represents a broad cross-section of fantasy-related fiction—not just "plain" fantasy but many of the recognized sub-types as well, including high fantasy, low fantasy, Gothic, "dark fantasy," experimental works, and other fringe works not immediately classifiable into separate categories. The 500 essays represent works by 341 authors, including novels, trilogies, series and collections. Even a representative sampling included in the survey would be prohibitive, but authors receiving major coverage (i.e., many short stories and/or novels surveyed) include Philip Jose Farmer, Harlan Ellison, Ursula Le Guin, August Derleth, Arthur Conan Doyle, Robert Aickman, Poul Anderson, L. Frank Baum, Peter S. Beagle, Max Beerbohm, Robert Bloch, Jorge Luis Borges, Ambrose Bierce, James Branch Cabell, Ray Bradbury, Edgar Rice Burroughs, Lord Dunsany, William Hope Hodgson, E.T.A Hoffmann, Washington Irving, Franz Kafka, Stephen King, Fritz Leiber, etc. In addition to the author surveys are 19 subject essays which clarify broad topic areas related to the fantasy genre; these range from articles on theories of fantasy (contemporary, European, Romantic), fairy tales, Arthurian legend, the Faust figure and eroticism and the supernatural, to witchcraft, religious fantasy in the nineteenth century,

German fantasy, and the fantasy pulps. Also included are a chronology of modern fantasy, a bibliography of fantasy anthologies, and an index. The author essays range from 1,000 to 10,000 words, probably averaging 2,500, and were written by a staff of 102 extremely knowledgeable fantasy fiction researchers and academics. The topic essays also were assigned to recognized experts in the various subject areas. Each author essay is followed by a bibliographical listing of other secondary materials. The Magill fantasy reference set seems to be somewhat more representative of the "popular" and the "classic" forms of fantasy than the SF set is representative of "high" and "low" forms of science fiction, and is correspondingly more useful across a wider spectrum of research and readership. This survey is the single most important critical survey of fantasy published to date, and is highly recommended as a core acquisition around which a collection of fantasy criticism and reference volumes can be built.

49. Magill, Frank N., ed. *Survey of Science Fiction Literature*, 5 vols. Englewood Cliffs, NJ: Salem Press, 1979. 2542p. MIN, SRB.

The *Survey of Science Fiction Literature* multivolume reference set is a landmark work in the SF field. The critical appraisals average about 2,000 words each, and were written by more than 100 knowledgeable SF experts, critics and scholars. There can be, perhaps, a minor quibble about the half-dozen "bibliographical references" at the end of each essay, for in many cases the references are little more than a list of several book reviews. That in itself is not a problem, because up to the late 1970s, book reviews were the bulk of all critical material published on SF. The problem is that many (if not most) of the bibliographical reference lists seem to have just the entries which may be found for each of the books in H.W. Hall's SF book review index (item 225). In other words, little original work was done to include any new bibliographical information in this important set. The scope of the set—513 essays—is quite broad, but title selection was not designed so the books would be immediately useful to most of the potential research audience who presumably will be using the reference set. Title selection apparently was made with an eye to "legitimizing" the SF field and enlarging it by including foreign language material, marginal SF works and mainstream novels which broaden the acceptability and respectability of SF. Students and teachers, the most likely candidates for using this set, needed an essay collection concentrating on "classic" and "generally obtainable" titles in a field for which it is chronically near-impossible to maintain a stable reading list of in-print and easily-obtainable titles. Much of the mainstream or near-mainstream material (such as *Nineteen Eighty-Four, The Inheritors, Lord of the Flies*, etc.) is very well documented elsewhere; the precious space available in this set should not have been used to further criticize that which has been discussed almost to death in dozens or hundreds of other reference volumes. Arrangement is alphabetical by book title, another serious mistake; alphabetical grouping by author would have allowed much more efficient use of the material. But despite imperfections in planning, research and execution, this set is an important research tool because it is the only reference of its kind in existence for the SF field, and because it contains a vast amount of information. Any library maintaining almost any size SF research collection will want to consider the set; it is now one of the most indispensible major research sources for SF studies.

50. Magill, Frank N., ed. *Science Fiction Alien Encounter*. Pasadena, CA: Salem Press (Salem Softbacks), 1981. 376p.

Alien Encounter is a Magill Survey with all the strengths (which are considerable) *and* all the weaknesses (also considerable) of the SF and fantasy surveys published by Salem Press. The intent was to provide convenient groupings of essays dealing with particular SF subject areas, but these "convenient groupings" do nothing except re-anthologize essays originally published in the five-volume SF survey set. A notice on the copyright page states, "Some of this material has appeared previously in *Survey of Science Fiction Literature*," a misleading statement which seems to indicate some of the material may be new—in fact, every one of the essays included in this volume is taken from the five-volume set. This means if a library with the five-volume set acquires this book, it has nothing more than another volume with 75 essays reprinted from material already on its shelves. Rather than recycle the same essays in a series of new volumes (in a less durable softcover format, no less), Magill should have produced one volume with a comprehensive theme index directing the reader to the appropriate essays in the five-volume set. For smaller libraries, unable to afford the five-volume set, this book offers a viable alternative for acquiring a book of SF essay-reviews; for libraries with a copy of the original survey, purchasing the books in this projected series would be a waste of resources.

51. Malone, Robert. *The Robot Book*. New York: Push Pin Press, 1978. 159p. MIN.

Robots are a staple theme in SF literature and film, so a reference book on robots that is SF-oriented can be a valuable reference tool. *The Robot Book* traces the development of robots from ancient descriptions of mechanical devices to "waldoes," bionics and machine intelligence. The author relates the technological development of robots to the use and depiction of robots in science fiction, and for that reason the volume is a useful interdisciplinary study of robotics and SF in literature/film. Profusely illustrated, including film stills and SF magazine covers, the book is a useful adjunct to the study of machines, robots, androids, bionics and artificial intelligence as they have been depicted in mythology, fantasy and science fiction. A glossary and bibliography are included, but the lack of an index imposes severe restrictions on the use of the valuable and interesting information contained in this volume. Recommended for collections that support research into major themes in SF/fantasy.

52.   Malzberg, Barry N. *Engines of the Night: Science Fiction in the Eighties.* Garden City, NY: Doubleday, 1982. 198p. MIN.

Engines is an informal history and an SF-world-view from the point of view of an author whose career (as he points out himself in the book) probably is not typical of most writers in the genre. Straight histories have been done better by others (Aldiss, del Rey, etc.) but the book is not a history so much as it seems to be an attempt by the author to codify and clarify some of his thoughts on SF: what it is, where it came from, and where it seems to be going. The coverage is uneven, which is to be expected in an informal history done from a very personal point of view. Most helpful to those in need of historical and biographical material are the chapters on John W. Campbell, Cornell Woolrich and Mark Clifton. Campbell, certainly, has never been forgotten, and considering his generally acknowledged position as the single-handed creator of SF's 1937-1949 "golden age," he probably never will; but Clifton and Woolrich, except for recent university press short story collections, have been unceremoniously shunted aside by the genre, and information on them is relatively scarce. Other portions of the book are not quite as helpful, and a few of the oft-repeated premises—such as the success or failure of a book depending entirely on its print run—seem questionable. But Malzberg approaches every subject with entertaining wit, cynicism and irony, which are deadly in combination with his clear, lucid prose. *Engines* is not a priority acquisition for any particular SF-related subject area, but in cases where the core collection is thorough and secondary acquisitions are needed to supplement the primary coverage, Malzberg's book is recommended. For other Malzberg-related materials see item 298.

53.   Maruyama, Magoroh, ed. *Cultures Beyond the Earth: The Role of Anthropology in Outer Space.* New York: Random House, 1975. 206p.

Cultures Beyond the Earth was an early attempt by one segment of the academic establishment to explore the application of science fiction ideas, themes, or points of view (interstellar colonization, the study of alien social structures, etc.) to a science—in this case, anthropology. The attempt was a failure. The essays and pseudo-fiction in this volume are extremely pedantic and display an astonishing lack of familiarity with the most basic SF ideas. Several of the articles are blatantly self-serving to the anthropology field when in fact the processes described likely would fall under the auspices of professionals more suited to the work under discussion. Concepts accepted and understood 30 years ago by an audience of average intelligence are here treated as virgin territory which must be laboriously explained even to other academics and professionals who might be expected to be more receptive, more understanding, and more familiar than the "average reader" with what the contributors are trying to do. The book is of little use either to scientists or science fiction readers, and is not recommended for acquisition.

54. Moskowitz, Sam. *Seekers of Tomorrow: Masters of Modern Science Fiction.* Cleveland and New York: World Publishing, 1966; New York: Ballantine, 1967 (450p.); Westport, CT: Hyperion Press, 1974. AOW, MIN, RSF, SRB, TYS.

Sam Moskowitz is one of the true historians of science fiction, especially in the areas of fandom and magazine publishing. His extensive knowledge of SF fandom and magazine publishing, however, allows him to delve into biography and criticism with mixed results. This collection of 22 "biographical and critical studies" was intended (at the time of publication) to be both a broad and in-depth survey of numerous SF authors "acclaimed as the leading creators of science fiction in the last twenty-five years," and the authors examined include E.E. Smith, John W. Campbell, Jr., Murray Leinster, Mort Weisinger, John Wyndham, Eric Frank Russell, L. Sprague de Camp, Lester del Rey, Robert Heinlein, A.E. van Vogt, Theodore Sturgeon, Isaac Asimov, Clifford Simak, Fritz Leiber, C.L. Moore, Henry Kuttner, Robert Bloch, Ray Bradbury, Arthur C. Clarke and Philip Jose Farmer. There is a "round up" chapter dealing with SF and religion which surveys a number of writers who have produced some religion-oriented SF and fantasy. Without question, there is a vast amount of trivia, minutiae and historical fact about fandom, and about late nineteenth century and early twentieth century magazines, in this book. The problem is critical evaluation, which is often weak and occasionally misdirected. In the Heinlein chapter, for example, Moskowitz states, "Somehow, Heinlein has overlooked the fact that successful authors are not misfits in modern society. They may be different but they *are* accepted, frequently in a sickeningly lavish fashion. He is still not aware that he no longer needs to justify himself vicariously." This quote illustrates not only prejudicial supposition about Heinlein's state of mind, thoughts, beliefs, feelings and motives—none of which Moskowitz could be aware of without extensive input from Heinlein—but also the imprecise use of at least two words, a problem that plagues Moskowitz throughout much of his work. Title and author indices allow reasonable access to the information in the book. Anyone using Moskowitz as a critical reference must consider cross-checking his opinions with other critics. The book was once an

important   source of information about major SF writers, but has been
superseded by the Bleiler biocritical volumes (items 12 and 13), the Cowart/
Wymer *Dictionary of Literary Biography*, and the Magill surveys (items 48
and 49).

55. Mullen, R.D. and Darko Suvin, eds. *Science Fiction Studies: Selected
Articles on Science Fiction 1973-1975.* Boston: Gregg Press, 1976. 304p.
RSF, SRB.

Notwithstanding the burgeoning academic interest in SF of the past 20
years, there are still only two major American SF academic/scholarly journals, of which *Science Fiction Studies* is one. This critical anthology is a
collection of articles previously published in early numbers of *Studies*.
Offerings are suitably broad-based, representing many subject areas and
points of view, though the articles are grouped into five general categories:
science fiction and literary theory, SF and Marxism, nineteenth century science fiction, six twentieth century writers (Arthur Clarke, Robert Graves,
Nabokov, Lem, Le Guin and Spinrad), Philip K. Dick and Ursula K. Le
Guin. Several of the pieces included in *Studies* are "round robin" exchanges,
so the number of contributors to this first collection of articles is somewhat
misleading. Critics, writers and other participants in some of the exchanges
include Lem, Russ, Rottensteiner, Blish, Le Guin, Franklin, Suvin, Knight,
Scholes, Philmus, Reynolds, Samuelson, and Watson, among others. A table
of contents is provided, but there is no general index. Although the articles
to be found in *Studies* tend to be of more value to students or researchers
working at the graduate level, several essays (notably those on selected
twentieth century writers) may be of interest to undergraduate students. The
book is not a high priority acquisition, but it is a reasonably good addition
to collections with a broad general scope in SF criticism and analysis.

56. Mullen, R.D. and Darko Suvin, eds. *Science Fiction Studies, Second
Series: Selected Articles on Science Fiction 1976-1977.* Boston: Gregg
Press, 1978. 335p. SRB.

Science Fiction Studies was the second major American SF journal (the
first was *Extrapolation*, established in 1959). This collection of articles previously published in *Studies* apparently was selected to represent a wide
range of subject matter and varying levels of critical interest. Several articles are of primary interest only to academics in limited fields of study, e.g.
"Iambulus' *Islands of the Sun* and Hellenistic Literary Utopias," while
others are directed toward a general audience. Some of the articles which
first appeared in *Studies*—such as Samuelson's "The Lost Canticles of Walter M. Miller, Jr."—are near-definitive treatments of their subject areas. The
articles in this volume are grouped into four general subject categories: sci-

ence fiction before Wells; Morris, Wells and London; science fiction since Wells; and the sociology of science fiction. Critics represented include many who are recognized as belonging to the ranks of the most respected academicians analyzing SF today: Samuelson, Suvin, Parrinder, Ketterer, Elkins, Berger and Plank, among others. A table of contents provides access by article title, but the book might have profited tremendously from a general index. *Studies*, second series, is a solid contribution to SF criticism, and like the first series, the book is recommended for libraries maintaining a reasonably thorough collection of general critical studies of SF.

57. New Dimensions Foundation. *Moving Into Space: The Myths & Realities of Extra Terrestrial Life.* Berkeley, CA: And/Or Press, 1978; New York: Harper & Row, 1980. 301p.

While not strictly a nonfiction book about science fiction, *Moving Into Space* may be of more than passing interest to the science fiction reader or researcher because in some ways the book is a catalogue of possibilities that less than half a century ago were considered, everywhere except in the SF genre, to be absolute impossibilities. The book also is a gauge with which to measure the scientific and popular acceptance of ideas that were seriously entertained only within the confines of the SF community until fairly recently—the construction of space stations and space colonies, reception and decoding or translation of signals from other civilizations, the wholesale transfer of industrial and manufacturing capabilities into space, and so on. Contributors include scientists and science writers well-known to most SF readers, such as Buckminster Fuller, Gerard K. O'Neill, Robert Anton Wilson, G. Harry Stine, Timothy Leary and Jacques-Yves Cousteau. *Moving Into Space* is not a primary research instrument for SF, but is a valuable source for contemporary speculations on social and technological possibilities and their after-effects—rather like no-nonsense and as-common-sensical-as-possible extrapolations of backgrounds, settings, and ideas that are treated in fictional form as part of the underlying structure of science fiction. Recommended primarily as an "SF associational" acquisition for larger collections with a sub-emphasis on practical or realistic applications for ideas pioneered in the SF genre.

58. Nicholls, Peter. *The Science Fiction Foundation—A Report; March 1976.* London: The Science Fiction Foundation, 1976. 22p.

The Science Fiction Foundation *Report* is a stapled booklet, printed offset from typewritten copy, which was meant, apparently, to be a combination public relations and marketing device. It contains an introduction, a brief history of the Foundation, and miscellaneous notes such as a list of the aims of the Foundation, information about a lecture agency, and explanations of the newly introduced James Blish award. From its inception, the Foundation SF journal has been the major British forum for review and criticism of SF films and books—the publication is more or less an English version of the American publication *Extrapolation*, except that essays appearing in *Extrapolation* are often more pedantic and therefore less accessible to the general reader. This report booklet has little research value except as a source for information about the Science Fiction Foundation.

59. Nicholls, Peter, and Charles Barren, eds. *Foundation—Numbers 1-8 March 1972-March 1975.* Boston: Gregg Press, 1978. SRB. (Each number is separately paginated but the volume contains approximately 786 pages.)

As one of the three major academic science fiction journals, and the only British journal of the three, *Foundation* is an important contribution to review and criticism in the SF field. This hardcover volume is a photo-offset reproduction of the first eight numbers. Editorial work was done by Nicholls and Barren, with additional editorial contributions by Kenneth Bulmer, George Hay, Malcolm Edwards, Christopher Priest and Ian Watson. A sampling of contributors to the journal would include such writers as John Brunner, John J. Pierce, Larry Niven, Darko Suvin, James Blish, A.E. van Vogt, James Tiptree, Samuel Delany, Brian Aldiss, Brian Stableford, and Ursula Le Guin, among others. As with the other academic journals, the articles occasionally approach the esoteric, but most are useful contributions. One particularly noteworthy feature of the first eight numbers of the journal is a continuing series of autobiographical essays by prominent SF authors. The first of these was contributed by John Brunner; others were provided by Blish, van Vogt, L. Sprague de Camp, Poul Anderson, etc. (though Anderson declined to contribute autobiographical material and instead provided an article/essay on SF as entertainment, instruction or both). The book reviews maintain a consistently high level of critical excellence. Though a complete and thorough indexing would be useful (every name reference on every page rather than simple title-author-subject indexing by article or review), *Foundation* still is an excellent source of SF criticism.

60. Nicholls, Peter, ed., with contributions by David Langford and Brian Stableford. *The Science in Science Fiction.* New York: Knopf, 1983. New York: Crescent Books, 1987. 208p.

The Science in Science Fiction is an impressive and colorful coffee-table book bearing, in some respects, very little relationship to science fiction. It is, in effect, a catalog of the scientific concepts and devices often used (or described or invoked or mangled) in SF novels. Devices, motifs and concepts catalogued include terraforming, energy, planetary colonization, the generation starship, the ramscoop starship, immortality, cyborgs, matter transmission, robots, artificial intelligence, holocaust/catastrophe, time travel, and so on. Many of the concepts are nicely explained and most are illustrated with photos, drawings, diagrams, or cover and interior artwork from SF magazines. Many of the art reproductions are in full color. In the text accompanying each device or concept, parallels are drawn between the pure theory itself as regarded by science and the use of these devices in well-known SF novels. There is even one section reserved especially for "Where science fiction gets it wrong," a catch-all for particularly outdated or wrongheaded concepts still perennially popular in the SF genre. The book is well done, interesting and attractive; considering that it was compiled by Nicholls, with significant contributions from Langford and Stableford, it is not surprising that the book is a first-rate effort, complete with index and bibliography. But the most practical *use* for the book is as "motif encyclopedia" or general browsing volume for those who like SF trivia displayed and explained by SF experts with impeccable credentials and a thorough grounding in the theory and application of a wide range of sciences. Recommended as a secondary or supplemental acquisition for collections already containing a solid core of general reference and critical volumes.

61. Palumbo, Donald, ed. *Erotic Universe: Sexuality and Fantastic Literature.* Westport, CT: Greenwood Press, 1986. 305p.

Sex in science fiction and fantasy is only beginning to receive the attention it deserves—and, no doubt, the attention it will receive in due course. *Erotic Universe* is a collection of 15 articles which explore different aspects of sexuality in SF/fantasy. The articles are divided into four groups: Theory; Themes; Feminist Views; and Fanzines. The number of articles per section is approximately equal for each of the first three divisions; only one essay appears in the "Fanzines" section. A partial list of contributors includes Marlene Barr, Judith Bogert, Brooks Landon, Judith Spector and Leonard G. Heldreth, among others. Topics examined include homosexuality in SF and fantasy, sexual comedy in SF/fantasy, sex with aliens, and the relationship between Kirk and Spock in some of the *Star Trek* fiction fanzines (a relationship that runs the gamut from friendship to homosexuality in the fan-generated fiction). As might be expected in the "Feminist Views" section, fiction by Joanna Russ, Marge Piercy and Ursula K. Le Guin is analyzed or commented upon in some context in more than one essay per author. The subject matter should be able to generate interest in the book and the essays it contains, though the scholarly treatment sometimes makes a very emotional act seem quite devoid of any significance other than the social or psychological symbolism selected for mummification in each article. Fantasy has long been recognized as a highly erotic form of literature, though attention to sexuality in SF, until recently, has been confined mostly to passing references to brass brassieres, phallic spaceships and aliens with an incomprehensible penchant for kidnapping nubile young earth women. Serious research into sexuality in SF is all but nonexistent in book form, so despite the ponderous nature of some of these explorations, *Erotic Universe* is recommended for collections supporting research into major themes and motifs in SF/fantasy. Includes an index and an annotated bibliography.

62. Pringle, David. *Science Fiction: The 100 Best Novels*. London: Xanadu Publications Ltd., 1985. 224p.

As Pringle states in his introduction, about 50 of his choices for the "hundred best novels" are true SF classics and are widely regarded as such; the rest are personal favorites selected by the author because they struck him as very good books when he read them while growing up. The book is a useful volume, and provides brief (two-page) yet knowledgeable appraisal of 100 novels, but the book could be misleading to the new SF reader and disappointing to the experienced reader. A survey of the 100 "best" might be expected to include some classic or influential novels such as *Stranger In A Strange Land*, but Heinlein is represented instead by *The Puppet Masters*, *The Door Into Summer* and *Have Space Suit—Will Travel*. Though perhaps not as representative of accepted classics as it might be, the book nevertheless contributes some useful commentary on books that often don't receive a great deal of attention. The expected "true" classics are covered: *Nineteen Eighty-Four*, *The Martian Chronicles*, *Farhenheit 451*, *Dune*, *The Dispossessed*, *A Clockwork Orange*, *A Case of Conscience*, *A Canticle for Leibowitz*, *The Sirens of Titan*, etc. However, many good books which are not well known even within the genre are included in Pringle's list, such as *Heroes and Villains* and *Woman on the Edge of Time*. The beginning date was arbitrarily set at 1949, so all novels included in the survey were published between 1949 and 1984. The book is indexed, it is a helpful collection of commentary on a wide range of post-World War II SF, and the volume is recommended for libraries with moderate to extensive holdings in general SF criticism.

63. Rabkin, Eric S., Martin H. Greenberg and Joseph Olander, eds. *The End of the World*. Carbondale, IL: Southern Illinois University Press, 1983. 204p.

In the post-nuclear-war age the catastrophe—both the natural and manmade varieties—has been a mainstay of the SF field, but even so, this critical anthology is the first volume systematically to explore "the end of the world" as a complex and important SF theme. Critics include Gary K. Wolfe, Robert Plank, Robert Galbreath, W. Warren Wagar and Brian Stableford. These five critics have contributed six lengthy articles; because the essays are somewhat longer than average, they cover proportionately more of the topic area within the scope of each individual contribution. Approximately an even division between practical access criticism and less accessible theoretical studies, the articles range from formal inquiries into transcendentalism in "end of the world" fiction to highly personal interpretations of "the lone survivor" as an element of apocalyptic and catastrophe fiction. The introduction, by Eric Rabkin, is such a thorough (if brief) survey of the subject theme that it acts almost as a seventh article; Rabkin touches on the "end of the world" theme in numerous sources, including the Bible and the poetry of Marvell and Wordsworth, as well as classic treatments of the theme—*Sleeping Beauty*, Clarke's "The Nine Billion Names of God" and Poul's *Tau Zero*. Notes are contained in an appendix, and the book has a select bibliography of fiction and nonfiction as well as an index. Recommended as a supplementary acquisition for undergraduate or graduate level collections of SF criticism that already contain a strong core of basic titles.

64. Rabkin, Eric S., Martin H. Greenberg and Joseph D. Olander, eds. *No Place Else; Explorations in Utopian and Dystopian Fiction.* Carbondale, IL: Southern Illinois University Press, 1983. 278p.

Essays which examine utopian fiction generally analyze only the "classics," leaving students and fans of more recent utopianesque fiction with few secondary sources. *No Place Else* helps to correct this problem by providing a useful mixture of articles dealing with the recognized landmark utopian/dystopian novels as well as more recent popular SF novels with unmistakable utopian characteristics. The articles are not general surveys; most of the essays focus on selected major aspects of a particular novel. Works chosen for analysis in this volume include *The Coming Race, Erewhon, We, Last and First Men, Brave New World, The Shape of Things to Come, Walden Two, 1984, Player Piano, Fahrenheit 451, Lord of the Flies, The World Inside* and *The Dispossessed*. Several of the articles are quite technical, but the analysis of utopian fiction has a longer history than the analysis of popular fiction—and utopian writings have existed in their "pure" form far longer than SF—so some sophistication in utopian criticism is to be expected. Readers interested in more recent utopian/dystopian writings within the SF publishing tradition may be disappointed to find the book is less an "access" volume for those just becoming interested in utopian/dystopian fiction than it is a mid-level critical analysis presuming in the reader a fairly broad familiarity with utopian writings and utopian criticism. The book is recommended for collections emphasizing utopian/dystopian fiction and criticism or for a collection intended for broad-based general research needing good representative sources for the utopian theme. The book is indexed and should be useful at the undergraduate or graduate level.

65. Riley, Dick, ed. *Critical Encounters: Writers and Themes in Science Fiction.* New York: Frederick Ungar, 1978. 184p. MIN, SRB.

Critical Encounters is an excellent introduction to single-author criticism for students at the high school or undergraduate college level. Riley has collected nine articles, the majority of which deal with one author and one book (or one major aspect of a single author's work) and which provide not only some criticism and explanation, but in many cases a great deal of biographical material about the author under discussion. Authors examined include Isaac Asimov, Ray Bradbury, Frank Herbert, Ursula Le Guin, Arthur Clarke, Samuel Delany, Theodore Sturgeon and Robert Heinlein. The single exception to the "one author" essay format is an article on themes explored by women SF writers. Regrettably, the book has no index. In some respects, the selection of only high-profile SF authors is a weakness—Asimov, Heinlein, Bradbury, etc. are "over criticized" in the genre, and other good writers continue to be ignored—but in other ways, the popularity of the recognized leading talents examined here may allow the essays to appeal to a broader range of students already familiar with, and knowledgeable about, SF. *Critical Encounters* is not a priority acquisition, but is recommended where budgeting will allow the expansion of holdings in general SF criticism at the high school or undergraduate level of study.

66. Rogers, Alva. *A Requiem for Astounding.* Chicago: Advent, 1964. 224p. AOW, MIN, RSF, SRB.

Rogers' tribute to *Astounding* has been unfairly criticized in some publications for not being a different type of book. In the introduction, the author states that the book is not a critical work, but is, instead, "...a nostalgic excursion into the past," and that describes the book well. It is almost a month-by-month survey of the first 30 years of the publication of *Astounding*, and as such is a valuable specific magazine reference. The book has three brief introductions, one each by Rogers, Harry Bates and John W. Campbell, Jr., as well as an "editorial" by F. Orlin Tremaine. The prose style of the general text is not as polished as it might be (for example, van Vogt's story "Slan" is described as "tremendously sensational") but the almost story-by-story survey could be extremely useful to someone researching *Astounding* without direct access to copies of the first 360 issues of the magazine. Rogers separates his commentary into sections by year dates—The Beginning: Clayton's Astounding 1930-1933, The Tremaine Era: First Phase 1933-1935, etc. Numerous cover and interior illustrations from magazines are reproduced. There are minor mistakes/omissions, such as an index entry that reads simply, "Pierce, John R. (see also," but within its limitations, *Requiem* serves exactly the purpose Rogers intended—it is a biased, uncritical and sentimental magazine survey. Though its lack of critical perspective keeps the book from being a priority acquisition, it could serve as a useful supplement to holdings which emphasize early SF magazines and SF magazine fiction.

67. Rose, Lois and Stephen Rose. *The Shattered Ring: Science Fiction and the Quest for Meaning.* Richmond, VA: John Knox Press, 1970. 127p. AOW.

The Shattered Ring is a general survey of "meaning" in science fiction. The emphasis is on "general" and the exegesis in predominantly religious (Lois and Stephen Rose have written books and articles on religious themes, and founded and edited a magazine on church and urban problems). Works examined range from novels by A.E. van Vogt to C.S. Lewis, Sturgeon, Delany, Zelazny, Disch, Ballard, Heinlein and Asimov. There is no attempt to apply any critical standards to the works discussed—the emphasis is not on technique or literary ability but on the transcendant meaning of the devices and conventions that are the common coin of literary borrowing and appropriating within the genre. The Roses identify modern SF as post-Campbellian SF, and credit Campbell with ushering in the "classic period" of science fiction which began in the years 1937-1939. They include Olaf Stapledon among the "new talent" that emerged after Campbell's editorial ascendancy, yet many of Stapledon's major works were published in the pre-Campbell era (*Last and First Men* in 1930; *Odd John* in 1935; *Star Maker*, published in 1937 but obviously written before Campbell had time to establish, with his editorial policies, the SF "modern era"). The most useful discussions are presented in the last chapter of the book, where specific novels are analyzed for their use of mythic elements. Some of the statements made by the Roses may be of value to researchers working on the undergraduate level, but the authors occasionally fall victim to non sequitur and broad overstatement. The volume is not indexed. The book is not recommended as an important acquisition; if the budget allows, it can serve as a useful supplement to existing sources of religious exegesis of SF.

68. Rottensteiner, Franz. *The Fantasy Book: An Illustrated History from Dracula to Tolkien.* New York: Collier, 1978. 160p. MIN, SRB.

Rottensteiner's historical survey of "fantasy" actually encompasses fantasy, fantastic or weird fiction, gothic, horror and supernatural fiction, all of which share some common elements but which also exhibit important differences. Some authors, such as Walpole, Hoffmann and Potocki, are treated at length, and a "themes and characters" section presents capsule histories of the development of major sub-genre divisions such as werewolf, golem and vampire fiction. Other topics, generally well-covered, include fantasy magazines, book publishers, imaginary worlds, sword and sorcery, and fantasy for children. Rottensteiner's book is particularly valuable for the European point of view—a definite contrast to the American viewpoint, which often is an insular and restricted tunnel-view based solely on the fact that the U.S. is the largest SF/fantasy market—and the multi-national treatment of the development of fantasy in its various forms. The book includes 200 illustrations, 40 in color. There are minor omissions, such as names mentioned in the text which are not included in the index, but the omissions are not numerous or substantial enough to damage this excellent fantasy overview significantly. Most SF histories also deal with fantasy in some form, but Rottensteiner's book is recommended for any collection with a strong enough emphasis on fantasy to require a separate illustrated historical treatment of the subject.

69. Scholes, Robert and Eric S. Rabkin. *Science Fiction: History, Science, Vision.* New York: Oxford University Press, 1977. 258p. MIN, RSF, SRB.

Science Fiction: History, Science, Vision is widely recognized as one of the most important and influential volumes of SF history/criticism to emerge in SF's modern era. The book is divided into three sections with the first section presenting a brief but remarkably detailed literary history that includes compact evaluations of numerous authors including Edgar Allan Poe, Edgar Rice Burroughs, H.G. Wells, Yevgeny Zamyatin, Karel Capek, Olaf Stapledon, Aldous Huxley, Hugo Gernsback, E.E. Smith, A.E. van Vogt, Stanley Weinbaum, John W. Campbell, Isaav Asimov, Robert Heinlein, Theodore Sturgeon and others. Section two, "Science," surveys major scientific advances and the effects of those advances on literary thought, as well as the use of scientific knowledge (or lack of such use) in specific SF and fantasy novels. The "Vision" section examines myth and myth-making, fantasy, utopia, imaginary worlds, imaginary beings, and other major themes, motifs and devices commonly used in SF/fantasy. In the final chapter, ten representative novels are briefly but thoroughly examined: *Frankenstein; 20,000 Leagues Under the Sea; The Time Machine; We; A Voyage to Arcturus; Star Maker; Childhood's End; A Canticle for Leibowitz; The Left Hand of Darkness; Shockwave Rider.* Included are an extensive bibliography and an index. Though somewhat technical in the literary analyses, the book can be of some use at most levels of study and is recommended as a basic and important acquisition for any SF reference or criticism collection.

70. Slusser, George E., Eric S. Rabkin and Robert Scholes, eds. *Bridges to Fantasy*. Carbondale, IL: Southern Illinois University Press, 1982. 231p.

Interest in fantasy seems to be increasing—indeed, much of the apparent expansion of the SF genre in recent decades might be better termed an expansion of interest in fantasy that masquerades as SF—and this critical anthology addresses problems with the definition, theory, structure, perception, genesis and development of fantasy as the form currently is manifest in literature and film. The 13 articles offer informed conjecture and scholarly commentary on narrowly defined topics ("Power Fantasy in the Science Fiction of Mark Twain") as well as large general topics ("The Search for Fantasy: From Primitive Man to Pornography"). Contributing critics include Harold Bloom, Larry McCaffrey, Marta E. Sanchez, Arlen J. Hansen, David Clayton, Roger Sale, G.R. Thompson, Robert A. Collins, John Gerlach, David Ketterer, George R. Guffey, Jack P. Rawlins and Gary Kern. Very few of the articles are of use or interest to a general SF/fantasy audience, though there are one or two exceptions; "Confronting the Alien: Fantasy and Antifantasy in Science Fiction Film and Literature," despite the imposing title, is a cogent and thought-provoking exploration of SF and fantasy elements as they are used in such films as *Invasion of the Body Snatchers, The Thing* and *2001*, but most of the articles require extremely detailed and specialized knowledge to appreciate. The book is indexed, and the collection is recommended as an excellent addition to SF/fantasy holdings which support graduate or post-graduate inquiry into the structure and mechanics of fantasy.

71. Slusser, George E., Eric S. Rabkin and Robert Scholes, eds. *Coordinates: Placing Science Fiction and Fantasy*. Carbondale, IL: Southern Illinois University Press, 1983. 209p.

The nominal purpose of *Coordinates* is to "establish basic coordinates for these two genres" (science fiction and fantasy) and to "permit the reader to assess the critical act itself, and to judge the adequacy of any given attempt to bracket and fix the basic problems of science fiction and fantasy." These difficult goals are achieved, at least in part, by the range of articles; several are one-work or one-author studies (two articles deal directly with Rider Haggard's novel *She* and one with editorial changes in Bradbury's *Fahrenheit 451*) while others are inquiries into general ideas, themes, or motifs which have some significance in SF or fantasy. Leslie Fiedler's article is one of the best ever published on the problem of applying sophisticated critical techniques to types of popular fiction which often represent the exact opposite of literary sophistication. Other works examined include *Atlas Shrugged* and *Triton* and a contribution by Gary K. Wolfe examines the implications of "autoplastic" (man adapting himself to his environment) and "alloplastic" (man adapting the environment to his needs through technological manipulation) themes in SF. *Coordinates* develops a range of ideas and approaches at a level of interest that makes the volume of use both to undergraduate and graduate research. As a group or "book unit," the essays actually tell more about what yet must be done to place the "coordinates" outlined in the introduction, but the work is here well-begun. The book is recommended as a useful addition to collections of general critical volumes.

72. Slusser, George E., George R. Guffey and Mark Rose, eds. *Bridges to Science Fiction.* Carbondale, IL: Southern Illinois University Press, 1980. 168p.

The purpose of this collection of critical essays is "to suggest connections between science fiction and other aspects of Western culture," according to the introduction. This goal is achieved with a mixture of subject matter and approach which includes SF in relation to "medieval cosmological discourse, classical empirical philosophy, contemporary philosophy of science, fairy tale, epic, and gothic fiction." This "shopping list" of topic areas may sound somewhat imposing to a student just beginning a pattern of research into SF, but several of the essays are thoughtful considerations of general subject areas such as the similarities between SF and the fairy tale or the near-impossibility of creating truly "unknowable" aliens in science fiction. Contributors include Harry Levin, Gregory Benford, Eric S. Rabkin, Patrick Parrinder, Kent T. Kraft, Stephen W. Potts, Robert Hunt, Thomas H. Keeling, Carl D. Malmgren and Thomas A. Hanzo. There is only one single-author study, an essay on Philip K. Dick's *The Man in the High Castle*; other essays consider such matters as the SF story as "truncated epic" and the similarities and differences between SF and the gothic tradition. A sampling of article titles might best show the diversity represented in the collection: "SF and the Gothic," "Fairy Tales and SF" and "Empirical Views of God from Locke to Lem." Though the book has a broad array of articles, all written specifically for the First Eaton Conference on Science Fiction and Fantasy Literature, it contains a high percentage of complex material requiring substantial familiarity with the subject matter, and so must be recommended—if highly recommended—for collections supporting research at the graduate or post-graduate level.

73. Smith, Nicholas D., ed. *Philosophers Look at Science Fiction.* Chicago: Nelson-Hall, 1982. 204p.

Looking at science fiction as a form of literature ideally suited to exploring philosophical considerations is not new, but using a genre fiction as a vehicle for academic speculation never has been popular among general readers because some academicians have a tendency to take their special areas of interest very seriously and then apply that specialty very rigorously to SF with a heavy-handed methodology. This collection of articles on SF as its possibilities are assessed by philosophy professors avoids some of the most serious problems usually encountered by academic treatments of the genre. One contribution ("On Again, Off Again," by Lee F. Werth) is written as a piece of fiction presented as truth told in fictional form because the (fictional) author didn't believe it possible to present the (real) story as fact. The structure of the story mimics the form used by countless stories and novels in the fantastic genres, and is an interesting and entertaining exercise in finding philosophical relevance in a genre fiction infamous for its overuse of cliched story elements. Other essays consider the philosophical problems inherent in time travel; the concept of causation and human understanding of nature (natural law) and its effect on writing SF; alternative linguistic concepts and communication with alien intelligence; the possibility that an alien language might have no translatable reference in English; the viability of the language developed by Delany for *Babel-17*; and several other subjects. The contributors to this book are quite familiar with SF—both the good and the bad aspects—and the articles pose interesting questions and provide enlightening points of view. The subject matter and treatment, however, are often complex, sometimes unduly so, and the volume is likely to be of little use to SF research on the undergraduate level. Those with the greatest interest in this volume of "speculative philosophy," in fact, may be other philosophers and not a general SF research audience at all. The volume has no index, so even for the rare occasions when a specific author or story is addressed in an article, there is no easy research access.

74. Suvin, Darko. *Metamorphoses of Science Fiction.* New Haven, CT: Yale University Press, 1979. 317p. MIN.

More than any other volume of SF criticism published to date, *Metamorphoses* develops a compact and credible theory of poetics, history and lineage for science fiction. The book is divided into three sections—poetics, "older" SF history and "newer" SF history, though the more recent history stops at the interwar period between the two world wars. Suvin identifies H.G. Wells as the turning point in the development of SF as a distinct and identifiable genre, and postulates violent technological intrusion on the staid, conservative, and complacent Victorian era (symbolized by many of Wells' best-known works, including *The War of the Worlds* and *The First Men in the Moon*) as the beginning of the hybrid fiction that would dominate the "paraliterature" or "subliterature" that would become twentieth century SF. Suvin's theories are widely inclusive and often somewhat vague, and throughout the book he suggests perhaps a dozen other books that should be written to explore aspects of SF he must cover in a few paragraphs. Though unquestionably a valuable contribution to SF scholarship, the book is so technical, and relies so heavily on foreign-language words and phrases, that its chief use and value probably will be to motivate other SF scholars and historians to develop their own theoretical frameworks for the evolution, development and value of the SF genre. The book is not likely to be of much help to students or general readers working below the graduate level, but should be a priority acquisition for libraries maintaining SF research materials at the graduate or post-graduate levels. Included in the volume are a detailed bibliography and an index.

75. Thiessen, J. Grant. *The Science Fiction Collector.* Three vols. Altona, Manitoba, Canada: Pandora's Books, 1981. Each number separately paginated, but the three volumes contain a total of approximately 776 pages.

J. Grant Thiessen, a Canadian bookseller, published 14 issues of an SF collector's magazine between 1976 and 1981. Some of the issues were titled *The Science Fiction Collector* and some were titled *Megavore: The Journal of Popular Fiction.* The magazine started out as a fanzine but quickly established itself as a premiere collector's publication containing articles, checklists, indexes, and other bibliographical data on collectible paperbacks, pulp magazines, pseudonymous books and similar subjects for which accurate and well-researched data can be extremely difficult to locate. The three hardcover volumes of this limited edition set, containing all issues of the now-defunct publications *Collector* and *Megavore*, represent a treasury of obscure bibliographical information on a wide variety of subjects, from the Ace double paperbacks and the DAW printing codes to the Health Knowledge magazines and erotic SF books. Many issues of *Collector/Megavore* were printed on newsprint paper and may not be able to tolerate excessive use or long-term storage under unfavorable conditions. Each issue has a table of contents, but the volumes lack a comprehensive index. The three-volume set is recommended for collections which emphasize bibliography and index for SF, paperback books, and magazines.

76. Warner, Harry, Jr. *All Our Yesterdays; An Informal History of Science Fiction Fandom in the Forties.* Chicago: Advent, 1969. 336p. AOW, RSF, SRB.

Histories of science fiction fan activity, or fandom, can provide unique and helpful insights into the SF fan hobby, and ultimately into the genre itself. Warner's *All Our Yesterdays* is not a definitive history of fandom in the 1940s, but it is as close to such a history as has yet been published. The goal, as outlined in the foreword, was to "deal basically with some of the important events of the forties," and this Warner has done. A glossary of oft-used SF fan terms is provided, and the volume begins with an overview and survey of "fanish" activities as they pertained to numerous pre-1940s, and some pre-twentieth-century, authors. Many of the chapters are clusters of capsule biographies of writers, editors, and fans who were major and minor figures in fandom. Included are surveys of previous fan histories, early SF reference books, press associations, conventions, national fandom, regional fandom, fanzines, and foreign fan activities. The volume is indexed and contains a great deal of biographical information on SF and fandom figures for whom very little such information is available. The book is especially helpful because the author maintains a reasonable perspective throughout, avoiding overstatement of the importance of incidents or events, and his critical judgments are sound and trustworthy. The book is highly recommended for any collection with any emphasis on fan history or activities.

77. Weinberg, Robert. *The Weird Tales Story.* West Linn, OR: Fax Collectors Editions, 1977. 134p. MIN, RSF, SRB.

A history and collection of fond reminiscences by several contributors, *The Weird Tales Story* is at once a fascinating, well-researched history of an influential magazine and a poorly organized piece of nonfiction. Much of the material the book contains is useful and interesting, but entire segments—for example, Chapter Four, "The Stories," which is little more than an issue-by-issue description of stories, many not worth describing—are of little use. Of great interest are essay "memoirs" by WT contributors such as Edmond Hamilton, Wallace West, H. Warner Munn, Frank Belknap Long, Carl Jacobi, Robert Bloch, Joseph Payne Brennan, Lee Brown Coye, and others. An editorial from WT is reprinted in full, along with numerous cover and interior illustrations, contents pages from the magazine, "teaser" or "coming next month" notices and excerpts from letter columns. Robert Weinberg is a noted authority on *Weird Tales* in particular and the pulp magazines in general, but this history of WT could have been far more useful to the serious researcher and general reader alike if it had been somewhat better organized and if it had incorporated an index to provide access to the information. The book apparently was intended for the uncritical collector who wants more information about his or her collecting specialty, no matter how badly organized or presented, though the book must be recommended as a supplemental acquisition for collections with an emphasis in magazine history or pulp magazine fiction and authors.

78. Williamson, Jack, ed. *Teaching Science Fiction: Education for Tomorrow.* Philadelphia: Owlswick Press, 1980. 261p. AOW, MIN.

Williamson's SF teaching anthology is more useful than most SF teaching aids because in many ways it is less specific. The book essentially is a collection of suggestions and helpful essays by people who have taught SF and who understand the problems, not the least of which is the intermittent availability or sporadic "shelf life" of most SF novels, even many of the accepted "standards" or "classics" in the field. Williamson's book does not tell which books or stories to teach; it simply provides workable teaching suggestions and strategies for teaching whatever fiction is to be incorporated into a science fiction literature course. There are three sections: "The Topic," "The Teachers" and "The Tools." Within the divisions are essays devoted to a wide range of topics, including women and SF, SF and the science teacher, philosophy and human problems through SF, film SF, syllabus description, SF and religion, SF and psychology, and so on. There is a bibliography of reference sources, a bibliography of major SF/fantasy books, and an index. There are some minor problems with the index, such as names out of alphabetical order, misspellings, etc. A partial listing of contributors includes Carl Sagan, Ursula Le Guin, Isaac Asimov, Leon Stover, Robin Wilson, Thomas Clareson, the Panshins, Susan Wood, Barry Longyear, Mark Hillegas, Kate Wilhelm, Vonda McIntyre, James Gunn and Neil Barron. Other SF teaching aids placed on the market from time to time offer dubious help, such as lists of questions, but so many writers, teachers and critics have contributed their experiences, suggestions and expertise to Williamson's teaching anthology that it is the best general SF teaching aid in existence and should be in any collection of SF pedagogic materials.

79. Wolfe, Gary K. *The Known and the Unknown: The Iconography of Science Fiction.* Kent, OH: Kent State University Press, 1979. 250p. MIN, SRB.

The Known and the Unknown is one of the most important SF studies yet published. Most SF studies fall into one of three categories: single author studies, general histories, or examinations of a particular sub-genre of SF such as utopian fiction. *The Known and the Unknown* is a study of recurring symbols or images in SF which Wolfe calls "icons." The occurrence, meaning and use of these icons is traced through numerous stories and novels, most of which are representative examples taken from the Gernsbackian through the Campbellian eras. The specific icons detailed in Wolfe's study include the image of the barrier; and the icons of the spaceship, the city, the wasteland, the robot and the monster. These seem to be the basic images accepted by the reading public as the most important or "core" components of the SF formula, but there are others—some more complex, such as time travel, and some simpler, such as the "alien" or the "stranger"—which could be studied profitably in the same light. Wolfe's study is ground-breaking in several respects, not the least of which is his thorough debunking of the "spaceship as phallic symbol" pseudoliterary myth that has plagued SF for virtually the entire span of its post-Freudian existence. Of interest also are speculations on the use of myth, the "cult of rationality," and as complete and reasonable an explanation of the "sense of wonder" as may be found anywhere in the scholarly literature on SF. The book is indexed, and should be available for use in any library that maintains a collection of SF related studies.

80. Wymer, Thomas L., Alice Calderonello, Lowell P. Leland, Sara Jayne Steen and R. Michael Evers. *Intersections: The Elements of Fiction in Science Fiction.* Bowling Green OH: Bowling Green University Popular Press, 1978. 130p. MIN.

There is some possibility *Intersections* could be used as a basic text for an SF course, but there is an even better likelihood that its best use would be as a text in a creative writing course emphasizing SF. The important elements of fiction—plot, character, setting, point of view, language, tone, theme and value, symbol and myth—are discussed on a relatively elementary level using numerous examples which are drawn from science fiction. The examples apparently were selected to be well-known, easily recognized and as readily accessible for teaching purposes as any SF works are likely to be, given the speed with which paperbacks can go in and out of print. Discussions range widely and often touch on non-SF literature (Homer, Hemingway, Joyce, Proust, Melville) as well as SF or SF-related literature (Stapledon, Wells, Verne, Shelley, Silverberg, Ballard, Blish, Pohl). A bibliography of the short fiction and poetry cited is included, as well as a key to anthologies and collections containing stories cited; there is a bibliography of SF nonfiction and reference books, but no index. The book is an excellent "beginner's" look at the building blocks of fiction which must be incorporated into SF to make good storytelling possible, but probably is more useful at the high school level than for undergraduate college work.

Section 2
Author
Studies

81. Bendau, Clifford P. *Colin Wilson: The Outsider and Beyond.* San Bernardino, CA: Borgo Press, 1979. 63p. MIN.

Colin Wilson is only of marginal interest to the fan or student of science fiction. The two SF novels *The Mind Parasites* and *The Space Vampires* are Wilson's major contributions to the SF field. Most of his other works (novels, nonfiction, biography, collections of essays, etc.) are unrelated to SF/fantasy. Much of Bendau's study is an explanation of the philosophical underpinnings that support Wilson's writings—collectively, Wilson's work, and particularly the system of philosophy behind it, is called the "new existentialism." Less than a page of commentary in this booklet is devoted to *Parasites* and two pages to *Vampires*. Treatment of many books covered in this study is quite abbreviated; after 30 pages of introduction to Wilson's philosophy, the author's books are examined in groups according to publication date. *The Outsider and Beyond* is an excellent short introduction to Wilson's work, but because the subject author has not been a major contributor to the SF/fantasy field, this monograph is more likely to be of use in collections emphasizing contemporary mainstream literature than in specifically SF/fantasy-oriented collections. For other Wilson-related material see item 146; see Appendix I for an evaluation of the Borgo Press SF/fantasy author critical series.

82. Brizzi, Mary T. *Philip Jose Farmer*. Mercer Island, WA: Starmont House, 1980. 80p. MIN, SRB.

Brizzi notes that Farmer has authored 40 novels, and in her conclusion she credits him with being one of the "brightest stars in the science fiction sky." But her coverage of Farmer is sparse at best. One chapter (very short) is devoted to a chronology; one to a biographical sketch; and one each to "The Lovers," *Night of Light*, the World of Tiers series, "Riders of the Purple Wage," the Riverworld series, and a wrap-up discussion of several works. Criticism in the book is restricted to explanations of many of the obscure allusions, and there is a tendency to dash off statements that are not well-explained or well-supported. Because there is so little true criticism of the fiction of most SF authors, a volume such as this one should be an accessible, readable introduction to the subject author, but too many critical "booklets" turn out to be just lists of reasons why a critic happens to like a subject author's work. Some carelessness is evident—for example, Brizzi uses unexplained descriptions, such as "polytropical paramyths," which are likely to be more confusing than clarifying to the undergraduate and fan readers who are the obvious "target audience" for these critical booklets. The book has serious flaws, but still is important because of the general lack of unified and methodical criticism on Farmer. See Appendix I for an evaluation of the Starmont House SF/fantasy author critical series.

83. Bucknall, Barbara J. *Ursula K. Le Guin*. New York: Frederick Ungar, 1981. 175p.

Le Guin belongs to that small group of SF writers that enjoys (or at least receives) the lion's share of the book-length critical evaluations afforded the SF field. Bucknall's general exploration adds another volume to the SF critical canon, and another volume to the growing body of Le Guin criticism, without contributing substantially to the understanding of Le Guin's fiction. Large sections—in some cases, five to ten pages at a stretch—are little more than lengthy plot summaries. The book begins with a brief foreword, a chronology, and an introductory chapter of general biography, and subsequent chapters examine the Hainish cycle; the Earthsea trilogy; *The Left Hand of Darkness; The Lathe of Heaven* and *The Word for World is Forest; The Dispossessed;* and a selection of short stories. There is a short "Summing Up" chapter, a separate list of notes, a bibliography and an index. The two novels *The Left Hand of Darkness* and *The Dispossessed* receive somewhat more coverage than other Le Guin novels. Much of the criticism of the Hainish books is an explanation of the Norse myths which are the source patterns for many of the events in the novels, especially *Rocannon's World*. It is, perhaps, a hopeful sign that the book seems to be directed at the student or academic who knows virtually nothing about SF—the author feels constrained to provide parenthetical insertions explaining the Hugo and Nebula awards—but the survey of Le Guin's fiction has been done better by others, and Bucknall does not deepen or extend the exploration in any way. For other Le Guin-related material see items 45, 119 and 134.

84. Cannon, Peter. *The Chronology Out of Time: Dates in the Fiction of H.P. Lovecraft.* West Warwick, RI: Necronomicon Press, 1986. 33p.

The methods used for compiling this chronology of dates in Lovecraft's fiction are explained in the introduction, but still there is a notable omission—a hint as to why an internal chronology of Lovecraft's fiction might be useful. A writer generally does not approach his writing from the standpoint of providing an all-encompassing and consistent chronology. Even the most famous instance of pre-planned chronology—Heinlein's "future history" framework—has discrepancies. But working under the assumption that the internal chronology of Lovecraft's fiction might be useful in some interpretive or critical respects, the Cannon Lovecraftian chronology is well done. One nice touch is the use of "Lovecraft's own words wherever possible" rather than colorless descriptive phrases to explain the dates. This chronology is an extremely specialized reference source and is likely to be of interest only to libraries or individuals who maintain an exhaustive reference collection on Lovecraft or supernatural horror. For other Lovecraft-related material see items 127, 184 and 215.

85. Carter, Lin. *Tolkien: A Look Behind the Lord of the Rings.* New York: Ballantine, 1969. 211p.

The cover copy of *A Look Behind the Lord of the Rings* (which is never the best gauge of the utility or value of a book in any case) is extremely misleading. The book was subtitled, possibly by an overzealous copywriter, as "a joyous exploration of Tolkien's classic trilogy and of the glorious tradition from which it grew." In fact, less than half the book has anything at all to do with the trilogy, and most of that half is devoted to lengthy plot synopses of the trilogy and *The Hobbit.* Carter has written exactly what the title states: a volume that represents a look *behind* the LOTR, a surprisingly thorough examination of the epic, mythology, Homer, Vergil, and other source texts and source authors used by Tolkien to fashion the philosophical underpinnings of LOTR. Carter yields, occasionally, to the temptation to make broad, sweeping statements which are indefensible on most grounds, e.g., "Tolkien is merely telling a story, and it has no overtones of symbolic meaning at all" or "In such a world it is not at all surprising that, when men invented writing and began putting down stories, his first literary adventures came out as fantasies." Authorial utterings are rarely the best guides to what a text means—Faulkner once called one of his novels a "potboiler," but that doesn't make it so—and because of the nature of fiction, virtually *any* story can be classified as a "fantasy," which means Carter's statement about fantasies is closely akin to saying water is wet. Despite the shortcomings, Carter's survey is a good introduction to the "pre-Tolkien" fantasy authors, devices, materials, and traditions which were used so expertly by Tolkien to create his popular fantasies. The general reader, interested only in the fantasies themselves, may have little use for the book, but readers and researchers intent on finding out more about the texts and traditions which contributed to the literary mechanics of Tolkien's "sub-creations" will find the book extremely valuable. Included in the volume are two appendices: a brief checklist of critical material on LOTR and a select bibliography, though there is no index. For other Tolkien-related material see items 35, 95, 104, 105, 123, 140 and 199.

86. Clareson, Thomas D. *Robert Silverberg.* Mercer Island, WA: Starmont House, 1983. 96p. MIN.

Silverberg is one of the most important twentieth century SF authors, though his fiction has yet to be evaluated at book length. (Taplinger scheduled a collection of critical essays on Silverberg several years ago for their Writers of the 21st Century series, but the project apparently was cancelled.) The dearth of Silverberg criticism alone makes this Starmont booklet a useful and important volume, but the fact that Clareson is one of the two most knowledgeable Silverberg critics in the field makes this Reader's Guide a milestone contribution to SF scholarship (the other major Silverberg critic is Brian Stableford). Clareson's book begins with a chronology of events in Silverberg's life and publication dates for his major works. The criticism is divided into six chapters or sections: Silverberg's early works, his "transitional" period, the "dark side" of his fiction, surveys of 11 novels, short fiction, and the beginning of the Majipoor cycle. The treatment of individual books is, by necessity, relatively brief, but critical evaluation is precise. Silverberg has been an important force in SF for more than three decades, and until someone does a full-length study, Clareson's survey will remain the major landmark in Silverberg studies. For other Silverberg-related material see items 163, 173 and 200; see Appendix I for an evaluation of the Starmont House SF/fantasy author critical series.

87. Collings, Michael R. *The Many Facets of Stephen King.* Mercer Island, WA: Starmont House, 1985. 190p.

It is to be expected that very popular writers will be the first to be treated extensively in critical analyses, so it is not surprising that the Stephen King book-and-film industry should spawn a Stephen-King-criticism industry. The purpose of *Facets*, Collings states, is to look at King's fiction from many different directions and in a non-chronological progression, but the tone of the introduction makes it very clear the book will make few evaluations—the purpose is laudatory rather than exploratory. Collings has done a great deal of King-related research, and has uncovered numerous thematic connections between King's columns in a college newspaper and his later novels and short stories, but he does little with the connections except point them out. It would seem that Collings plans to write many more books of King criticism to add to the ones he has authored already, and he refers constantly to his other books—both those already extant and those he apparently intends to write. Much of the criticism in this book is random, and peppered with misconceptions which arise from criticism that is wholly uncritical. For example, Collings suggests that King's use of a real person's name (David Bright) in *The Dead Zone* and a real college (Harrison College) in *Firestarter* "accentuates the realistic tone of the novel," but such accentuation presupposes the reader will be familiar with Bright and Harrison and, therefore, aware that the names are "real" rather than borrowed or fabricated. Few of King's mass market readers will know—or care—that the names are real rather than fictitious. There is some interesting biographical material in the book, especially in regard to the order in which King's novels were written, but the few strengths of the book are not enough to overcome the structural weaknesses. For other King-related materials see items 39, 89, 90, 128, 142 and 147; see Appendix I for an evaluation of the Starmont "Stephen King" critical series.

88. Collings, Michael R. *Piers Anthony.* Mercer Island, WA: Starmont House, 1983. 96p.

Critical studies are an important form of taking an author seriously, yet critical studies of authors of contemporary popular fiction must have a reasonable perspective above and beyond the criticism and analysis. Collings' volume of criticism of Piers Anthony lacks some of the perspective it needs to make it as useful as it should have been. The fiction surveyed in the study includes *Battle Circle*; the Aton novels; the Omnivore novels; *Macroscope*; the Cluster trilogy and the Tarot trilogy; the four Xanth novels; and selected short fiction. Collings often piles one quote upon another until the quotes control the text—and he often makes judgments of questionable value, such as a declaration that controversies concerning Anthony's reputed stubbornness have developed in Anthony a "toughness and independence of conception and execution that otherwise might not have been possible." Anthony has not worked through a second and parallel career lacking controversy, so there is no way to know if such a pronouncement is true. Collings writes about such things as "inverting the reader's expectations" by allowing the reader to see more humanity in a character as the novel progresses. This is a normal fiction-writing device, and is nothing to be singled out as an "inversion of reader expectation." Collings creates paper tigers only to banish them with a flourish, and his criticism and analysis are the poorer for it. The criticism in this booklet cannot be recommended on its own merits, but the book does contain much plot synopsis, description, and overview which could be of some help to those who would like to know more about Piers Anthony's fiction. See Appendix I for an evaluation of the Starmont House SF/fantasy author critical series.

89. Collings, Michael R. *Stephen King as Richard Bachman.* Mercer Island, WA: Starmont House, 1985. 168p.

Stephen King as Richard Bachman has the distinction of being the only book-length critical evaluation of the King novels published under the Bachman pseudonym, yet the book offers little of use or interest to anyone seeking to understand King's fiction and place it in some sort of cultural perspective. The criticism in this book vacillates awkwardly between two unhelpful attitudes—an argumentatively defensive posture on one hand, and embarrassingly uncritical praise for everything King writes on the other. Collings' ideas and conclusions are muddled: on one page he states that *Rage* is essentially plotless, and a few pages later he states that *The Long Walk* has a plot which is "more streamlined" than the plot of *Rage.* The volume, which deals exclusively with the five Bachman novels, devotes a chapter to each, and unendingly turns over every rock, examines with great interest what lies underneath—and then unblushingly praises it. If the Starmont books are to be taken at face value, then Stephen King apparently makes no mistakes, is breathtakingly original in every aspect of his writing, does absolutely nothing which might have been done differently or better, and, in fact, seems to be the one perfect writer ever to live and write in an imperfect world. The lack of perspective makes this book all but useless. Comprehensive collections of King criticism will need the book for the sake of completeness, but collections emphasizing quality and utility of critical explorations will not. For other King-related materials see items 39, 87, 90, 128, 142 and 147; see Appendix I for an evaluation of the Starmont "Stephen King" critical series.

90. Collings, Michael R. and David Engebretson. *The Shorter Works of Stephen King.* Mercer Island, WA: Starmont House, 1985. 202p.

This volume must be considered a marginally useful addition to King criticism because it provides plot synopses and commentary on most of King's short fiction, especially a number of items not readily available to the average reader/collector. Some of the commentary is not as useful as it might have been, and many of the plot synopses are done in an amateurish man-

ner, as if the critic were horrified at the idea of giving away an ending—in
fact, some of the synopses actually end with E.C.-comics-style "Heh heh,
that's all, kiddies" statements and ellipses. An entire page of the book is
missing (p. 38 is blank), and nonsense statements plague the text. "Anyone
who has ever stood in the middle of a Nebraska cornfield, unable to see
anything but tall, green, waving corn in every direction, knows the inexplicable fear that such a situation can generate" opens one sub-chapter of commentary; just why and how a Nebraska cornfield generates inexplicable fear,
or why a cornfield but not a wheatfield should be able to generate fear, or
why a Nebraska cornfield should be able to generate fear but not an Indiana
cornfield, are not explained. The authors of this study rely on the idea of
King-as-horrormaster to do their work for them. Their explanations are the
half-explanations of the elders in a mystical pseudo-discipline (King wor-
ship) who are initiating the neophytes, not the explanations and analyses of
critics who seek meaning, structure, value, or other attributes of fiction
wherever it is to be found. Nearly every story discussed in this volume is
judged to be somehow an "exception" to the King-rule of unrelenting fright
and horror. After the reader hears about the dozens of exceptions—from
mainstream fiction and SF to fantasy, mystery and symbolic fiction—he
may begin to wonder if there is enough material left over to form a body of
fiction which provides the general rule. Libraries attempting to keep a
"completist" King criticism collection will buy this book in any case, but
those exercising more care in acquisition may want to determine if the plot
synopses alone are reason enough to acquire the book. For other King-
related materials see items 39, 87, 89, 128, 142 and 147; see Appendix I for
an evaluation of the Starmont "Stephen King" critical series.

91.   Diskin, Lahna. *Theodore Sturgeon.* Mercer Island, WA: Starmont
House, 1981. 72p.
   No book-length study of Sturgeon's fiction exists (an ironic circumstance
in view of the fact that Sturgeon has been recognized for four decades as
one of the top stylists in the field), and that makes this Reader's Guide an
important contribution to SF criticism. The first four chapters are devoted to
the novels *The Dreaming Jewels, More Than Human, The Cosmic Rape* and
Venus Plus X, and the fifth examines about two dozen of Sturgeon's 200+
short stories. Included in the volume are a chronology and indices listing
primary works (fiction), primary works (non-fiction), and secondary materials. All three indices are annotated and are especially useful because the
separate short stories in the Sturgeon collections are briefly described. Much
of the criticism, especially of the short fiction, consists primarily of plot
synopsis and simple description of the works rather than evaluation or
analysis. But more of Sturgeon's fiction is discussed in this booklet than in

any other single source, so in spite of minor shortcomings, Diskin's book is an important source of information on one of the most respected and admired writers in the SF/fantasy genre. See Appendix I for an evaluation of the Starmont House SF/fantasy author critical series.

92.   Dozois, Gardner R. *The Fiction of James Tiptree, Jr.* New York: Algol Press, 1977. Unpaginated (32). San Bernardino, CA: Borgo Press, 1983. MIN.

Dozois' survey of Tiptree's fiction was written before the publication of the first Tiptree novel, and at a time when it still was assumed that Tiptree was a man. It was the first study of Tiptree, but the first six pages, containing a mixture of known biographical data about Tiptree and a great deal of groping-in-the-dark speculation, became so much useless wordage when Tiptree let it be known "he" was a woman. The survey is brief, but the critical judgments are sound and well-expressed. It is an anomaly that even the best and worthiest SF authors have not been properly evaluated in book-length surveys—major names like Heinlein and Asimov will rate two or more critical volumes each, but most SF authors have yet to be the subject of adequate unified surveys. The short survey or "mini-book" seems to be the most popular vehicle for single-author analysis in the SF field today. Because of the shortage of reliable critical materials on most SF authors, this booklet on Tiptree is a major contribution to SF criticism. It badly needs to be revised, expanded, and updated to include Tiptree's entire canon (Tiptree/Sheldon is now deceased), but to date it is the best single essay on Tiptree in existence. For other Tiptree-related material see item 130.

93.   Ellik, Ronald and William Evans. *The Universes of E.E. Smith.* Chicago: Advent, 1966. 272p. RSF, SRB.

Universes is a double concordance. The first part is a concordance to the Lensman novels, and the second is a concordance to the Skylark novels. E.E. Smith's novels generally are considered to the be genesis of space opera, so this book is an important study aid for research into E.E. Smith's fiction. Included are an explanation of Smith's "classification system" for categorizing "all animal life encountered in the Lensman universe," brief introductions to the Lensman and Skylark novels, genealogical charts for the characters, a bibliography of primary and secondary materials, and a "page concordance" (all page references in this book are to the original versions, so the page references are an aid for readers who have access only to the more recent paperback editions). The introduction is by James H. Schmitz. There are some illogically pedantic entries—such as an escape plan alphabetized as "Able, Operation" rather than "Operation Able"—but *Universes* is the single greatest compilation of information about the Skylark and Lensman books, and is recommended for collections emphasizing the "space opera" subgenre of SF.

94. Fonstad, Karen Wynn. *The Atlas of Pern.* New York: Del Rey/ Ballantine, 1984. 169p. London: Corgi Books, 1985.

Concordances and atlases for fantasy worlds are becoming popular in their own right, but in some ways can be a necessity for understanding the complicated geography, chronology, genealogy, and other aspects of multi-volume series books with complex societies. The Pern atlas has a section with regional maps, then four sections containing maps which explain different Anne McCaffrey novels or groups of novels, plus notes, selected references, and an index of place names. The volume consists not only of maps but has also a great deal of text explaining a multitude of concepts, place names, processes, social customs, and chronologies of events. Many of the maps in this volume are extremely detailed, and diagrams provide visual reference for geographic areas, dwellings, and even the dragons of McCaffrey's popular series. Because the atlas was prepared with the permission, cooperation and assistance of McCaffrey, the volume should provide a useful overview and general reference not only for fans but for anyone contemplating critical evaluation of McCaffrey's fiction. The book can be appreciated on its own merits as a nicely produced "borderline art book" as well, though it is a specialty item, directed primarily at hardcore McCaffrey fans and is not really organized as a pure reference volume. Recommended primarily for fans, collectors, and library collections emphasizing genre fantasy by contemporary popular authors.

95. Foster, Robert. *The Complete Guide to Middle-Earth: From the Hobbit to the Silmarillion.* New York: Ballantine/Del Rey, 1978. SRB, TYS.

For a body of work as large and complex as Tolkien's, a glossary can be a useful quick reference tool for keeping characters, names, dates, locations, geographical features, concepts, genealogy and other facts in perspective. Foster's guide is more than adequate for the purpose, in some cases providing more information than a reader may be able to assimilate effectively (though this is not necessarily Foster's fault—it is a problem of the richness, complexity, depth and detail to be found in Tolkien's work). While proceeding through the Tolkien canon, a reader who uses the Foster glossary can maintain a more complete view of characters, chronology and geography in Tolkien's epic masterpiece. A helpful feature of the Foster book is a concordance which relates the chapters and page numbers of the Ballantine and the revised Houghton-Mifflin editions of the Tolkien books. Several genealogical charts are included. Character entries include birth and death dates, and all entries have notations identifying the work or works in which the character or other entry may be found. In cases where Tolkien himself provided information on the origin or meaning of a word, that information is included in the entry (e.g., Mordor="black land"). Besides simple identification of characters, places, events, and so on, the glossary provides a tremendous amount of historical information which places many of the entries in an historical framework that can be easier to understand than searching out bits and pieces of the information scattered throughout several novels. Foster's book is highly recommended for collections emphasizing modern fantasy in general or Tolkien's fiction in particular. For other Tolkien-related material see items 35, 85, 104, 105, 123, 140 and 199.

96. Frane, Jeff. *Fritz Leiber*. Mercer Island, WA: Starmont House, 1980. 64p. MIN, SRB.

It would have been impossible for Frane to examine all of Leiber's fiction in the space of 50 pages—a fact which Frane himself notes in the book—but he does an excellent job of examining the major accomplishments in the Leiber canon. The first eight chapters comprise: a chronology; an introduction with biographical information; and discussions of *Conjure Wife; Gather, Darkness;* the Change War stories; *The Wanderer* and *A Specter is Haunting Texas;* the Fafhrd and Gray Mouser stories; and general themes and several short stories. Chapter nine is an annotated primary bibliography complete with extensive synopses and lists of short stories included in collections; and the last chapter is a very detailed annotated secondary bibliography contributed by Roger Schlobin. Leiber is yet another neglected SF/fantasy writer who, paradoxically, is recognized as a master of the form; Frane's book is a readable, knowledgeable and engaging first step toward reducing the level of that neglect. See Appendix I for an evaluation of the Starmont House SF/fantasy author critical series.

97. Franklin, H. Bruce. *Robert A. Heinlein: America As Science Fiction.* New York: Oxford University Press, 1980. 232p. MIN.

In perceptive acuity and clarity of expression, Franklin's study is the best of the three extant book-length critical appraisals of Heinlein. The Olander and Greenberg volume (item 118) is a collection of unrelated articles; the two Borgo Press booklets by Slusser (items 132 and 136) cover too much material in too short a space; and the Panshin book (item 120), though a groundbreaking effort, was the first volume of criticism on Heinlein, and therefore is now the most out-of-date. Franklin's book makes a more obvious effort to place Heinlein in the social, political and technological milieu that seems to have influenced his fiction. Franklin divides Heinlein's novels and short stories into five groups: the pre-war fiction; 1947-1959; the 1960s; the 1970s; and Heinlein's first novel of the 1980s (*The Number of the*

Beast—). An introductory biographical chapter is the best and most extensive biographical sketch on Heinlein currently in print, and is the result of original research by Franklin in the area near Heinlein's childhood home. Franklin's interpretation of Heinlein may be excessively political, but in this case the author under examination has been so apparently hyper-political himself that a political view is understandable if not more or less mandatory. For good or ill, Heinlein is the third of the "big three" SF authors of all time—Verne, Wells and Heinlein—and has had more influence on the shape and direction of modern SF than any other twentieth century author. Besides a vast body of work, most of which remains perpetually in print, Heinlein is credited with virtually creating most of the modern SF markets (TV, film, slick magazine, juvenile book publishing, etc.). Most criticism of Heinlein's work concentrates on faults, which are variously identified as objectionably excessive political content, militarism, the typical "Heinlein mouthpiece" character, and so on, but Franklin's study balances criticism of excesses with praise of accomplishments better than other published works of Heinlein criticism. Large libraries, and those with extensive collections of SF criticism, will need all existing volumes of Heinlein criticism; those with more restricted holdings may want to choose the Panshin volume for undergraduate work and the Franklin book for students and researchers working at higher levels. For other Heinlein-related materials see items 24, 118, 120, 129, 132 and 136.

98. Gordon, Joan. *Joe Haldeman.* Mercer Island, WA: Starmont House, 1980. 64p. MIN, SRB.

Joe Haldeman has not been a prolific author, so the limited space in a "booklet" of criticism is not as restrictive as it might be for other authors. Gordon discusses four novels and a short story collection in separate chapters: *War Year, The Forever War, Mindbridge, All My Sins Remembered* and *Infinite Dreams.* The introductory chapter presents a variety of biographical information interspersed with long quotes from an interview with Haldeman. The book suffers slightly from a "pre-positive" point of view— obviously, a critic must believe there is something positive to be gained from a study of an author's fiction, or the effort would be essentially useless, yet to be too openly adoring implies a strong possibility that mistakes or weaknesses will be ignored. The evaluations of Haldeman's fiction are lengthy and reasonably thorough. This Starmont Reader's Guide is the first source of organized commentary on Haldeman; though the book is now several years out of date, it is still the basic text for Haldeman criticism and analysis. See Appendix I for an evaluation of the Starmont House SF/ fantasy author critical series.

99. Haining, Peter. *The Dracula Centenary Book.* London: Souvenir Press, 1987. 159p.

A central element of the horror tradition is the Dracula mythos, a modern mythology with intermingled components of legend and fact. In this centenary book, Peter Haining examines all aspects of the Dracula tradition. Chapter One is a biography of Bram Stoker; Chapter Two is an account of the recent discovery of the original manuscript of Stoker's famous novel; other chapters are devoted to explanations of the specific legends and myths incorporated into Stoker's book, the historical figures whose lives contributed to the legend (Prince Vlad and Countess Bathery), and surveys of the films and actors that have contributed to the growth of the Dracula film cult. The volume is profusely illustrated and includes six appendices: a short essay on Transylvania superstitions, a checklist of incidents from the thirteenth to the twentieth centuries involving apparent incidents of vampirism, a short essay by Bela Lugosi ("I Like Playing Dracula"), a list of Dracula films, an essay by Dr. David H. Dolphin which offers some scientific explanations for symptoms commonly associated with vampirism, and the names and addresses of six British and American Dracula societies. Haining is a widely recognized expert on the horror genre, and *The Dracula Centenary Book* is a valuable contribution to horror film and fiction scholarship, though it suffers from two serious omissions: it has neither an index nor a checklist of major novels incorporating elements of the Dracula theme.

100. Hammond, J.R. *An H.G. Wells Companion: A Guide to the Novels, Romances and Short Stories.* New York: Barnes & Noble, 1979. 288p.

H.G. Wells is remembered chiefly for his science fiction (or "scientific romances"), at least among the general reading public, but his reputation today rests principally upon a very small number of his books. Hammond's *Companion* may help the average reader (or average SF reader) to realize more of the full extent of Wells' literary achievements. The book begins with a brief preface, a chapter of background and biography, and a chapter on Wells' literary reputation. Part II is a dictionary containing the titles of all the "novels, romances, short stories and fictional essays," and brief descriptions of where these works were first published, whether they were later reprinted in collections, etc. Part III is a critical survey of the short stories. Beginning with Part IV, Hammond provides descriptions, plot summaries, and critical evaluations of 23 romances in essays of two to four pages each, and Part V is a similar survey of 30 novels. Part VI is a "Key to Characters and Locations" (characters and locations "having a significant role in the novels and stories") and several appendices provide lists of film versions of Wells' works; references; a select bibliography (works, letters, bibliography, biography, criticism); and an index. The novels of primary interest to the SF reader are listed/evaluated in Part IV (*The Time Machine, The Island of Dr. Moreau, The Invisible Man, The War of the Worlds, When the Sleeper Wakes, The First Men in the Moon, The Food of the Gods, In The Days of the Comet, Men Like Gods, The Shape of Things to Come*, etc.), but besides providing numerous types of useful access to Wells' fiction, the book may allow even those interested only in a limited area of Wells' output to appreciate the size and diversity of his complete body of work. Highly recommended for any library serving research in general SF studies, H.G. Wells, or "key author" research on major SF writers. For other Wells-related material see items 34, 108 and 139.

101. Holland, Thomas R. *Vonnegut's Major Works.* Lincoln, NE: Cliff's Notes, 1973. 58p. MIN.

The Cliff's Notes Vonnegut survey is adequate, if somewhat mechanical, and in general serves the purpose for which it was intended. It is, however, out of date, and badly needs updating to include Vonnegut's more recent works. The plays and novels discussed in the booklet include *Player Piano; The Sirens of Titan; Mother Night; Cat's Cradle; God Bless You, Mr. Rosewater; Slaughterhouse Five; Happy Birthday, Wanda June;* and *Breakfast of Champions.* The survey is repititive, and some aspects—such as the one-paragraph "round up" discussions of major themes and the elementary "questions for review"—are unimaginative academic fluff-work which accomplish little except to provide enough of the required material to fill up a given amount of space. Surveys as dull and mechanical as this one do little to encourage the appreciation of any form of literature, and may do more harm than good by allowing students to believe a colorless collection of synopses can explain the "meaning" or "value" of a body of work as rich and complex as Vonnegut's fiction. The use of this booklet should be discouraged whenever possible. When available in paperback, the Reed survey of Vonnegut (item 124) is the preferred book. For other Vonnegut-related materials see items 112, 124.

102. Hollow, John. *Against the Night, The Stars; The Science Fiction of Arthur C. Clarke.* New York: Harcourt Brace Jovanovich, 1983. 197p.

Hollow's study of Calrke is extremely methodical, spanning the entire body of Clarke fiction from the early short stories and novels to *2010.* In fact, the coverage of short fiction is not only broad but quite thorough and extensive, and is one of the great strengths of this critical survey. Hollow gathers into his critical fold virtually all Clarke's work, including the "adventure novel for adolescents" *Dolphin Island* and the non-SF novel *Glide Path.* The study is, in part, an intensive search for influences. Clarke's fiction does not lack influences—some of which Hollow finds himself, others he identifies with help from Clarke's essays and introductions, and still others were previously catalogued by other critics. The shopping list of direct influences includes Stapledon, Hilton, and Wells, among others, the problem being that almost exactly the same influences could be cited for any SF writer who began his or her career before 1970. Wells is invoked throughout, almost to the point that Clarke seems to be offered as a contemporary stand-in for Wells; both Clarke and Wells wrote short stories titled "The Star," for example, and these are examined together in a "parallel analysis." The criticism is generally even-handed and not given to flights into the abstruse and theoretical, so the book is recommended as a good author study at the undergraduate level. Includes a bibliography of Clarke's books (short stories are listed only as contents identification for collections) and a bibliography of selected criticism (not annotated). There is no index. For other Clarke-related material see items 116, 137, 201, 252 and 253.

103. Ketterer, David. *Imprisoned in a Tesseract: The Life and Work of James Blish.* Kent, OH: Kent State University Press, 1987. 410p.

Ketterer's literary biography of Blish may be taken as a model for future biographies of SF writers. Until the publication of this volume (and Warrick's volume on Philip K. Dick), the only SF writers to be awarded the distinction of full-length biographical and critical treatment were Asimov and Heinlein (not including critical anthologies, the Borgo and Starmont "booklets," or the lavish treatment afforded "cult figure" writers such as Lovecraft or Burroughs). Ketterer's book far surpasses previous efforts, and sets a new standard for the SF field. The biography is divided into three sections: Science Fiction Futures; Historical Models; and The Nub of Fantasy. The notes are contained in a separate section, and the book includes a primary bibliography, a secondary bibliography, and an index. The research for *Imprisoned in a Tesseract* was meticulous and impeccable; sources include letters, and various chapters list and discuss not only the well-known works, such as *A Case of Conscience*, but unpublished works and unfinished fragments as well. There are numerous photos, including a pencil sketch of Blish, a photograph of his notes for the short story "How Beautiful with Banners," and magazine cover reproductions. The primary bibliography is arranged chronologically and includes not only Blish's SF work, but detective, western, jungle, and sports stories, as well as other types of material. The Ketterer literary biography is the best SF author biography published to date, and is an essential acquisition for any collection with a subject emphasis in SF author criticism and biography. For other Blish-related materials see items 7, 8 and 138.

104. Kilby, Clyde S. *Tolkien & The Silmarillion.* Wheaton, IL: Harold Shaw, 1976. 89p. RSF.

In his last years Tolkien strictly limited the number of people who could meet with him and otherwise place demands on his time. Clyde Kilby was one of the few who was allowed access to Tolkien during those final years. This small book is an account of the summer Kilby spent assisting Tolkien, reading through his papers and making suggestions for works that might be immediately publishable. It is an informal account of Kilby's summer as friend, confidant and "editorial and critical assistant" (the quote marks denote Tolkien's own description of Kilby's duties), and yet within the space of 90 pages Kilby provides a portrait of Tolkien as man, teacher, scholar and writer; a preliminary chronology of Tolkien's major works; numerous letters written by Tolkien and sent to Kilby; brief and tantalizing descriptions of works still unpublished at the time; and consideration of Tolkien as a Christian writer and as a member of the famous informal writers' club The Inklings (which group included C.S. Lewis and Charles Williams). The book is an excellent supplement to the Tolkien biographies, and an important addition to any collection with extensive Tolkien holdings or a subject area emphasis in modern fantasy or biographies of modern fantasy writers. For other Tolkien-related materials see items 35, 85, 95, 105, 123, 140 and 199.

105. Kocher, Paul Harold. *Master of Middle Earth: The Fiction of J.R.R. Tolkien.* Boston: Houghton Mifflin, 1972. New York: Del Rey/Ballantine, 1977. 233p. AOW, RSF, SRB, TYS.

Tolkien's fantasies are a complex literary achievement which can be read and accepted on many different levels. Anyone who discovers Tolkien, and immediately determines that he or she would like to understand more than just the top layers of Tolkien's narratives, will need some assistance in the form of a bioliterary introduction which explores beneath the surface meanings and obvious parallels in Tolkien's work. Kocher's book is generally recognized to be the best current "guide" to Tolkien, though a glance at the table of contents can be misleading. There are seven chapters, apparently devoted to several general topic areas, but the chapters range widely through the entire Tolkien canon, including the novels, short stories, criticism and poetry. Kocher constructs (or perhaps uncovers) Tolkien's elaborate system of convictions about how fiction should operate, and provides examples of how those convictions were translated into epic fantasy. Tolkien's work is viewed from several useful points of view, including philology, linguistics, philosophy, and theology. Some aspects of biography, and how Tolkien's life may have affected his art, were a mandatory inclusion, but Kocher treads lightly in biographical territory, a practice Tolkien himself recommended. If there is a flaw in Kocher's work, it is a tendency to delve too deeply or range too widely for the reader unfamiliar with Tolkien's work to follow easily. Overall, the volume is a good mix of the scholarly and the popular—there are moderately extensive notes, for example, but they are contained in a separate section for optional consultation. The book is indexed, and is the best available general introduction and guide to Tolkien. The book is recommended for collections with particular emphasis in Tolkien or modern fantasy. For other Tolkien-related materials see items 35, 85, 95, 104, 123, 140 and 199.

106. Leatherdale, Clive, ed. *The Origins of Dracula: The Background to Bram Stoker's Gothic Masterpiece.* London: William Kimber, 1987. 239p.

Count Dracula and the concept of vampirism form one of the most important wellsprings of modern horror. Leatherdale's study of the sources which contributed to Stoker's *Dracula* is a "source text sampler" which presents relevant chapters or pages from books consulted by Stoker during the research phase of the writing of his gothic horror masterpiece. Information on Stoker's exact research sources was unknown for more than 70 years; historical parallels had been firmly established (Vlad the Impaler, the Countess of Bathory, etc.), but the discovery of the original manuscript of *Dracula*, and the research notes for the novel, have contributed substantially to an understanding of the conscious choices made by Stoker in his transformation of history, legend, superstition and myth into purposeful and powerful fiction. Subjects surveyed by the 17 selections include burial customs, vampirism, the history of Transylvania, torture, werewolves (lycanthropy), and somnambulism/mesmerism/hypnosis, among others. Authors represented by the excerpted material: Sabine Baring-Gould, Herbert Mayo, Rushton M. Dorman, Emily Gerard, and others. An appendix provides the complete list of sources for *Dracula* from Stoker's research notes. More than a dozen black and white photos are included. The main introduction, and separate chapter introductions, help overcome the fragmental nature of text selections which cover a wide range of topics and a period of several hundred years. Though detailed source studies generally are not of interest to students or researchers working on the undergraduate level, Leatherdale's anthology contributes substantially to a clearer understanding of one of the novels upon which the entire horror genre is based, so the book must be recommended for any collection with extensive resources for horror fiction research.

107. Lupoff, Richard A. *Edgar Rice Burroughs: Master of Adventure.* New York: Canaveral Press, 1965; New York: Ace, 1968; revised edition, 1975. 317p. AOW, SRB, TYS.

Lupoff is a recognized Burroughs expert and his volume *Master of Adventure* is generally accepted to be one of the best critical appraisals ever done on Burroughs. The hardcover edition, when it can be obtained, is more desirable for library use, but the Ace paperback edition contains corrections and some expanded information not in the first hardcover edition. Coverage of Burroughs is so thorough, and the bibliographic research so meticulous, the book serves three purposes—biography, critical evaluation and bibliography. Information on copyright dates, editorial expurgations, editions, and other bibliographic details is extensive, but unfortunately the broad range of bibliographic information is not presented in a separate bibliographic listing. There is a bibliography of works cited, though the volume lacks an index. Lupoff's book is an important addition to any collection which emphasizes Burroughs or modern heroic/epic fantasy. For other Burroughs-related materials see items 125 and 212.

108. McConnell, Frank. *The Science Fiction of H.G. Wells.* New York: Oxford University Press, 1981. 235p.

McConnell's book on Wells concentrates on the "science fiction"—that is, the "scientific romances," most of which were published in the two decades 1895-1914—the works for which he is primarily remembered despite a lifetime of book-writing which included every kind of book from novels and collections to encyclopedias and an autobiography. In the first chapter McConnell establishes the background and social context into which Wells was born, and the latter chapters examine specific novels. McConnell states that Wells' realistic works should be read alongside the scientific romances because the themes, if not settings and action, are quite similar: "his theme was obsessively that of middle-class man's chances for survival in a world which through the accumulated weight of technology and the inexorable pressures of evolutionary history threatens his life." Despite the occasional description of one of the realistic novels, however, the focus in this monograph is on the scientific romances or "SF" Wells produced in his early years as a writer. *The Time Machine* and *The Island of Dr. Moreau* are called "evolutionary fables," and other works in the Wells SF canon which are examined at length include *The Invisible Man, The War of the Worlds, The First Men in the Moon, The Food of the Gods,* and *In the Days of the Comet.* A final long chapter considers the later books and Wells' gradual change from a novelist to a social propagandist. McConnell's book is suitable for use at the undergraduate level or above, and is recommended for any collection with a need for general background research sources for science fiction, or specific research volumes on the most important nineteenth and twentieth century SF authors. For other Wells-related material see items 34, 100 and 139.

109. McNelly, Willis E. *The Dune Encyclopedia.* New York: Berkley Books, 1984. 526p.

The Dune Encyclopedia is at once both more and less than a companion or concordance to the *Dune* books. It begins with basic information taken from Herbert's popular novel series, but that information is fleshed out, elaborated upon, embroidered, detailed and footnoted. There are chronologies, succession lists, and even some illustrations. In many cases, too much information is given. Entries for Arrakis, for example, include five pages on "Arrakis, Astronomical Aspects of"; four pages on "Arrakis, Atmosphere of before the Atreides"; five pages on "Arrakis, Ecological Transformation of"; four pages of "Arrakis, Geology"; and two pages of "Arrakis, Oxygen Saga." The book does serve as a concordance of sorts, but many of the entries would be difficult for an "uninitiated" reader to locate. Such an extensively interpolated concordance goes far beyond the bounds of a reference book and becomes a fictional experience in its own right. Thus the book may have more use—and appeal—for dedicated *Dune* fans than for critics, researchers, or general readers who would like to take a word, character or idea from the *Dune* context and find out more about it. Now that Herbert is deceased and no more Herbert-authored *Dune* books will be forthcoming, *The Dune Encyclopedia* will serve as one more brick in the construct of Herbert's desert-world mythology; the brick was not contributed by Herbert himself, but for dedicated fans that fact will hardly matter. The book is for readers who respond favorably to immersion in the words, concepts, characters and conflicts of the *Dune* novels; it has little utility as a reference or research tool. For other Herbert-related materials see items 33 and 114.

110. Mathews, Richard. *The Clockwork Universe of Anthony Burgess.* San Bernardino, CA: Borgo Press, 1978. 63p. MIN.

The preface to Mathews' study of Burgess makes it quite clear what direction the monograph will take—in the space of a single paragraph it is declared that Burgess "may very well be the greatest living English novelist" and he is described as "more flexible and more brilliant than many of his more highly-touted contemporaries among American authors." Almost defensive in tone, the study examines at some length (three to eight pages each) the novels *A Vision of Battlements, Time for a Tiger, The Enemy in the Blanket, Beds in the East, The Doctor is Sick, A Clockwork Orange, The Wanting Seed* and *One Hand Clapping*; other works are mentioned in briefer contexts. Burgess is not generally recognized as an SF writer (in the same way that Sinclair Lewis and George Orwell are not generally recognized to be SF writers *per se*), though of his futuristic novels, *A Clockwork Orange* is considered a classic science fictional exploration of violence and social/ psychological conditioning in a dystopianesque mode. The regularity with which the title of Burgess' one "classic SF" novel is invoked may be some- what out of proportion to its actual importance within the SF field, but a good SF research collection should have some research materials pertaining to Burgess and *Clockwork*; Mathews' study is a reliable introduction to Burgess for small to medium collections, though larger collections may need one of the existing book-length Burgess studies for more expansive coverage. See Appendix I for an evaluation of the Borgo Press SF/fantasy author critical series.

111. Mathews, Richard. *Worlds Beyond the World: The Fantastic Vision of William Morris.* San Bernardino, CA: Borgo Press, 1978. 63p. MIN.

William Morris, nineteenth century Renaissance man—designer, printer, poet, political activist, author—generally is considered to be the originator of the modern fantasy genre. Mathew's survey of Morris' fiction is divided into five sections, and specific sub-sections are devoted to separate short stories and novels: "The Story of the Unknown Church," "Lindenbourg Pool," "A Dream," "Gertha's Lovers," "Svend and His Brethren," "The Hollow Land," "Golden Wings," *A Dream of John Ball, The House of the Wolfings, The Roots of the Mountains, News From Nowhere, The Glittering Plains, The Well at the World's End, The Wood Beyond the World, Child Christopher and Goldilind the Fair, The Water of the Wondrous Isles,* and *The Sundering Flood.* Coverage is broad but as thorough as could be expected with so many works to cover in so short a space. The volume includes a short list of biographical and critical sources. The booklet is poorly designed—there is no table of contents and no index, so locating the discussion of a particular work is a mildly inconvenient matter. Mathews' commentary, explication and critical evaluations are masterful and precise; the booklet, because of the broad coverage in a compact text, is an excellent introduction to the subject author, though the book is likely to be most use- ful above the undergraduate level. The volume is a highly recommended acquisition for collections emphasizing nineteenth century fantasy or fantasy authors. See Appendix I for an evaluation of the Borgo Press SF/fantasy author critical series.

112. Mayo, Clark. *Kurt Vonnegut: The Gospel from Outer Space.* San Bernardino, CA: Borgo Press, 1977. 64p. MIN.

Vonnegut is not particularly fond of being called an SF writer, but he cannot seem to resist using many of the devices and themes commonly (and strongly) associated with SF. Mayo's study seeks to interpret Vonnegut's fiction as a literary phenomenon significant both to SF and the mainstream, and is therefore more successful than some other critics in making his analysis comprehensible (not to mention relevant) to the "average" reader; many Vonnegut "studies" assume no significant SF connection because the author's fiction is "too good" to have genre origins. As Mayo points out, Vonnegut first published his short stories in the SF pulps (perhaps more accurately the SF "digests") and switched to the mainstream only after he had spent years learning and perfecting his craft. The two unifying ideas in this analysis are descriptions: the philosophy behind Vonnegut's fiction considered as "naive vision" and the structure of the novels as "Gestalt fiction." These ideas limit the discussion somewhat arbitrarily, but Mayo still adequately covers a sufficient number of novels/works (from *Player Piano* to *Slapstick* and including some short stories and plays) to make the booklet a readable and useful introduction to Vonnegut's fiction. The "biography" is limited to a three-sentence paragraph on the last page, and a bibliography lists the published books through *Slapstick* (1976). For other Vonnegut-related material see also items 101 and 124. See Appendix I for an evaluation of the Borgo Press SF/fantasy author critical series.

113.   Miesel, Sandra. *Against Time's Arrow: The High Crusade of Poul Anderson.* San Bernardino, CA: Borgo Press, 1978. 64p. MIN.

Poul Anderson's fiction has a strong infusion of mythology, and Miesel uses the mythic elements as one part of a two-part critical analysis. The other part of the analysis is a consideration of Anderson's work as a multifaceted treatment of the concept of entropy. The criticism is often vague and unfocussed, and coverage is limited. Despite the space available in 61 pages of text, Miesel discusses only *Operation Chaos, The Broken Sword,* "The Queen of Air and Darkness," *World Without Stars, The Night Face,* "Goat Song," "Tomorrow's Children," *The Enemy Stars* and *Tau Zero.* Other works are mentioned briefly. As with most of the more prolific SF authors, this Reader's Guide is more a brief critical "sampler" than a survey, and in fact has an air of being the first part of a longer and more thorough work. There is no table of contents and no index, and the separate sections are not titled by the worked discussed—such chapter heads as "Fetters of Madness" and "The Ultimate Emptiness" make it difficult to locate discussions of individual works. The volume includes a bibliography of Anderson's works. The book is long on synopses and rambling associations and short on useful criticism, but in view of the lack of major critical sources on Anderson, it must be recommended as an important contribution to SF criticism. See

Appendix I for an evaluation of the Borgo Press SF/fantasy author critical series.

114.   Miller, David M. *Frank Herbert.* Mercer Island, WA: Starmont House, 1980. 70p. MIN, SRB.

With a series sub-title like "Reader's Guides," it might be expected that individual volumes would provide introduction and preliminary access on the undergraduate level, but such is not the case for the *Frank Herbert* volume. Miller has produced a book which reads like a detailed outline for a dissertation rather than an aid to the study, comprehension and appreciation of a body of fiction. The book is liberally strewn with phrases such as "Prince Irulan's headnote, rather than being narratively proleptic, is grandly sententious" and "...a fulcrum upon which the macro-organism of sentience teeters in the imperative process of maintaining dynamic homeostasis." Such phrasing sends more readers to the dictionary than it does to the primary work. Varying levels of critical complexity and intricacy are necessary to serve the diverse needs of readers with different levels of critical acumen, but when criticism is so self-aware as to be divorced from the fiction it describes, becoming an end in itself, it no longer serves its intended purpose. Miller's prefatory material includes a chronology and brief biographical fact sheet. There are lists of characters, and the novels are discussed in turn with—unsurprisingly—more discussion devoted to the *Dune* volumes than to the others. Herbert's short stories are glossed over in less than two pages; there is an annotated primary bibliography, an annotated secondary bibliography, and an index. There is so little criticism on SF authors that even a disjointed and self-indulgent volume with a too-heavy reliance on stilted critical jargon has some value, but in this case of this Reader's Guide the general reader cannot expect much guidance. For other Herbert-related materials see items 33 and 109; see Appendix I for an evaluation of the Starmont House SF/fantasy author critical series.

115.   Mogen, David. *Ray Bradbury.* Boston: Twayne/G.K. Hall, 1986. 186p.

Ray Bradbury, more than any other writer (with the possible exception of Vonnegut), is identified both as a charter member of the unofficial SF/fantasy "author's guild," and yet an outsider whose achievements and recognition in the mainstream literary world make his SF/fantasy credentials suspect if not outright invalid. Mogen's study captures this career-dichotomy and reader-ambivalence eloquently in a well-ordered study structured around themes rather than individual works or chronological periods. The first three chapters deal with biography, the controversy surrounding Bradbury's mixed mainstream/SF reputation and the lack of full acceptance in

either camp, and Bradbury's literary style. Later chapters examine Bradbury's early "weird fiction," the Green Town novels (*Dandelion Wine* and
Something Wicked This Way Comes), realist fiction, detective fiction, other
media (films, drama, poetry), and a final chapter surveys Bradbury's overall
achievement. Because of his position as one of the major short story writers
of the twentieth century, Bradbury, more than any other SF-related author
(except, perhaps, Heinlein and Vonnegut), has been the subject of intensive
critical analysis; many of these studies have been book-length. Mogen's
study is less "novel" or "story" oriented than it is "theme" or "idea"
oriented; researchers seeking long critical analyses of specific works will
not find them here. The structure of the analysis allows examination in
numerous contexts, but rather than a unified analysis of, for example, *Dandelion Wine* from page 50 to page 70, various aspects of the novel are discussed at more than a dozen different points throughout the volume. This
can be inconvenient for those seeking single-work analyses, but is a singu-
larly useful approach for a broad-spectrum author study intended to examine
many different themes or ideas to be found in the stories and novels in an
author's canon. The study is particularly helpful because it treats Bradbury
as an artist who works in many genres and media, and not one-
dimensionally as an SF/fantasy author. The book includes a select bibliography of primary sources, a select bibliography of secondary sources, and an
index. Mogen's book is the best full-length Bradbury study published to
date, partly because of the multi-media consideration, and is highly recommended for collections with SF author study emphasis supporting SF
research on any level. For other Bradbury-related material see items 117
and 131.

116. Olander, Joseph D. and Martin Harry Greenberg. *Arthur C.
Clarke.* New York: Taplinger, 1977. 254p. MIN, SRB.

Contributors to the Clarke volume in the Taplinger *Writers of the 21st
Century* series include Peter Brigg, Thomas D. Clareson, E. Michael Thron,
Betsy Harfst, Robert Plank, Alan B. Howes, Eugene Tanzy, David N.
Samuelson and John Huntington. The nine articles contained in the collection examine such diverse aspects of Clarke's fiction as aliens, mythic content, expectation and surprise in *Childhood's End*, the development of
Clarke's themes in his nonfiction, and the "myth of progress" in Clarke's
fiction. Unsurprisingly, the book/film *2001* and the novel *Childhood's End*
both are mentioned often, but the critical survey actually is more wide-
ranging than might be expected. Clarke, perhaps more than most SF writers
whose status as scientists puts their fiction squarely on the "hard science"
end of the SF spectrum, deals with religious issues ("The Nine Billion
Names of God," "The Star," *Childhood's End*), and this aspect of his writ-

ing is not ignored in the book even though there is no single essay with
religion as its central focus. Clareson's essay is particularly useful, survey-
ing the idea of "cosmic loneliness" through the entire body of Clarke's fiction and nonfiction from the 1940s to *Rendezvous with Rama*. This collection of articles is a landmark contribution to Clarke criticism. For other
Clarke-related material see items 102, 137, 201, 252 and 253; see Appendix
I for an evaluation of the Taplinger *Writers of the 21st Century* series.

117. Olander, Joseph D. and Martin Harry Greenberg. *Ray Bradbury.*
New York: Taplinger, 1980. 248p. MIN, SRB.

Though Bradbury has been considered a major SF/fantasy author for several decades, criticism and analysis of his fiction has been piecemeal until
fairly recently. This volume was the first to collect a representative sample
of critical approaches to a satisfying variety of different aspects of his fiction. The eight articles were contributed by Willis E. McNelly and A. James
Stupple, Gary K. Wolfe, Edward J. Gallagher, Marvin E. Mengeling, Eric S.
Rabkin, Lahna Diskin, Steven Dimeo, and Hazel Pierce. Topics discussed
by the critics include Bradbury's use of the "frontier myth," the thematic
structure of *The Martian Chronicles*, Bradbury's attitudes toward science,
technology and religion, Bradbury and the Gothic tradition, children in
Bradbury's fiction, etc. Considering that this pioneering effort to gather a
large body of Bradbury criticism between two covers was to have only a
certain amount of space, the novel *The Martian Chronicles* receives perhaps
a bit too much coverage—but in all fairness, the book is one of the three or
four best-known Bradbury titles, so perhaps the wordage was not too unrea-
sonably distributed. The bibliography, by Marshall B. Tymn, is extensive,
and includes such items as teleplays written by Bradbury; there is also a
bibliography of "selected criticism" listing 28 articles, one booklet (in the
Borgo Press series) and one book (a collector's edition containing an assort-
ment of previously unpublished work). As the first major anthology of critical analysis of the fiction of Ray Bradbury, this volume is part of the foundation of an SF collection which emphasizes author studies. For other
Bradbury-related materials see items 115 and 131; see Appendix I for an
evaluation of the Taplinger *Writers of the 21st Century* series.

118. Olander, Joseph D. and Martin Harry Greenberg. *Robert A. Heinlein.* New York: Taplinger, 1978. 268p. MIN, SRB.

Heinlein, perhaps the pre-eminent SF author and for many years known
as the "dean" of American science fiction, was a logical choice for one of
the early volumes in the Taplinger series despite the fact that Heinlein has
received more bioliterary attention than any other SF writer (exclusive of
Wells, Lewis, Huxley, Orwell, Burgess, and other contributors to the field

who are not primarily SF authors). The articles explore a suitably diverse range of topics, including Heinlein's juvenile novels, the Future History stories, *Stranger in a Strange Land*, sexuality in Heinlein's work, political and social elements in his fiction, the Lazarus Long character, etc. The book contains nine articles by some of the most respected of the currently active SF critics and historians (the article on the juvenile novels was contributed by Jack Williamson). Some of the essays—such as the one by Ronald Sarti—take positions opposing the generally accepted view of Heinlein and his fiction; most avoid extremely abstruse or rarefied "theoretical" issues and thus are immediately useful to the widest possible range of potential readers on almost any level of comprehension. As with all the Taplinger volumes, the Heinlein collection is recommended as part of the core title structure for a collection which includes author studies of the major SF writers. For other Heinlein-related materials see items 24, 97, 120, 129, 132 and 136; see Appendix I for an evaluation of the Taplinger *Writers of the 21st Century* series.

119.   Olander, Joseph D. and Martin Harry Greenberg. *Ursula K. Le Guin.* New York: Taplinger, 1979. 258p. MIN, SRB.

The nine essays in this volume explore a variety of facets of Le Guin's fiction, from touch as a theme and metaphor to the use of shadow as a motif, evolutionary and political theory, use of the psychological journey, anarchism and utopian tradition in *The Dispossessed*, and androgeny, ambivalence, and assimilation in *The Left Hand of Darkness*. The essays vary in complexity, but because of Le Guin's great popularity the collection should be useful in libraries, including high school libraries, with even modest SF/fantasy holdings. Marshall B. Tymn compiled a Le Guin bibliography which appears as an appendix to the book, and the volume also contains a biograpical note on Le Guin and an index. Contributors include Margaret P. Esmonde, Peter Brigg, Peter S. Alterman, Philip E. Smith II, N.B. Hayles, Thomas J. Remington, Sneja Gunew, John H. Crow and Richard D. Erlich. The volume is recommended for any collection emphasizing author studies of contemporary SF and fantasy writers. For other Le Guin-related materials see items 45, 83 and 134; see Appendix I for an evaluation of the Taplinger *Writers of the 21st Century* critical series.

120.   Panshin, Alexei. *Heinlein in Dimension: A Critical Analysis.* Chicago: Advent Publishers, 1968. 204p. AOW, MIN, RSF, SRB.

Panshin's critical survey of Heinlein is an important contribution to SF criticism because it was the first book-length evaluation of a twentieth-century science fiction writer. The research for the volume was meticulous; Panshin apparently read every word of Heinlein's fiction at least once before writing the book, even ferreting out obscure material originally published in the magazines and never reprinted. The critical evaluations seem occasionally somewhat harsh but are generally sound, and Panshin provides some biographical information about Heinlein in his book. The surveys of short fiction are particularly interesting and useful, and incidentally provide a wealth of information on magazines and magazine publishing at the time Heinlein began writing (1939) and through the decade of the 1940s. If there is a general weakness in Panshin's criticism, it is a tendency to overindulge in first-person criticism, though in the introductory material he specifically states the book is "a personal reaction to Heinlein's writing." As writer, editor, critic and SF historian himself, Panshin has the knowledge, experience and ability to engage in SF criticism without hedging, but it must be remembered that this volume was a groundbreaking effort. A certain amount of apology and defensiveness are to be expected. Panshin divides Heinlein's writing into three distinct periods: The Period of Influence (roughly 1939-1942), The Period of Success (1947-1958), and The Period of Alienation (1959-1967). Other chapters deal with such technical matters as construction (story elements, context, people, problems, attitudes), execution (style, plot, etc.), content, and Heinlnein's nonfiction. In a brief conclusionary chapter, Panshin calls his book an "interim report" on Heinlein, and that statement turned out to be quite prophetic—Panshin's survey ends with *The Moon is a Harsh Mistress*, and Heinlein has gone through at least one more phase of his extraordinary career, possibly two, since this book was published. Heinlein is perhaps the most important SF author of the twentieth century, and this book is a seminal study for that reason alone. Panshin's book belongs in almost any collection of critical material on SF in spite of the need for substantial update and expansion to cover the most recent phases of Heinlein's career. For other Heinlein-related material see items 24, 97, 118, 129, 132 and 136.

121. Patrouch, Joseph F., Jr. *The Science Fiction of Isaac Asimov.* Garden City, NY: Doubleday, 1974. London: Panther Books, 1976. 325p.

Patrouch's survey of Asimov's fiction is generally accepted to be the best critical analysis of Asimov to date. Patrouch divides Asimov's works into four chronological periods, and each section or discussion is prefaced by a listing of works included in that period classification. Primarily a popular rather than a scholarly evaluation, Patrouch's analysis is "comparative rather than absolute," according to the preface. Patrouch describes his analysis as "practical" criticism, and chose to analyze and compare on a practical "intramural" level rather than attempting the near-impossible task of defining the entire SF spectrum and establishing Asimov's exact position on the spectrum. The study is a useful, interesting and informative volume that provides much-needed access criticism for an author who has been instrumental in establishing SF as a major literary division in the twentieth century. First published in 1974, the book is now out of date; Asimov has continued to produce both fiction and nonfiction quite prolifically since that date, and a revised edition is becoming more a necessity with the publication of each new Asimov novel and collection. Included in Patrouch's book are a bibliography and an index. The book is recommended as an integral part of any collection, supporting SF research on any level, with an emphasis on volumes of critical appraisal of major SF authors. For other Asimov-related materials see item 6.

122.   Pringle, David. *Earth is the Alien Planet: J.G. Ballard's Four-Dimensional Nightmare.* San Bernardino, CA: Borgo Press, 1979. 63p. MIN.

Pringle examines Ballard's fiction in light of a "fourfold symbolism" theory—a group of four symbols which he believes are used throughout Ballard's fiction: water, sand, concrete and crystal. Pringle's theory, as he applies it, does not become a rigid framework with no flexibility of interpretation. An undercurrent of righteous scholarly anger over the American tendency to ignore Ballard's contributions to SF and general literature surfaces at several points, but the critical survey is very thorough, covering all the novels and an impressive number of the short stories. The four major sections include an introduction with biographical information; a chapter on the "fourfold symbolism"; a section on character and narrative point of view; and an examination of Ballard's two major themes—"imprisonment" and "flight." The novels and stories included in the survey are not criticized at length in any one chapter, but are mentioned or discussed as necessary in the appropriate sections. The booklet includes a bibliography of Ballard's books and a bibliography of criticism and secondary sources. Pringle's study is likely to become part of the cornerstone of Ballard criticism, and is a highly recommended acquisition for collections emphasizing author studies; in the U.S., particularly, Ballard is known—when he is recognized at all—as a "disaster" writer of the modern school, having novelistically destroyed the world several times with wind, drought, and crystalline metamorphosis. See Appendix I for an evaluation of the Borgo Press SF/fantasy author critical series.

123.   Ready, William. *Understanding Tolkien and The Lord of the Rings.* Chicago: Henry Regnery Co., 1968. New York: Warner Paperback Library, 1969. 96p.

Part biography and part literary analysis, *Understanding Tolkien* is an excellent introduction to the Tolkien canon, particularly the *Lord of the*

Rings trilogy. The book is relatively short, and yet is a readable and engaging starting-point for the reader or critic who seeks to understand more about Tolkien and his fiction. The comprehension level for Ready's bio-critical essay is relatively high, making the book an unlikely candidate for undergraduate research or casual-interest reading. The book is not as structured as it might have been, but that problem is not as serious as the lack of an index. With no index, the unstructured nature of the long and involved essay means its utility is considerably less than it should be because the information it does contain is not easily accessible. Of special interest are Ready's observations on the similarities and differences between Tolkien's fiction and fiction by C.S. Lewis and Charles Williams. The book is not indispensible, but would make a good supplementary volume for collections specializing in graduate or post-graduate fantasy research, or literary or biographical Tolkien research. For other Tolkien-related materials see items 35, 85, 95, 104, 105, 140 and 199.

124. Reed, Peter J. *Kurt Vonnegut Jr.* New York: Warner Paperback Library, 1972. 222p. New York: Thomas Y. Crowell, 1976. RSF, TYS.

Vonnegut is one of the most popular SF (or pseudo-SF) writers, and because his work also is accepted by the mainstream literary establishment, there are more full-length studies of Vonnegut than most other SF (or borderline SF) writer—with the possible exception of Orwell and Huxley. Reed's study is a good general or introductory survey of Vonnegut, though its scope is limited by its publication date and subsequent lack of coverage of Vonnegut's later works. Published in 1972, the study examines only the first six Vonnegut novels—*Player Piano, The Sirens of Titan, Mother Night, Cat's Cradle, God Bless You Mr. Rosewater* and *Slaughterhouse Five*. Each novel is analyzed in a chapter, and these chapters are followed by a short final section in which comparisons are made among the novels and conclusions drawn. The volume includes a brief selected bibliography but no index. For other Vonnegut-related materials see items 101 and 112.

125. Roy, John Flint. *A Guide to Barsoom: Eleven Sections of References in One Volume Dealing with the Martian Stories Written by Edgar Rice Burroughs.* New York: Ballantine, 1976. 200p. RSF.

As a general popular guide, Roy's *A Guide to Barsoom* is adequate, and its publication by Ballantine in a paperback edition may make it more readily available to readers than scarce and expensive limited-edition hardcover guides. The book begins with an introductory note about Burroughs and a list of the 11 Barsoom books. There are 11 chapters, some as essential as "A Geography of Barsoom, Including a Gazeteer-Index and Hemispheric and Polar Maps of its Surface" and some as esoteric as "Measurements on

Barsoom—Linear, Time, Monetary—and a List of Barsoomian Numbers."
Guides such as this one sometimes border on being in-group tracts appreciated more by devoted fans for their concentrations of trivia than by new
readers seeking information about a newly-discovered book, author or
series, and in some respects, Roy falls into that trap. The sheer amount of
accumulated information, however, cannot help being useful to anyone
researching Burroughs' Barsoom. There are some apparent inconsistencies
in the cataloguing method. The Lost Sea of Korus, for example, is listed as
"Korus, Lost Sea of" while Valley Dor is listed as "Valley Dor." This simply confirms that the book was intended more for those already initiated into
Burroughsian fiction than for the newcomer, but this criticism isn't too serious because the lists of terms are short enough that someone searching for a
specific term could scan the entire list. Besides some maps and diagrams, a
number of line-drawing illustrations are included. The book has some value
as a general guide to Burroughs' fictional world of Barsoom, but in the
main can be recommended only as a supplementary acquisition for collections with a strong emphasis on Edgar Rice Burroughs and his fiction. For
other Burroughs-related material see items 107 and 212.

126. Schweitzer, Darrell. *Conan's World and Robert E. Howard.* San Bernardino, CA: Borgo Press, 1978. 64p. MIN.

Like Schweitzer's Borgo Press volume on H.P. Lovecraft, this monograph on Conan and Robert E. Howard is an excellent introduction to its
subject area. The book is not a biography, though it obviously would be difficult to write an introduction to an author's fiction without some reference
to events in the author's life. Schweitzer provides some introductory biography, a credible chronology of the Conan stories and novels, and commentary containing—but not limited to—extensive synopsis of the stories. He
places Howard, his idiosyncrasies, his abilities, his accomplishments, and
his prejudices in the context of the age he lived in and the magazines and
audiences he wrote for, and Schweitzer is neither condescending or fanishly
slavish in his critical evaluations of Howard's work. It is clear that he is
thoroughly familiar with the conventions of "heroic" or "barbaric" fantasy,
and he explains, concisely and without hyperbole, Howard's use (and, in
some cases, his origination) of those conventions. *Conan's World* is an
excellent introduction to the Conan character and Howard's fantasy fiction,
not to mention one of the best single-author "introductory surveys" in the
Borgo series. The book is highly recommended for collections featuring
Robert E. Howard material, or primary and secondary holdings in heroic/
barbaric fantasy. For other Howard-related material see items 144 and 189;
see Appendix I for an evaluation of the Borgo Press SF/fantasy author critical series.

127. Schweitzer, Darrell. *The Dream Quest of H.P. Lovecraft.* San Bernardino, CA: Borgo Press, 1978. 63p. SRB.

This Borgo Press volume is one of the best in the Milford series. Schweitzer is intimately familiar with, and thoroughly knowledgeable about, Lovecraft and the entire horror fiction tradition, and he relates that tradition entertainingly to the reader while explaining Lovecraft's importantance to the horror genre and his influence upon it. Lovecraft's career is divided into the general topic areas Background; Early Horror Tales; Lovecraft and Lord Dunsany; Hauntings and Horrors; Nameless Hordes; Lovecraft at His Best; An Interlude with Disaster; Last Years; The Revisions; Lovecraft's Nonfiction; The Collaborations with August Derleth; and Conclusions. Each of Lovecraft's works is synopsized, criticized, and placed within the broader context of his entire canon. Much has been written about Lovecraft, and many of Lovecraft's fans and would-be critics are blind to his faults, but Schweitzer never lets his admiration for Lovecraft cloud his judgment of the writer's fiction. This book is an exceptionally thorough general survey (considering the space limitations) and should be included in any collection maintaining any degree of emphasis in horror fiction or H.P. Lovecraft. For other Lovecraft-related material see items 84, 184 and 215; see Appendix I for an evaluation of the Borgo Press SF/fantasy author critical series.

128. Schweitzer, Darrell, ed. *Discovering Stephen King.* Mercer Island, WA: Starmont House, 1985. 219p.

Schweitzer's volume of King Criticism is a poorly planned, poorly edited, and, in some cases, poorly written book of criticism which relies heavily on the tired old "commercialism versus art" argument. Several of the articles have an air of self-righteous anger, presumably over the fact that King is not fully accepted and endorsed by a unified and admiring literary establishment, and the authors of at least two of the articles mistake false analogy, absurdity, and tautology for profundity. Despite the shortcomings, which are many and serious, the book has several nice features, including a chapter (by Schweitzer) on collecting King with clearly explained book collecting principles which apply not only to King collecting but to the entire book collecting hobby. There is a chapter of synopses of King's novels and major short fiction, and a bibliography of King's work. The chapter on King's Bachman novels (by Don D'Ammassa), and the essay on the "death of a child" as a major theme in King's works, are particularly helpful and fascinating. Completist collections, where the goal is to obtain a copy of everything written about King, will need this book; those with restricted budgets may prefer to use their resources to acquire books on King with a higher percentage of useful criticism. For other King-related material see items 39,

87, 89, 90, 142 and 147; see Appendix I for an evaluation of the Starmont "Stephen King" critical series.

129.   Searles, Baird. *Heinlein's Works, Including Stranger in a Strange Land.* Lincoln, NE: Cliff's Notes Inc., 1975. 59p. MIN, RSF, TYS.

As a brief survey, *Heinlein's Works* serves its general purpose, but Panshin's *Heinlein in Dimension* (item 120) covers the same ground and covers it better. Because it was intended as a basic guide to Heinlein's fiction—and because Heinlein is far better known, both in and out of the SF genre, for his novels than for his short fiction—this booklet should have concentrated more on the novels. The only works discussed by this booklet that are not covered in Panshin's book are *Time Enough for Love* and *I Will Fear No Evil*, and these two long and complex novels are glossed over so quickly in Searles' booklet that the coverage is neither representative nor useful. There is a select primary bibliography but no secondary bibliography, despite the fact that Heinlein is one of the "fortunate few" SF writers to have been criticized, discussed and analyzed at great length. *Heinlein's Works*, because it is a Cliff's Notes volume, probably is more accessible to students (i.e., copies should be readily availabe on the Cliff's Notes rack at the campus bookstore), but the Panshin and Franklin (item 97) books are far better for any conceiveable study of the value, meaning, or mechanics of Heinlein's fiction. For other Heinlein-related material see items 24, 97, 118, 120, 132 and 136.

130.   Siegel, Mark. *James Tiptree, Jr.* Mercer Island, WA: Starmont House, 1985. 89p.

James Tiptree/Alice Sheldon (now deceased) was recognized as a major writing talent and premiere SF stylist almost from the publication of her first story. Her work has been predominantly in the short story form, and Siegel has chosen to examine most of Sheldon's work in groupings of stories defined by the published collections. After the chronology and introduction, the chapters are divided into examinations of *10,000 Light-Years from Home, Warm Worlds and Otherwise, Star Songs of an Old Primate, Up the Walls of the World* (novel), *Out of the Everywhere, Tales of the Quintana Roo*, and *Brightness Falls from the Air* (novel). There is a detailed primary bibliography, an annotated secondary bibliography, and an index. Siegel prepared the book after intensive research which included locating reviews and other material available only in fan publications, and he conducted an interview with Sheldon from which he provides numerous excerpts. This "reader's guide" represents the single most important source of methodical, balanced and well-informed Tiptree criticism now in existence, and also is recommended as one of the best volumes in the Starmont series. For other Tiptree-related material see item 92; see Appendix I for an evaluation of the Starmont House SF/fantasy author critical series.

131. Slusser, George Edgar. *The Bradbury Chronicles.* San Bernardino, CA: Borgo Press, 1977. 63p. MIN, RSF, SRB.

Ray Bradbury has been one of the few SF/fantasy writers to transcend the genre and find a reasonable level of acceptance among mainstream literary critics. Despite that acceptance, Slusser's study was one of the first monographs on Bradbury (several have been published since). Slusser's critical evaluations often ramble, but in this case, Bradbury's tendency to work in the short story rather than the novel form required a representative survey of short stories, so the commentary is fairly solidly focused on the subject author. The booklet is divided into six sections. The first is a brief introduction; "The October Country" examines Bradbury's early fiction; "The Vintage Bradbury" deals with fiction produced during the time-frame Slusser calls Bradbury's "vintage" period (1946-1955); "The Machineries of Joy" describes a type of Bradbury story Slusser calls "stories of collective eccentricity"; "Fahrenheit 451" is a two-and-a-half-page examination of that novel; and "Dandelion Wine & The Martian Chronicles" is a five-page overview of those two books. Included are a biographical note on Bradbury and a bibliography. *The Bradbury Chronicles* is more immediately useful to a wider range of students and readers than most of Slusser's studies, and is recommended as a good introduction to Bradbury's fiction. For other Bradbury-related material see items 115 and 117; see Appendix I for an evaluation of the Borgo Press SF/fantasy author critical series.

132. Slusser, George Edgar. *The Classic Years of Robert A. Heinlein.* San Bernardino, CA: Borgo Press, 1977. 64p. MIN, SRB.

The years covered by this study are, in general, the 1940s and 1950s. The booklet is divided into five sections: "Stories," "Novellas," "Two Novels of Intrigue" (*Rocket Ship Galileo* and *The Puppet Masters*), "A Heinlein Masterpiece" (*Have Space Suit—Will Travel*), and "Afterthoughts." The thrust of the criticism is a "subverted" view of plot elements and a Calvinistic label for all aspects of Heinlein's fiction that can be explained with a religious or pseudo-religious interpretation. Slusser spends too much of his time building nonexistent opposition so it can be conveniently debunked— for example, he adopts a condescending tone in regard to Panshin's three-part classification of Heinlein's work, even though Panshin never claimed his system to be anything more than a convenient method for dividing Heinlein's works into manageable units; Heinlein was, after all, obviously still quite an active author in 1968 when Panshin's study was published, and no one would have been more aware than Panshin of the fact that a contemporary writer, if he continues to write, may enter other career phases. Slusser also makes occasional careless mistakes in dealing with text (in one case he changes a milkshake to a "pie"). Libraries with large collections of SF criticism will want Slusser's booklet, particularly for useful supplementary commentary on Heinlein's short stories, but more restricted holdings may safely rely on the Panshin (item 120), Franklin (item 97) and Olander/Greenberg (item 118) volumes for the bulk of their Heinlein criticism. For other Heinlein-related material see items 24, 97, 118, 120, 129 and 136; see Appendix I for an evaluation of the Borgo Press SF/fantasy author critical series.

133. Slusser, George Edgar. *The Delany Intersection: Samuel R. Delany Considered as a Writer of Semi-Precious Words.* San Bernardino, CA: Borgo Press, 1977. 64p. MIN, SRB.

Slusser performs well in the "literary analysis" mode, but a Slusser analysis often is more interesting and useful to other critics than to the general reader who enjoys reading a particular author and makes the first tentative efforts to find out what an experienced critic has to say about that author. The greatest need for critical appraisal in the first stages of the general acceptance both of SF and SF criticism as legitimate literary territories in their own right is for general access to the fiction of major writers. While Slusser is ruminating over such concepts as "Contained in the modal auxiliary is an inflection toward prescription," the Delany reader or fan is left wondering why *The Delany Intersection* couldn't have been an introduction to, and a broad-based general survey of, a body of fiction regarded by many to be one of the finest in the SF field. There is nothing wrong with producing criticism that is primarily of interest to those working on the graduate or post-graduate level, but the first lengthy study of Delany should have been a bit more accessible. The major chapters of Slusser's book examine the trilogy *Out of the Dead City, The Towers of Toron* and *City of a Thousand Suns*; and the three novels *Babel-17, The Einstein Intersection* and *Nova*. A brief disclaimer states that the booklet does not have enough space to allow for discussions of *The Tides of Lust, Dhalgren* or *Triton*, though that seems more likely to be a problem with planning than space—many of the booklets in the Borgo Press series cover a surprising amount of material in the space of 60 to 75 pages. The booklet is an important contribution to Delany criticism, but is not likely to be very useful at the undergraduate level. See Appendix I for an evaluation of the Borgo Press SF/fantasy author critical series.

134. Slusser, George Edgar. *The Farthest Shores of Ursula K. Le Guin.* San Bernardino, CA: Borgo Press, 1976. 60p. MIN, RSF, SRB.

Slusser's criticism of Le Guin's fiction is more even-handed than many of his other single-author studies. In this critical appraisal he elects to use a "Taoistic" or "dynamics of polarity" approach to the fiction of one of the most popular contemporary SF/fantasy writers, and that choice is symptomatic of the general access problems exhibited by most of his critical explorations. The major novels are discussed at length: the Hainish novels (*Rocannon's World, Planet of Exile, City of Illusions*), *The Left Hand of Darkness*, the Earthsea trilogy (*A Wizard of Earthsea, The Tombs of Atuan, The Farthest Shore*), and *The Dispossessed*. The shorter works "The Word for World is Forest," "Vaster Than Empires and More Slow" and "Atlantis" are mentioned in passing, though the short stories in general are ignored. Slusser finds *The Lathe of Heaven* to be Le Guin's "worst" novel and it therefore receives little attention or treatment. Because of the different approaches, points of view, writing styles and levels of critical complexity displayed by the contributions to the Taplinger volume on Le Guin (item 119), it is the preferred volume; Slusser's contributions to Le Guin criticism are more likely to be appreciated above the undergraduate level. There is no table of contents for easy reference, although a biographical note and bibliography are included. For other Le Guin-related material see items 45, 83 and 119; see Appendix I for an evaluation of the Borgo Press SF/fantasy author critical series.

135. Slusser, George Edgar. *Harlan Ellison: Unrepentant Harlequin.* San Bernardino, CA: Borgo Press, 1977. 63p. MIN, RSF, SRB.

Slusser's criticism tends to move along the same lines, no matter what author he is discussing. Once he gets beyond the center-circumfrence analogy, and the tendency to uncover Calvinistic undertones wherever they may be hidden, he provides some useful evaluation and commentary. He divides Ellison's work into three aspects rather than several chronological divisions—"journalism," "fantasy" and "myth." Under the journalism heading he advances the theory that Ellison's ebullience, vulgarity, apparently superior attitude, tendency to undercut all types of evaluation, analysis and criticism, and his endless justifications as a dynamic and still-actively-evolving "framing" device for the fiction. Common sense would tend to indicate that for this type of elaborate framing concept to be valid the person involved would need to be a full-fledged popular culture icon—not on the order of a Harlan Ellison but at least on the order of an Elvis Presley—but despite the obvious problems and weaknesses with the theory, Slusser presents a convincing argument. The most immediately useful feature of the book is the fantasy section, which synopsizes and comments on 30 short stories. No full-length critical work on Ellison exists, so notwithstanding problems and imperfections, the booklet is an important addition to Ellison criticism. For other Ellison-related material see item 29; see Appendix I for an evaluation of the Borgo Press SF/fantasy author critical series.

136. Slusser, George Edgar. *Robert A. Heinlein: Stranger in His Own Land.* San Bernardino, CA: Borgo Press, 1976. 64p. MIN, RSF, SRB.

The thesis Slusser presents in *Stranger in His Own Land* is an interpretation of Heinlein's novels as examples of "ellipsis" and "subversion of standard conventions." His criticism is unnecessarily argumentative, and he tends to create false problems with the text by using descriptions that are not wholly accurate, then resolve the problem by stating a self-evident truth. Slusser often opts for the explanation that strains credulity rather than the one which seems to be the most likely—for example, if Heinlein gives a character a boyhood spent in Missouri, he is committing a "supreme act of literary narcissism" when the reason for the Missouri boyhood could be that Heinlein knows more about Missouri boyhoods than he does about Florida boyhoods or Rhode Island boyhoods. What Slusser indicates as a new idea (the "ellipsis" interpretation) actually is a common procedure in fiction-writing because it allows the author, and the reader, to skip over long segments of a story that might be boring to both parties. Slusser has some interesting things to say about Heinlein when he works more on direct and reasonable analysis and less on freewheeling associational interpretation. In an afterword, he predicts that any novels beyond *Time Enough for Love* will be "little different in purpose and design" from that novel; predictions are almost always useless, and this one is no exception. The booklet includes a one-paragraph Heinlein biography and a bibliography of Heinlein's books. As with most of Slusser's contributions to SF criticism, this volume is more a supplement to existing criticism than a groundbreaking effort in its own right. The Franklin (item 97) and Panshin (item 120) analyses of Heinlein's fiction have more substance and credibility. For other Heinlein-related materials see items 24, 97, 118, 120, 129 and 132; see Appendix I for an evaluation of the Borgo Press SF/fantasy author critical series.

137. Slusser, George Edgar. *The Space Odysseys of Arthur C. Clarke.* San Bernardino, CA: Borgo Press, 1978. 64p. MIN, SRB.

Even many of the accepted masters of the SF genre have yet to receive a comprehensive critical analysis of their fiction; Arthur C. Clarke, for many years, was one of those masters, though now there are several books on Clarke's fiction. Slusser's booklet was the first attempt at a unified commentary on a broad sampling of Clarke's work, yet the booklet is disappointing because 34 of the 64 pages are spent in introducing and "warming up" to the subject. The last few pages of the warm-up also discuss, briefly, some of Clarke's short fiction. The second half of the booklet discusses the novels *The Sands of Mars, Islands in the Sky, Childhood's End, 2001: A Space Odyssey, Rendezvous with Rama* and *Imperial Earth*. In oddly reverse-telescopic fashion, Slusser considers *Sands* and *Islands* at great length—12 pages. *Childhood's End* is covered in seven; *Space Odyssey* in four; *Rendezvous* in one; and *Imperial Earth* in just over two. Of most interest to contemporary readers are those books—among which are two of the most important and widely acclaimed genre classics in SF history—which receive least coverage. Slusser spends too much time formulating catchphrases, such as his identification of Clarke's "odyssey pattern," and not enough providing useful commentary. The two best books of Clarke criticism are the Hollow study (item 102) and the Taplinger collection of critical articles (item 116), and Slusser's study is simply a useful supplement to existing Clark criticism. The book includes no table of contents, no primary or secondary bibliography and no index. For other Clarke-related materials see items 102, 116, 201, 252 and 253; see Appendix I for an evaluation of the Borgo Press SF/fantasy author critical series.

138. Stableford, Brian M. *A Clash of Symbols; The Triumph of James Blish*. San Bernardino, CA: Borgo Press, 1979. 62p. MIN, SRB.

Most major SF authors are under-represented by thoughtful, intelligent critical analysis—in many cases, they are under-represented by critical analysis or appreciation in any form—and James Blish, despite widespread recognition as a major talent in the SF field, has been one of those writers whose fiction continues to be reprinted but who has been critically ignored until fairly recently. Brian Stableford's analysis of Blish's fiction represents a rich concentration of criticism, appreciation and analysis of Blish's work, and at the same time is a persuasive argument for the "booklet" style of criticism exemplified by the Borgo Press and Starmont House series. Short booklet-type publications often degenerate into Cliff's-notes-like surface introductions of the patently obvious; Stableford's book is a unified, methodical, and finely crafted exploration that touches on virtually every aspect of the subject author's body of work. The essay is divided into eight chapters: Foundation Stones; Tectogenesis and Pantropy; Cities in Flight; Experiments in Thought; Experiments in Adventure; Juveniles; After Such Knowledge; and Conclusions. Considering the brevity of the essay (p. 3-60), Stableford perhaps uses too much valuable time and space explaining theoretical concerns behind topics, such as religion and the philosophy of technological development, which tell more about the necessary background preparation for intelligent SF criticism than about the fiction of a particular author. But Stableford is thorough, rigorous, and fair in his evaluations, and he considers several areas (such as the juvenile fiction) which are slighted or ignored elsewhere. The Ketterer study (item 103) is the landmark Blish study, but this booklet is an extremely important source for detailed analysis of the fiction of James Blish. For other Blish-related materials see items 7, 8 and 103; see Appendix I for an evaluation of the Borgo Press SF/fantasy author critical series.

139. Suvin, Darko and Robert M. Philmus, eds. *H.G. Wells and Modern Science Fiction*. Lewisburg, PA: Bucknell University Press (represented by Associated University Presses, Cranbury, NJ), 1977. RSF, SRB.

Compiled from revised papers originally presented at a Wells symposium held at McGill Universivty in 1971, *H.G. Wells and Modern Science Fiction* has much more an international scope than most collections of critical essays on SF-related subjects. The 11 contributions achieve the goal, stated in the introduction, of "open(ing) up or extend(ing) inquiry into...large areas of Wells' affinities and influences." A contribution by a Russian critic, Tatyana Chernysheva, was translated into English for the volume by Suvin, and a Japanese contribution by Sakyo Komatsu was translated by the author with the assistance of Judith Merril and Tetsu Yano and a final revision by R.M. Philmus. Though the essays, concerned with topics such as the folk-tale, the use of the garden as a metaphor, *The Time Machine* as a structural model for SF, evolution as a theme, etc. all are respectable contributions to Wells criticism, two of the most useful items in the book are not essays. One item is a selective bibliography, with abstracts, of Wells' science journalism 1887-1901 (by Daniel Y. Hughes and Robert M. Philmus) and the second is an annotated survey of books and pamphlets by Wells (contributed by R.D. Mullen). The annotations for the second survey are intended to be "not evaluative as to literary quality, but factually descriptive as to content and reputation." The survey thus identifies interrelationships between Wells' works that might otherwise escape casual notice. The book is recommended for any collection emphasizing H.G. Wells or the development of SF through the Victorian era and into the first half of the twentieth century. For other Wells-related material see items 34, 100 and 108.

140. Tyler, J.E.A. *The Tolkien Companion*. New York: St. Martin's Press, 1976. 530.

Though done in a somewhat tongue-in-cheek style, and undoubtedly a work that takes some liberties with its subject matter, Tyler's *Companion* represents a useful collection of information about the *Lord of the Rings* trilogy. Tyler sets the tone in an introduction which details the way in which Tolkien "translated" the LOTR books and then allowed the world to believe he published the books as fiction because he felt most people would not believe the "truth." Words, names, concepts and events are explained, some at great length. Though much of the beauty, mystery and other-worldliness of the best epic fantasy lies in casual references to people and events long dead or long past, a companion or concordance to a particularly complex fantasy series—such as Tolkien's—can be helpful, especially for researchers or critics who may need to check an occasional character or place name. The general fan may enjoy browsing through the book at random because information on a given topic is presented in compact form rather than being scattered through vague references in several novels. Tyler's compendium is recommended for collections with emphasis on Tolkien or epic fantasy. For other Tolkien-related material see items 35, 85, 95, 104, 105, 123 and 199.

141. Underwood, Tim and Chuck Miller. *Jack Vance.* New York: Taplinger, 1980. 252p. MIN.

Jack Vance has had several interrelated careers, including SF/fantasy writer, mystery writer, screen writer and critic. Despite a career spanning more than 40 years, and hard-won status as one of the premiere writing talents in the genre, this collection is the first anthology of critical essays on Vance's fiction. Topics include the novel *The Dragon Masters*, Vance's early fiction, influences of Clarke Ashton Smith in Vance's work, Vance as a stylist, and the novels *The Eyes of the Overworld* and *The Dying Earth*. Contributors to the volume include Norman Spinrad, Peter Close, Arthur Jean Cox, Don Herron, Mark Willard, Robert Silverberg, Terry Dowling, Richard Tiedman and Poul Anderson. It is interesting to note that a number of the contributors to the Vance volume in the "Writers of the 21st Century" series are SF/fantasy writers themselves—a higher percentage than in any other volume in the series, a fact which emphasizes Vance's position as a highly influential "writer's writer" within the genre, though his work still is largely unappreciated in the academic world. The Vance volume of this critical series is a major source of commentary on one of the most influential and highly regarded authors in the SF/fantasy genre. For other Vance-related material see item 188; see Appendix I for an evaluation of the Taplinger *Writers of the 21st Century* critical series.

142. Underwood, Tim and Chuck Miller, eds. *Kingdom of Fear: The World of Stephen King.* San Francisco, CA and Columbia, PA: Underwood-Miller, 1986. 267p.

Most any serious contribution to King criticism will have some value, if for no other reason than the fact that King earned an incredible amount of popularity, and earned it incredibly quickly; King's popularity has cut across so many lines of social and economic demarcation that any book about him, whether bad or good, can be expected to sell. *Kingdom of Fear* offers a diverse group of essays on King, two of which are "forewords" and five are "introductions." Why a book should require so much introduction is not clear. The 12 articles cover a good range of topics with an approximately even division of the essays between the popular and the academic. The contribution by Harlan Ellison is an exceptionally lucid overview of film and television relative to King's work, and Herron's article is a pleasant and refreshing debunking of the "King can do no wrong" fan myth. The volume has a survey of King fiction transferred to film and TV, and essays on King as a children's writer (an aspect of his fiction overlooked, and perhaps not even thought to exist, before *The Eyes of the Dragon*); character in King fiction (characterization is widely accepted to be a major strength of King's work); and psychology in King's fiction, among other subjects. The book is laced liberally with pages that contain nothing but boxed quotes from King's fiction or from King interviews, and the beautiful job of book production, typical of Underwood-Miller, give the impression the book was produced primarily for the King-related market rather than the academic market. The quality of the criticism, however, makes it a viable offering for both segments of the book-buying public. For other King-related material see items 39, 87, 89, 90, 128 and 147.

143. Warrick, Patricia S. *Mind in Motion: The Fiction of Philip K. Dick.* . Carbondale, IL: Southern Illinois University Press, 1987. 222p.

Only in the latter years of the 1980s has SF author biography truly come into its own. By 1985, only Isaac Asimov and Robert Heinlein had been the subject of book-length studies; the door is now open, and one of the first and best efforts to come through the door (along with Ketterer's bioliterary study of James Blish (item 103)) is Warrick's book on Philip K. Dick. An acknowledged master of SF (who also has written "literary" fiction, some published and some still unpublished), Dick has contributed several novels to the list of generally accepted genre classics. In Warrick's study, separate chapters are devoted to major novels: *The Man in the High Castle, Martian Time-Slip, Dr. Bloodmoney, The Three Sitgmata of Palmer Eldritch, Do Androids Dream of Electric Sheep?, Ubik, A Scanner Darkly*, and the Valis novels. The final chapter, though not an identified "conclusion," is instead a survey of Dick's "moral vision." Warrick notes that it would be impossible to comment at length on all the published novels (34), but her selection of works for analysis encompasses a representative body of early and late fiction, including acknowledged classics. Though not all Dick's novels are analyzed in depth, many are mentioned in the context of their similarities to works which are discussed at length. Philip K. Dick, now deceased, was an important SF writer and a major candidate for bioliterary criticism and analysis by the "new generation" of academics who take SF as seriously as other academics take other literary fields. Warrick's biography of Dick's life and her analysis of his fiction represents some of the finest bioliterary work done on an SF author, and the book is recommended for any collection emphasizing biography and criticism of SF writers. For other material related to Philip K. Dick see item 214.

144.   Weinberg, Robert. *The Annotated Guide to Robert E. Howard's Sword & Sorcery.* West Linn, OR: Starmont House, 1976. 152p. RSF.

Robert E. Howard was one of the early "sword & sorcery" writers (he is sometimes credited with creation of the S&S genre), and this annotated guide is a useful survey of Howard stories and novels featuring series characters. Story surveys are for the characters Soloman Kane, Bran Mak Morn, James Allison, Turlogh Dubh, and Conan, with additional summary and comment on "The House of Arabu," a story in the S&S tradition but not a part of any of the Howard series. Each section has information on where a story was first published, a list of main characters for each story, a plot synopsis, and commentary. Weinberg is a well-known collector and acknowledged expert on pulp fiction; the research is accurate and the critical judgments trustworthy. Some annoying typos make for unintentional humor in the book, and Weinberg's writing could have profited from the attentions of an experienced editor—he often allows the violet-tinged, stilted, and pseudo-antiquarian linguistic awkwardness that passes for standard S&S prose to creep into his own commentary, thus making unnecessary substitutions such as "comes upon" for "meets" or "encounters." Minor irregularities aside, Weinberg's annotated survey is now a standard reference on Robert E. Howard's fiction, and belongs in any library collection emphasizing the S&S or heroic fantasy genre. For other Howard-related materials see items 126 and 189.

145.   Wendell, Carolyn. *Alfred Bester.* Mercer Island, WA: Starmont House, 1982. 72p.

In the SF field, several large reputations are based on a relatively small number of books. Alfred Bester is one of the most widely acclaimed masters of the genre, yet his reputation rests largely on one short story and three novels. The booklet-length critical appraisal is perfectly suited to an examination of the fiction of an author with a minimal output, and Wendell uses the form to good advantage. The introductory chapter covers the subject author's biography, his ideas about SF, and general themes in his fiction; and separate chapters explore *The Demolished Man, The Stars My Destination, The Computer Connection* and Bester's short fiction. There are four appendices: an annotated bibliography of Bester's SF; an annotated bibliography of his comments on SF; an annotated bibliography of the non-SF writings; and a secondary bibliography. The critical analysis is a useful and informative mixture of synopsis, description, explication and analysis. This booklet is the first complete survey of Bester, and is an important addition to a collection specializing in criticism of major SF authors. For other Bester-related material see item 24; see Appendix I for an evaluation of the Starmont House SF/fantasy author critical series.

146. Wilson, Colin. *The Haunted Man; The Strange Genius of David Lindsay.* San Bernardino, CA: Borgo Press, 1979. 63p. MIN.

David Lindsay is virtually unknown outside the SF/fantasy field; several of his novels remain unpublished, and even within the SF confines Lindsay is known primarily for his unusual fantasy classic *A Voyage to Arcturus.* Wilson spends several pages of this booklet on biographical material relative to Lindsay, but fully half the booklet is an extended synopsis of *Arcturus* and a point-by-point explanation of the symbols that crop up periodically throughout the novel. At the halfway point of the book, Wilson finishes with *Arcturus* and then spends the last pages shifting back and forth between *The Haunted Woman, Sphinx, The Adventures of M. de Mailly, Devil's Tor* and *The Witch.* Wilson has a tendency to drift off into philosophical constructs of his own making rather than systematically exploring Lindsay's fantastic vision thoroughly and methodically, but Lindsay's work can be difficult to appreciate and Wilson does an excellent job of separating what is admirable in Lindsay's fiction from the ponderous excesses that can confuse the reader or send him searching for books by other authors which contain more congenial prose. Wilson's introduction to Lindsay is the best general introductory survey now available for this "forgotten" fantasy author, and is recommended on that basis. For other Wilson-related material see item 81; see Appendix I for an evaluation of the Borgo Press SF/fantasy author critical series.

147. Winter, Douglas E. *Stephen King: The Art of Darkness.* New York: Plume/New American Library, 1986. 297p.

Like many other Stephen King critics, Winter is first a King fan and second a critic. In fact, in the introduction he calls the book a "critical appreciation," and if he is no less honest than other critics about his favorable position with regard to King's fiction, he is at least better able to keep his admiration for King under control so that his criticism is not reduced to the level of literary cheerleading. *The Art of Darkness* has a chronology of King's life, a chapter of biographical material, and chapters devoted to the explication and analysis of *Carrie; 'Salem's Lot; The Shining; The Stand* and *The Gunslinger; The Dead Zone; The Firestarter; The Mist; Cujo; Different*

Seasons; Creepshow; Christine and *Cycle of the Werewolf; Pet Sematary; The Talisman; Night Shift, Skeleton Crew,* and other short fiction; a round-up of unpublished works, projects scheduled for publication and works in progress; three appendices, one each for the King/Bachman books, short fiction, and film and television adaptations; a King bibliography; and an index. One of the important strengths of Winter's book is the sheer volume of quoted material from King. Many of these quotes apparently were available only to Winter because of his friendship with King, but he does not use the friendship in an attempt to win the reader's envy or admiration. The friendship also allows Winter a direct knowledge of the circumstances surrounding the composition of many of King's novels, a fact which occasionally contributes substantially to his criticism of King's work. Winter's study is the best single-critic volume published on King to date, and therefore is an important book in any collection of secondary materials on contemporary horror fiction. For other King-related materials see items 39, 87, 89, 90, 128 and 142.

148. Yoke, Carl B. *Roger Zelazny.* West Linn, OR: Starmont House, 1979. 111p. MIN, SRB.

Yoke, a long-time friend of author Zelazny, has written a readable, accessible introduction to Zelazny's fiction. There is little real criticism in this volume, but a great deal of synopsis and explanation. What criticism that exists in the book is a "surface" evaluation, though that isn't a weakness in every case—in this case, it simply means the book is more suitable for SF author studies on the undergraduate level than the graduate or post-graduate level. The introduction is short and very general, more a disclaimer than anything else, because it mentions such elements as theme, plot, characters, and style while pointing out that a full analysis would be impossible in a short work. Rather than covering a wide range of materials in a brief space (something which several of the Starmont and Borgo volumes do quite well), Yoke provides separate chapters with in-depth commentary on "A Rose for Ecclesiastes," *This Immortal,* "The Doors of His Face, the Lamps of His Mouth, *The Dream Master, Lord of Light,* "Home is the Hangman," the Amber novels, and a final round-up chapter that briefly mentions several novels and short stories. A bit more critical evaluation might have been useful and interesting, but the study still serves as a major body of Zelazny criticism and a knowledgeable introduction to Zelazny's fiction. For other Zelazny-related material see item 187; see Appendix I for an evaluation of the Starmont House SF/fantasy author critical series.

Section 3
General
Bibliographies

149. Alpers, Hans-Joachim, Werner Fuchs, Ronald M. Hahn, Wolfgang Jeschke. *Lexikon der Science Fiction Literatur* (2 vols.). Munich: Wilhelm Heyne Verlag, 1980. 1,252p. MIN.

Foreign language SF reference publications are of value mostly to bibliographers for use in clearing up problems about the existence of translated editions of SF authors' works. Libraries and individuals specializing in bibliography and the collecting of foreign editions may need this two-volume treasure trove of information about American, British and European SF writers whose work has been translated into German, but it is not likely to be of much use to the general reader or researcher. The information contained in these two books is so clearly delineated even a reader with no familiarity with the German language can extract useful data from the listings. Volume 1 has general introductory and historical sections, several chapters dealing with major themes and motifs (utopia/dystopia, space opera, militarism, monsters/aliens, invasions, global catastrophe, etc.), and the main alphabetical listing of biographical material on authors. Bibliographic listings for each author provide the German titles, publishers, year dates of publication, and original English titles of books translated into German. Volume 2 has a listing of books published by German publishers (anthology and collection entries include story titles, authors, and English titles for the stories), award listings, bibliography and index. The two-volume set is an indispensible reference for beginning a bibliographic search into German editions of translated English language SF, but that also makes it a specialty item of interest only to libraries maintaining collections that include foreign language SF reference books.

150. Bleiler, E. F. *The Checklist of Science Fiction and Supernatural Fiction.* Glen Rock, NJ: Firebell Books, 1978. 266p. MIN, SRB.

The Checklist of Fantastic Literature, published in Chicago in 1948, was one of the most important contributions to SF bibliography in the first half of the twentieth century. *The Checklist of Science Fiction and Supernatural Fiction* is an extensive revision of the 1948 bibliography. Weak or marginal titles were dropped from the original list, new titles added, and subject matter codes introduced. The book includes published titles through 1948, and the bibliography is intended, in the compiler's words, "...to provide first edition and subject matter information on adult, English language fantastic fiction (including translations) from 1800 to 1948." A few exceptions were made for important contributions to fantastic literature originally published before 1800. The main body of the book is a listing by author; individual entries include pertinent information on pseudonyms, titles, publishers, publication dates, number of pages, an indication whether or not a book is illustrated, and code letters and numbers which refer to a list of theme/motif types. There is a supplementary listing by title. The period before World War II can be very difficult to research, and Bleiler's checklist provides the best available access to SF and related material from 1800-1948. The theme/motif information alone is a significant contribution to SF research; examples of specific themes and motifs in the Bleiler listing are suspended animation, parallel worlds, hollow earth, immortality and reincarnation. Bleiler's checklist is an essential acquisition for any collection emphasizing SF bibliography or research of SF-related fiction in the nineteenth and early twentieth century.

151. Clareson, Thomas D. *Science Fiction Criticism: An Annotated Checklist.* Kent, OH: Kent State University Press, 1972. 225p. AOW, RSF, SRB, TYS.

Thomas Clareson was one of the first American adacemics to embark on a teaching, research and publishing career which would assist countless others in their appreciation of science fiction and their research into the subject. This annotated checklist provides access to items (including articles, essays, book reviews, etc.) which are concerned with direct discussion of the SF genre. Material was divided into nine categories: General Studies; Literary Studies; Book Reviews; The Visual Arts; Futurology, Utopia, and Dystopia; Classroom and Library; Publishing; Specialist Bibliographies, Checklists and Indices; and The Contemporary Scene. There is an author index of entries and an index of authors mentioned. Most of the annotations are very brief but provide adequate descriptions of the contents or intention of each item, often employing quotes from the item. Obviously the checklist had to be a selective one—there would have been far too much material to have included everything. The approximately 800 entries are representative of the resources that were available at a time when the number of SF classes was expanding rapidly all across the U.S., and teachers were desperately in need of something to help them and their students locate articles, books, reviews, and other research materials for the genre. Clareson's book was the first of what later evolved into a continuing series of SF resource bibliographies compiled by other academics and published by Kent State University Press, one of the leading academic publishers of bibliographies and study materials for science fiction research. The Clareson checklist is one of the most important modern SF resource checklists or bibliographies, and should be included in any collection with holdings emphasizing general SF resource bibliography.

152. Currey, L.W. *Science Fiction and Fantasy Authors: A Bibliography of First Printings of Their Fiction.* Boston: G.K. Hall, 1979. 571p. MIN, SRB.

Currey's first edition bibliography is the first American bibliography of its type published for the collector who wishes to be able to identify the first printings of books by fantasy and science fiction authors. The volume is well-researched, authoritative, and is useful as a title checklist as well as a first-printing bibliography. Authors are listed alphabetically and titles are arranged alphabetically within the author listings. Novels and collections of short stories are listed first under each author entry, then selected nonfiction by the author, associational material (such as plays adapted by another author from one of the subject author's works), edited fiction, and reference materials about the subject author. Coverage is particularly thorough—the Fredric Brown entry, for example, includes his mystery/detective titles as well as his science fiction books. A number of obscure writers are included for completeness, but the volume was published in the 1970s and now needs updating to include entries for contemporary authors, especially those whose first editions are becoming more and more collectible. Stephen King has only three titles listed, and a number of major SF authors who have emerged since 1979 should be included in an updated edition. Even if no new edition ever becomes available, this bibliography still sets the standard for bibliographical research in the SF field, and will continue to be useful for the tremendous amount of bibliographical information it contains.

153. Day, Bradford M. *The Checklist of Fantastic Literature in Paper-bound Books.* Denver and New York: Science Fiction & Fantasy Publications, 1965; New York: Arno Press, 1974, 128p. Salem, NH: Ayer Co. Publications. AOW, RSF, SRB, TYS.

Bradford M. Day is one of the pioneering figures in twentieth century bibliography of fantastic literature, and the *Checklist* was one of his pioneering efforts. The book has a listing by author, with approximately 800 entries, and a listing by title with perhaps 2,300 entries. The scope of the Day checklist is a bit broad, including, as it does, some adventure fiction with only slight fantastic content, but the vast bulk of the listing—possibly 75 percent or more—is considered SF or fantasy. Reprinting out-of-print SF reference books is a good idea, but Arno Press made two mistakes with the Day checklist: Day's pioneering efforts to provide a checklist for fantastic literature have been partially superseded by the revised and updated Bleiler volume (item 150) and the extremely comprehensive Reginald index (item 160), and Arno chose to publish a photo-offset reproduction of an existing copy of the book (it was originally published from typewritten originals, with all the attendant problems of republication in a third-generation photo-offset format, including difficult-to-read light areas). The book no longer serves the purpose for which it was originally intended, and is now a supplemental comparison volume largely of interest to bibliographers and specialist collectors.

154. Dikty, Alan S. *The American Boys' Book Series Bibliography 1895-1935.* West Linn, OR: BBC Publications, 1977. 167p.

Although not concerned primarily with science fiction *per se*, the Dikty "boys' book" bibliography still is an important SF research source for those interested in juvenile SF, fantasy and fantastic adventure fiction, particularly the Tom Swift series. The main listing is somewhat awkwardly arranged; the beginning of each entry is not separated, indented, or otherwise differentiated for easy scan, but the entries include name of series, author (or house name), number of volumes, year range of publication, brief description of series, series type or genre, title list, publisher, and descriptions of the bindings used on the books. Appendix I is a cross-reference of author and series, and Appendix II a cross-reference of publisher and series. The bibliography lists approximately 4,700 titles. Though the compiler admits in the introduction that the index probably is not complete, it is the most exhaustive and detailed bibliography extant which deals with this specialized genre of juvenile literature. Recommended for collections emphasizing bibliography or research sources for juvenile SF/fantasy literature.

155. Glut, Donald F. *The Frankenstein Catalog: Being a Comprehensive Listing of Novels, Translations, Adaptations, Stories, Critical Works, Popular Articles, Series, Fumetti, Verse, Stage Plays, Films, Cartoons, Puppetry, Radio & Television Programs, Comics, Satire & Humor, Spoken & Musical Recordings, Tapes and Sheet Music Featuring Frankenstein's Monster and/ or Descended From Mary Shelley's Novel.* Jefferson, NC: McFarland & Co., 1984. 525p. MIN.

One of the most important and enduring of all SF themes has been the Frankenstein mythos, and yet this comprehensive index to "Frankensteiniana" is a relatively recent addition to the field of bibliography. Many photos and film stills are included in the book, and aside from the numerous category listings of Frankenstein-related material, a title and name index provide easy access to the entries. The categories covered by this bibliography represent an unusually broad spectrum of popular culture, as indicated by the category listings in the volume's sub-title. The bibliography is well-arranged and annotated in detail. Though the volume deals with a limited topic, and is very much a specialty research tool with limited use, the subject for which it provides almost unlimited access is a major wellspring of cultural mythology, not just in the U.S. or in English-speaking countries but all over the world. Frankenstein was not the only historical starting-point for science fiction or horror literature, nor was it the earliest, but in view of the role Shelley's creation has assumed in modern SF and horror mythology, Glut's bibliography represents an important cross-cultural record of the power and significance of the technological mythology represented by Frankenstein. The volume is recommended for collections specializing in bibliography, the mythological aspects of SF, and interdisciplinary studies of popular culture.

156. Hancer, Kevin. *The Paperback Price Guide.* New York: Harmony Books, 1980. 430p. New York: Harmony Books, 1982. 390p.

Price guides are strictly an "associational" item for SF studies, partly because paperback price guides contain a great deal of information not related to SF. However, the listings by publisher do provide series numbers for paperbacks, and can be useful for determining bibliographic details about some books. The Hancer volumes include some dates in the listings, information on edition size (digest or mass market), an indication of subject matter (for example, some of the Saint novels are straight mysteries and some have elements of SF), and other useful information. There are also numerous black and white cover illustrations and a section of color plates. The second edition has an author cross-reference.

157. Jaffery, Sheldon R. *Horrors and Unpleasantries: A Bibliographical History and Collector's Price Guide to Arkham House.* Bowling Green, OH: Bowling Green University Popular Press, 1982. 142p.

An "anecdotal bibliography," according to the compiler's own comments, *Horrors and Unpleasantries* actually is a bibliographic collector's catalogue of Arkham House titles. Because the company was one of the earliest specialty publishers for collector's editions of horror, fantasy, supernatural, and macabre fiction, Arkham House editions have become highly collectible and much sought after. Jaffery's lengthy annotations provide useful historical information on Arkham House publications, including date of publication, an approximate print run, and an estimate of current collector's value. Three appendices are included: a list of Arkham House titles planned or announced but never actually published; a list of "sponsored" books published by other companies but actively promoted and catalogued (sold) by Arkham House; and a suggested horror literature core collection checklist of Arkham House titles. The book also contains a short essay by Gerry de la Ree explaining the probable fate of the two-volume set *The Illustrated Lovecraft* that was planned but which never appeared. The main title listing is chronological in the order the books were issued by Arkham House. There is no appendix with alphabetical title listing, and the lack of such a listing is a moderately serious shortcoming for an otherwise extremely well-researched annotated bibliography. Recommended for collections emphasizing bibliography, book collecting, or horror/supernatural literature.

158. Magill, Frank N., ed. Compiled by Marshall B. Tymn. *Survey of Science Fiction Literature: Bibliographical Supplement.* Englewood Cliffs, NJ: Salem Press, 1979, 1982. 183p.

As the title indicates, this volume is a bibliographical supplement to the five-volume Magill *Survey of Science Fiction Literature.* The intent of the book is to extend the bibliographical listings presented after each entry in the survey; though the book contains some useful information, there are two flaws which severely limit the utility of the work. The first, and most fundamental, problem was the exclusion of this material from the original survey. The "bibliographical listings" in the original survey were little more than book review listings cribbed directly from Hall's *SF Book Review Index* (item 225) with perhaps a small percentage of additional listings thrown in. While the bulk of the contributors to the five-volume survey (over 100 of them) were busy researching and writing the articles, one person (at least) should have been assigned the task of developing bibliographical listings suitable for a set of the scope and magnitude (not to mention cost) of the original survey. The second serious flaw is arranging the material in this book alphabetically by title rather than alphabetically by author. When SF research is undertaken, it is more often done as a research activity or exercise in finding out as much as possible about an author, not as much as possible about a single book, so the title listing makes this book (and the original survey) more cumbersome and difficult to use than was necessary. Tymn's supplement does extend the survey's bibliographical listings, but it does so in a way that, in some cases, is quite redundant. For example, there are six Robert Silverberg novels with separate listings—and under each listing is a reference to an article in *Voices for the Future* (in many of the listings it is the *only* entry). Under an alphabetical-by-author listing, this reference would have been included once rather than six times, and should have encompassed a brief reference to the novels mentioned or examined in the article. Very little original research was done for this book; most of the entries were taken from established SF bibliographies (Tymn is co-compiler for the occasional *Year's Scholarship in SF and Fantasy* bibliographies), leaving hundreds or perhaps thousands of reviews unmentioned and inaccessible to the students who could put the information to some use (up through 1980 and perhaps beyond, book reviews form the single most important untapped resource for critical material on SF authors, and Hall's book review index—despite its status as a basic SF research source—lists only a tiny percentage of the SF book reviews in periodicals outside the SF magazines). This volume must be recommended, despite the crippling limitations under which it was compiled, because it is a supplement to the largest existing collection of critical analysis and evaluation of SF, but librarians should be aware of the extremely narrow field it covers.

159. Rabiega, William A. *Environmental Fiction for Pedagogic Purposes.* Monticello, IL: Council of Planning Librarians, 1974 (Exchange Bibliography #590). 21p. MIN, RSF, SRB, TYS.

Environmental, or more precisely, "catastrophe," fiction has been a staple of the SF genre for decades. In this annotated bibliography, Rabiega divides environmental fiction into the categories "Environmental Catastrophe," "Extraterrestrial Environments," "Near Future Environments" and "Far Future Environments." The categories seem somewhat rigid and artificial in theory, yet in practice can include virtually anything. For example, "The Menace from Earth," a short story by Heinlein, is given as an example of stories concerning extraterrestrial environments (in this case, the moon), but the same classification could be applied to almost any SF story set on the moon. Obviously it would not be feasible to list every SF story ever written which uses the moon for a background or setting. There are no reasonably rigid yet reasonably flexible guidelines for inclusion in this list—and to be useful to a contemporary reader or researcher in any case, considerable time and effort would have to be expended to update the list. Recommended only for collections with a major sub-emphasis in theme/motif indexing.

160. Reginald, Robert. *Science Fiction and Fantasy Literature, Vol. 1;*
Indexes to the Literature. Science Fiction and Fantasy Literature, Vol. 2;
Contemporary Science Fiction Authors II. Detroit, MI: Gale Research, 1979.
1141p. AOW, MIN, SRB.

The two volumes of *Science Fiction and Fantasy Literature*—because of
the sheer volume of information they contain—comprise one of the half-
dozen most important reference sources in the science fiction and fantasy
fields. The collection of indexes, listed alphabetically by author, is massive;
the biographical volume contains a wealth of information about SF and fantasy authors, some of them relatively unknown outside the genre (and many
who are not well-known even *inside* the genre), and many of the biographical entries are long autobiographical essays contributed by the authors themselves. The expansiveness and all-inclusiveness of the work is simultaneously a strength and a weakness. It is a strength because of the amount of information; it is a weakness because perhaps as many as half the authors
represented produced a single book, and a large majority of these authors'
single contributions to SF and fantasy (or borderline SF/fantasy) were published prior to 1950. Copies of these books will range from difficult-to-find
to virtually nonexistent outside some very specialized private collections
which are inaccessible to the general public. This reduces the utility to the
general reader or student and probably raises the acquisition cost of the
Reginald books considerably. A combination general and special reference
book often turns out to be inadequate for either the generalist or the specialist, but in this case the two aspects are combined to good effect; a library
with any pretensions about maintaining even a basic collection of SF reference materials will need a copy of this book. That is not to say the book is
perfect and requires no improvement, for there are in fact a number of
annoying mistakes. An example is a cross-reference directive under "Mothe
Fenelon, Francois de Salignac de la" (p. 377) to "see Fenelon, Francois,"
but no entry under "Fenelon, Francois" exists. There are numerous dead-end
cross-references, but the mistakes and omissions are almost impossible to
find unless the user is looking specifically for a particular cross-reference.
In any case, the mistakes are not important or numerous enough to detract
substantially from the work's usefulness. It is one of the few reference
works in the SF/fantasy genre that can be considered indispensible.

161. Sargent, Lyman Tower. *British and American Utopian Literature*
1516-1975: An Annotated Bibliography. Boston: G.K. Hall, 1979. 324p.
MIN.

Utopian and dystopian fiction has been considered an SF associational
genre for many years, probably because most utopias must be dislocated
from contemporary reference (islands, undiscovered valleys, etc.) and suc-

cessful dystopias (*Brave New World, 1984, This Perfect Day, Player Piano*) generally are set in a future in which humans have become subservient to a government which uses technological controls to maintain power. Lists of books obviously a part of the utopian/dystopian literary tradition were fragmentary and incomplete before Sargent published his bibliography, and upon publication it became the standard utopian/dystopian bibliography. The main body of the book consists of a chronological listing of books (and representative short stories) judged to be within the confines of the utopian/dystopian definition. There is a list of secondary materials (books) on utopian literature, a list of articles on the subject, and a list of unpublished materials (mostly unpublished theses and dissertations). The volume includes author and title indices to the chronological listing. The primary entries are succinct but informative, giving year date of publication, title, author, publishing information, a brief description of the contents, and a location code to tell where at least one copy of the book may be found. The chronological list begins with Thomas More's *Utopia* and ends in 1975. Sargent's bibliography is highly recommended for any collection specializing in SF and related bibliography or utopian/dystopian literature.

162. Searles, Baird, Martin Last, Beth Meacham and Michael Franklin. *A Reader's Guide to Science Fiction.* New York: Avon, 1979. 266p. New York: Facts on File, 1980. MIN.

Science fiction may well be the most over-documented genre fiction in existence, and *Reader's Guide to Science Fiction* is yet another author survey of the SF field. The author evaluations are understandably brief, but overall are well-written and informative. It is the book itself which was poorly planned. For example, an entry on Richard Shaver is included, though the entry states, "None of Shaver's work is available at this time"—yet major authors, such as Kurt Vonnegut, are excluded from the listing. Entries on authors whose work is only marginally SF or very difficult to find (William Hope Hodgson, Austin Hall, Homer Eon Flint) are included, but authors of acknowledged classics in the genre (Ward Moore, Laurence Schoonover) are excluded. Arthur Byron Cover's entry mentions his second novel and a collection of short stories, though it says nothing about his first—and, arguably, his best—novel. An appendix which lists series material also is erratic. Le Guin's fantasy trilogy is listed but not her three interrelated SF novels (usually called the "Hainish novels"); Tanith Lee is represented by an author entry, but none of her series material is listed in the series appendix. The volume includes a list of prize-winning SF novels and stories, a suggested basic reading list, and a brief history of SF. Somewhat arbitrary and now quite dated, the book is of questionable value and is not recommended; its most valuable asset is the author summaries, and these are done better and at much greater length in such volumes as the Nicholl's SF encyclopedia (item 232).

163. Silverberg, Robert. *Drug Themes in Science Fiction.* Rockville, MD: National Institute on Drug Abuse, 1974. 55p. MIN, RSF, SRB, TYS.

Research Issues No. 9, *Drug Themes in Science Fiction*, was published by the National Institute on Drug Abuse as part of a series intended to provide researchers with bibliographical access to the broad range of information available on the drug problem. Silverberg provides a preface, a general overview, and an annotated bibliography of short stories and novels using drugs as an important theme. The bibliography is divided into three segments—the Primitive Period (1900-1935), the Predictive Period (1935-1965), and the Contemporary Period (1965-). Entries include brief descriptions such as "drugs as mind expanders" or "drugs as mind-controllers." Published in 1974 and now somewhat out of date, the bibliography is the only existing bibliography of drug-related SF and so is a valuable contribution to thematic bibliography in the SF field. The use and effects of drugs has been an important theme in twentieth century science fiction, and this list badly needs expansion and updating. Recommended for collections with an emphasis in bibliography.

164. Spaink, A., G. Gorremans and R. Gaasbeek. *Fantasfeer: Bibliografie Van Science Fiction en Fantasy in het Nederlands.* Amsterdam: Meulenhoff, 1979. 279p. MIN.

Foreign language bibliographies are particularly difficult to obtain, and they present special problems in use—obviously, most of the book and magazine references in a foreign language bibliography will not be available for reference. Specialty bibliographies are normally of use only for serious bibliographical research (the truly die-hard collector also may be able to put a good foreign language bibliography to use), and are not recommended for libraries needing general reference materials. *Fantasfeer*, a bibliography of science fiction published in the Netherlands, has a combined alphabetical listing by title and author, and two appendices—a list of SF series and a list of pseudonyms. Story titles are numbered, English titles are provided as necessary for English language novels and short stories translated into Dutch, and each entry provides original year date of publication, and code designations and title cross-references for the Dutch book or books in which a story appeared. Compilation or proofreading (or both) apparently was careless and many of the code cross-references are faulty, but someone using the book to research a single-author bibliography should have no trouble weeding out the faulty references, even if he or she doesn't know a word of Dutch. The book is recommended only for collections specializing in foreign language bibliographies.

165.   Tymn, Marshall B. *A Basic Reference Shelf for Science Fiction Teachers.* Monticello, IL: Council of Planning Librarians, 1978 (Exchange Bibliography #1523). 13p. MIN.

Tymn's *Basic Reference Shelf* booklet (8½ x11, stapled) is an annotated bibliography of SF-related reference materials suggested for use by teachers. Though the booklet was useful when it was first published, it has been superseded by far more comprehensive bibliographies. Entries are generally very short, except in the case of very important works such as Tuck's encyclopedia (item 240). Critical judgments on the value and utility of the SF reference works listed are sound, but in the years since the publication of this booklet there has been nothing short of a virtual explosion of academic interest in SF and in the publication of well-researched scholarly reference works. The booklet is now outdated and is not recommended.

166.   Tymn, Marshall B., and Roger C. Schlobin. *The Year's Scholarship in Science Fiction and Fantasy: 1972-1975.* Kent, OH: Kent State University Press, 1979. 222p. SRB.

The *Year's Scholarship* volumes, published periodically, provide the best available bibliographic information for books, articles, and other secondary sources for SF research. Materials are divided into four categories: general studies, bibliography and reference, author studies and bibliographies (with sub-groupings for collective and individual studies), and teaching and visual aids. The bibliography is arranged by author in the main body of the book, and the volume is indexed by author and title. A table of contents provides immediate access to the single-author studies. The *Year's Scholarship* series began as a listing in *Extrapolation*, and in 1972 Thomas D. Clareson expanded the previous journal listings to complete the volume *Science Fiction Criticism: An Annotated Checklist* (item 151). In 1975 Marshall Tymn published in *Extrapolation* a checklist of SF scholarship for 1972 and 1973, and that list became the core for this volume. Listings include both scholarly and popular articles, books, and dissertations, and the teaching and visual aids list has descriptions of handbooks, films, cassettes and filmstrips. The Tymn-Schlobin reference is the only ongoing full-range SF bibliography in existence, and as such is one of the most important bibliographic tools in the field.

167.   Tymn, Marshall B., Roger C. Schlobin and L.W. Currey. *A Research Guide to Science Fiction Studies: An Annotated Checklist of Prim-*

ary and Secondary Sources for Fantasy and Science Fiction. New York: Garland, 1977. 165p. SRB.

Research Guide was one of the early attempts to provide an annotated bibliographical guide to science fiction criticism and reference materials. It is a broad-based and wide-ranging bibliography, despite its 165 pages, because it includes such non-SF general sources as *The World Bibliography of Bibliographies.* Separate category listings include Anonymous and Pseudononymous Literature, Title Changes, Classification, Biography, Anthology Indices, Magazine Indices, and so on. In some cases, the subject categories are broken down into such specialized topics that a category may contain only one entry. Much of the "coverage" supplied by this volume is of questionable value; anyone capable of determining that a book or article ought to be written about a specific SF/fantasy topic surely is capable of checking standard non-SF references (*Bibliography of Bibliographies, Humanities Index, Dissertation Abstracts,* etc.) without being told to do so. If all the non-SF references containing material of some value to SF researchers were to have been included, the volume might have been 500 pages rather than 165. Some of the annotations are too brief and do not provide information that should have been included; Slusser's *Bradbury Chronicles,* for example, is labeled a "useful study" in a three-line annotation, but no mention is made of the lack of an index in Slusser's book—and an index is an extremely useful feature in any single-author study or general nonfiction book. The book does include author and title indices, and despite the severe limitations, contains much useful information including a list of doctoral dissertations on science fiction and fantasy novels, authors, film, and associated subjects.

168. Wells, Stuart W., III. *Science Fiction and Heroic Fantasy Author Index.* Duluth, MN: Purple Unicorn Books, 1978. 186p. MIN, SRB.

Typos and misspellings are a special problem in a reference work, and the frequency and severity of such problems in this volume substantially reduce its value and utility. It is primarily a collector's listing of SF and fantasy books, but the assumptions and lack of attention to detail mean that the average collector already will have a better working knowledge of his collecting field than can be learned from this book. In effect, a specialty reference cancels its own value with fewer mistakes than would be the case with a general reference. The introduction states, "This index covers the type of books that you read and collect. It contains the information that you want to know about a book for reading or collecting." Aside from an introduction which assumes a complete and perfect knowledge of the needs of all collectors everywhere, the main body of the index has a number of entries which are out of alphabetical sequence. Many names and titles are misspelled: Frank R. Stocton, Thomas Pychon, Nick Bodie Williams, John B. Priestly, *The Johan Kit,* Gary Wolf, Frederick Pohl, Lawrence Yep, Frank O'Rouke, Ben Orkaw, C.J. Cutliffe Hyne, Hugo Gernsbach, Laurence Schooner, and so forth. The book might serve adequately as a preliminary checklist so long as the collector keeps the mistakes and limitations in mind. Though considerably more expensive, the Currey (item 152) and Reginald (item 160) volumes are much to be preferred over this carelessly done bibliography.

169.   White, Anthony G. *Urban Futures: Science Fiction and the City.* Monticello, IL: Council of Planning Librarians, 1973 (Exchange Bibliography #418). 5p. MIN.

Although the theme anthology is extremely popular in SF publishing, "theme access" to the genre can be difficult, as no comprehensive theme-motif indexes have yet been published. White's booklet (8½ x11, stapled), though restricted by its 1973 publication date, is useful for locating short stories and novels which use the city as an iportant aspect of theme development. There are only 26 entries, with novels predominating, but the booklet could form the core of an updated, expanded "urban future" motif listing. As the booklet stands now, it is simply an outdated list of short stories, novels and series that use the very vague and ill-defined "urban future" idea as a theme or motif in some form. The idea of "the city" or even "the future of the city" is hopelessly broad as a category, and perhaps needs to be broken down into sub-categories to be of real use for research in theme/motif interrelationships. The annotations, however, are useful because they describe the general outlines of novels and short stories which may be difficult to locate. Recommended only for collections where theme/motif indexing is one of the major collecting sub-emphases.

Section 4
Author
Bibliographies

170. Ashley, Mike. *Barrington J. Bayley*. Essex, England: Beccon Publications, 1981. Unpaginated (6).

Barrington J. Bayley is a "mid-range" SF author—that is, he has not produced a large body of work and he is not well-known or critically acclaimed, but his work cannot be casually dismissed. This booklet lists the handful of Bayley's published short stories in the 1950s and a dozen novels published in the 1970s, and includes the titles of works finished but not yet published as well as works in progress. Living authors still actively writing are particularly difficult subjects for bibliographers, and it generally falls to the amateur/semi-professional bibliographer to maintain in-progress listings for living authors. Ashley is well equipped for compiling an SF bibliography, being the author, editor or compiler of several SF reference books, and this unpaginated booklet listing works by and about Bayley should be of some use to collectors, researchers and other bibliographers. Libraries may find the stapled booklet format awkward to handle, but any collection specializing in the difficult area of SF bibliography should have some reasonable method for handling booklet-type materials, and this Bayley booklet is recommended as a good addition to such special collections.

171. Bilyeu, Richard. *The Tanelorn Archives: A Primary and Secondary Bibliography of the Works of Michael Moorcock 1949-1979*. Manitoba, Canada: Pandora's Books, 1981. 108p.

One of the most difficult research problems involving contemporary

authors is the problem of bibliography. That problem is greatly compounded
when the author is both prolific and collectible. In Moorcock, most of the
really difficult bibliographical problems intersect—he is a contemporary
author still publishing new material, he is a prolific contributor to several
media, he is collectible, and he has used numerous pseudonyms. Generally,
the best SF author bibliographies are published by Underwood-Miller and
G.K. Hall, but *The Tanelorn Archives* is an exception. It is thorough and
comprehensive, and was compiled with the active assistance of the subject
author. Included are listings for books, short fiction, non-fiction, editorials,
reviews, fan publications, letters, comic books and comic strips, music,
films and related material, and manuscripts. Both fiction and non-fiction
influenced by Moorcock's work are listed in separate indices, as well as
"associational" items such as art portfolios containing illustrations of Moorcock's works and games based on Moorcock's fiction or characters from his
fiction. The book listings are complete and include all printings plus information on each title's position in a series (where applicable). There are only
two minor cavils: the table of contents is done in alphabetical order (no real
problem, merely a curiosity) and there is no separate listing of titles in
series. There are several dozen book cover illustrations in the bibliography.
Of particular interest to completist-collectors who have encountered problems collecting all the printings of Avon and DAW paperbacks is an appendix explaining the numbering of print runs for those companies. This book,
though inclusive of Moorcock's work only to 1979, is the standard Moorcock bibliography.

172. Blackmore, Leigh. *Brian Lumley: A New Bibliography*. Penrith, Australia: Dark Press Publications, 1984. 53p.
     This Brian Lumley bibliography is a perfect example of "bibliographical
overkill." Most of the categories of information are fairly standard: books in
English, fiction and nonfiction, contributions to periodicals, reviews, poetry,
published letters, material included in books by other authors or editors,
translated works, works lost or destroyed or abandoned, reference works
about Lumley, bibliographies, criticism in books or periodicals, book
reviews, and miscellaneous data. There is a chronology of unusual and
probably unnecessary parallel construction, one chronology for fiction and
another for poetry—it would have been more common-sensical and less
confusing to have compiled a single   chronology with two separate fiction
and poetry groupings under each year date. Indexes to the bibliography are
provided as separate title, name and periodical indexes. A minor mistake
was the lack of indicators for the nationality of the translations. *Die Herrs-
chaft der Monsters* is obviously a German translation, but a (German),
(French) or (Italian) indicator—or even a (G), (F) or (I) indicator—might

have been very helpful for some research purposes. Another shortcoming is the unnecessarily detailed information about Lumley's books. Bibliographic descriptions which tell the location of every blurb, the title page, the copyright page, the dedication, blank pages, and so on cannot be justified unless the author is highly collectible and his publisher has turned out numerous editions and printings which must be described for collecting purposes. Standard issue mass market paperbacks by Jove, Berkley, DAW, etc. should be easy for any collector to locate for decades to come; painstakingly detailed bibliographic descriptions of such books are a waste of time and effort. A section of Lumley's early fanzine artwork is included in the booklet. Despite the overzealous excesses, this booklet is the definitive Lumley bibliography, and is recommended for collections specializing in single-author bibliography where there are adequate arrangements for handling paperbound booklet materials.

173. Clareson, Thomas D. *Robert Silverberg: A Primary and Secondary Bibliography.* Boston: G.K. Hall, 1983. 321p.

G.K. Hall launched the first major hardcover series of SF and fantasy author bibliographies, and this Silverberg volume, compiled by Thomas D. Clareson, was an early volume in the series. The bibliography series, because it signalled a change in the willingness of major publishers to handle bibliographies of genre writers (rather than leaving such bibliographies to the fan and amateur presses), was an important milestone in SF reference publishing. Clareson, who is perhaps the foremost critic and historian in the SF field today, was the logical choice to do the Silverberg volume. He has done an excellent job of unearthing and presenting a great deal of information on Silverberg, but he apparently was hampered by two considerations not under his direct control—time and format. The bibliography contains a short-title list of Silverberg's works; separate primary bibliographies for science fiction and fantasy, miscellaneous fiction, and edited anthologies; and a bibliography of articles in fan and professional publications and introductions which give some of Silverberg's views on SF. The secondary bibliography lists book reviews and critical studies in chronological order. Several appendices provide listings of Silverberg's articles in the *Bulletin of the SFWA*; pseudononymous works listed by the pen name used; and awards and nominations. The book contains an absolute wealth of information on Silverberg, no mean feat when it is considered that Silverberg may be one of the most difficult contemporary SF writers to research. Yet the book review listing in this volume, one of the most important features, is seriously flawed; it contains references to a relatively small percentage of the reviews of Silverberg's books, and the format is chronological rather than alphabetical by book title. When a student decides to research reviews on a selected Silverberg book, he or she should be able to photocopy one page and proceed with the research. Instead, the reviews must be located separately in the index and photocopied from separate pages, because they are in chronological order. Clareson's bibliography is one of the best bibliographies ever compiled on an SF author, but G.K. Hall should not require contributors to the series to arrange the review indexes chronologically. In some respects, fan bibliographies are better than professional bibliographies because the fans compile the books to use; scholarly bibliographies often are compiled for other scholars to admire but for no other practical purpose. Where single-author bibliographies are needed for a collection, the Underwood-Miller bibliographies are the best; for authors not represented by one of the Underwood-Miller volumes (and Silverberg is one of those not represented), librarians will have to do the best they can. This book is the best Silverberg bibliography in existence, though portions were poorly planned and the book should be a better-constructed and better-researched volume than it is. For other Silverberg-related material see items 86, 163 and 300.

174. Covell, Ian *J.T. McIntosh: Memoir & Bibliography.* Polk City, IA: Chris Drumm, 1987. 32p.

This McIntosh bibliography is well-researched and includes the titles of several nonfiction works not listed in the standard SF author references. McIntosh (James Murdoch Macgregor) was not a prolific writer, he has authored perhaps two dozen books and a hundred short stories, so this bibliography is not lengthy, but it is more complete than any other existing McIntosh listing. Covell's compilation lists McIntosh's science fiction alphabetically, with additional listings for contemporary fiction and nonfiction. A chronological list of short fiction and one of books completes the bibliography. Also bound into the booklet is a memoir by McIntosh that was provided as a lengthy letter and edited "only slightly" by Covell. Reliable biographical information on SF writers can be difficult to find, and unlike some of the genre giants, McIntosh does not suffer from "interview overexposure." Though the Drumm publications are printed in booklet form, they are often—as in this case—major reference items for the subject authors. See Appendix I for an evaluation of the Drumm booklet series.

175. Dalby, Richard. *Bram Stoker: A Bibliography of First Editions.* London: Dracula Press, 1983. 81p.

As more research is undertaken in the SF/fantasy/horror genres, first edition bibliographies such as this Stoker bibliography will be required to serve the needs of researchers and collectors. The Stoker bibliography includes complete descriptions of all editions of Stoker's books, reproductions of the title pages of first editions, a variety of illustrations (including cartoons from the magazines contemporaneous with the publication of Stoker's works), a reproduction of a title page autograph inscription by Stoker, a survey of the author's short stories and serials, and a briefly annotated list of Stoker biographies and other publications of interest to the Stoker enthusiast. A title index completes the volume. Though the book is a small-format paperback, it would make an excellent addition to a collection specializing in Bram Stoker or in SF/fantasy/horror author bibliographies.

176. Drumm, Chris. *An Algis Budrys Checklist.* Polk City, IA: Chris Drumm, n.d. Unpaginated (16).

The Drumm checklist for Budrys, done with the cooperation and assistance of the subject author, includes nonfiction items which are not found in standard SF listings, and even includes such items as a novel which only exists in the form of a first draft. Also listed are film and book reviews written by Budrys, as well as listings for published letters. Useful notes provide starting points for specialized research into Budrys material known to exist but which was beyond the scope of the checklist and therefore is not covered in detail. A loose addenda sheet has a note from Budrys clarifying the politics and geography of Prussia, the nation of his birth as recorded in biographical essays about him, and a list of several non-SF mystery stories. For other Budrys-related material see item 16; see Appendix I for an evaluation of the Drumm booklet series.

177. Drumm, Chris. *A Hal Clement Checklist.* Polk City, IA: Chris Drumm, n.d. Unpaginated (8).

Checklists and bibliographies compiled by SF fans often are better and more useful than professionally done books because the fan-published form is less permanent and can be updated more economically and more often. The Drumm booklets are an example of well-researched fan checklists which are sometimes more helpful to the researcher than more scholarly efforts. The Clement checklist in the Drumm series is an eight-page booklet with an addenda sheet tipped in; the addenda page is not stapled or otherwise bound into the book, and that may cause some use and storage problems for libraries. Entries are chronological and numbered, and because of the brevity of the booklet there is no index. Clement has not produced a large volume of fiction in his writing career, but because of his classic novel *Mission of Gravity* he is considered to be one of the major twentieth century SF writers from the Campbell/*Analog* stable. Until more in-depth and scholarly work is done on Clement, this booklet should serve as an adequate checklist for those researchers and fans interested in the complete Clement canon. See Appendix I for an evaluation of the Drumm booklet series.

178.   Drumm, Chris. *A James Gunn Checklist.* Polk City, IA: Chris Drumm, 1984. Unpaginated (27).

Bibliographic listings in the Drumm booklet format can be difficult for libraries to store and retrieve for use, but the works of some of the authors represented in the series are not extensively documented elsewhere. The introduction to this booklet is by Stephen H. Golman. Gunn's writings are listed chronologically and identified as articles, short stories, books, etc. Some foreign editions of books (Spanish, French and German) are documented, as are some pieces of fiction which were dramatized on radio or television. Chronological entries are dated as recently as 1984, though indications are that the listings are not complete for that year. Appended to the listing is a letter from Gunn which gives extensive information about works in progress, forthcoming books, articles, and fiction, and other items of interest to the collector or bibliographer. An index is included, as well as a biographical note. For other Gunn-related material see item 32; see Appendix I for an evaluation of the Drumm booklet series.

179.   Drumm, Chris. *A John Sladek Checklist.* Polk City, IA: Chris Drumm, n.d. Unpaginated (26).

Chris Drumm's checklist booklets are very much in the fan tradition of publishing biographical and bibliographical information about SF authors just for the fun of it, but they also are a logical extension of the ongoing need for updated checklists. Drumm compiles his information from standard references and various other sources, and then "advertises" through his book catalogue (he is an SF book dealer) for additional information. He usually enlists the assistance of the subject author. In so doing, he often produces checklists which contain more bibliographic information about a single author than is available anywhere else. The Sladek checklist is an example of the type of checklist needed in the SF genre but often not available—a reliable, well-researched checklist for an author who doesn't get the attention or credit his work deserves. The list, obviously prepared with the consent, advice and assistance of the subject author, includes information not readily available elsewhere, such as title and pseudonym identification for non-SF stories lacking more definite bibliographical information. It is in the area of non-SF material for authors generally considered to be primarily "SF authors" that most standard SF references are weakest, and the Drumm checklists can be very helpful with non-SF material, information available only from the subject author, and recent work that has not had time to get into the standard hardcover references. See Appendix I for an evaluation of the Drumm booklet series.

180.   Drumm, Chris. *A Larry Niven Checklist.* Polk City, IA: Chris Drumm, 1983. Unpaginated (23).

The Niven checklist contains 140 numbered items plus numerous references to works in progress and completed works that will be published in the near future. 1983 is the last year covered in the chronological listing. Numerous foreign editions of Niven's books are cited, and many of the book notations include the name of the illustrator. There is an occasional annoying omission, such as the entry for an article in the *Herald-Examiner* which does not indicate the originating city for that newspaper. In the brief introduction, Drumm states that much of the checklist is based on Larry Niven's personal bibliography, and so is likely to be an extremely useful bibliographical supplement if not the definitive existing Niven checklist. See Appendix I for an evaluation of the Drumm booklet series.

181.   Drumm, Chris. *An R.A. Lafferty Checklist.* Polk City, IA: Chris Drumm, 1983. Unpaginated (29).

Drumm's Lafferty checklist begins with a note by Lafferty and then proceeds directly to a chronological listing of the author's writing beginning in 1959. The last year covered is 1983; there are 192 numbered entries, including several scheduled for publication in 1983 and a 1983 "update" listing seven books and booklets actually published in 1983. Extensive notes present long quotes, apparently from Lafferty-Drumm correspondence, explaining the circumstances of publication (or non-publication) of some works, and the inside back cover of the booklet is a bound-in addenda sheet with 20 additional entries. Lafferty is a brilliant but idiosyncratic writer, stylistically the "James Joyce of the SF field," and fans, researchers, and bibliographers will be particularly interested in the number of unpublished Lafferty items listed. For other Lafferty-related material see item 44; see Appendix I for an evaluation of the Drumm booklet series.

182.   Drumm, Chris. *A Tom Disch Checklist.* Polk City, IA: Chris Drumm, n.d. Unpaginated (25).

Tom Disch is another of the under-appreciated SF writers Drumm seems to specialize in, and this Disch checklist should be especially helpful in presenting the broad range of writing Disch has accomplished. Besides being one of the most-respected stylists writing in the SF genre, Disch is a prolific poet and contributor to newspapers and other non-SF publications. Undoubtedly there are omissions from this checklist—a bibliography, especially one dealing with a contemporary writer, hardly can be compiled without some omissions—but in spite of that problem, the booklet still contains an overwhelming number of entries. A letter by Disch, an addenda sheet and several notes by the compiler indicate material that was not included for one reason or another, but the supplementary commentary and notes should give the serious researcher at least a general idea what else Disch has written and where it may be found. See Appendix I for an evaluation of the Drumm booklet series.

183. Drumm, Chris, and George Flynn. *A Mack Reynolds Checklist: Notes Toward a Bibliography.* Polk City, IA: Chris Drumm, n.d. Unpaginated (24).

Mack Reynolds, now deceased, was one of the many "low profile" major SF authors of the past several decades. The specialty for which he is remembered is a "socioeconomic" type of fiction. Drumm's booklet has a chronological listing of Reynolds' fiction and an alphabetically arranged title index. The booklet is current through 1983. A loose addenda sheet and the stapled booklet format are likely to be a problem for libraries, though until comprehensive bibliographies for SF writers are more common, this booklet should fill the gap admirably for Reynolds' work. The booklet has no pretensions toward comprehensiveness—a serious problem with some fan-generated publications, partly because SF fans tend to have little or no interest in an author's non-SF work and partly because modern popular writers are particularly difficult to research. Reynolds, for example, contributed mystery fiction and miscellaneous nonfiction to magazines, but such non-SF material is not included here. Like other booklets in the series, this checklist is a reliable supplement to existing bibliographical materials and a good starting point for further in-depth bibliographical research. See Appendix I for an evaluation of the Drumm booklet series.

184. Joshi, S.T. and L.D. Blackmore. *H.P. Lovecraft and Lovecraft Criticism: An Annotated Bibliography Supplement 1980-1984.* West Warwick, RI: Necronomicon Press, 1985. 72p.

To be of any use to the researcher, this Lovecraft criticism supplement must be used in conjunction with the original *H.P. Lovecraft and Lovecraft Criticism.* The abbreviations used in the supplement are explained in the original volume, and most supplementary or explanatory material is contained only in the first volume. Criticism on Lovecraft is appearing more and more often, as are English language and foreign translations of Lovecraft's fiction. A supplement to the original bibliography certainly was in order, but it should have been better able to stand on its own as a separate publication. The first listing details new printings of books by Lovecraft, and additional lists identify contributions to periodicals; non-fiction; poetry; revisions and collaborations; letters; material included in books by others; apocrypha and other miscellany; books in translation; translated short fiction; translated verse; translated material in books by others; and Lovecraft criticism, book reviews, theses and unpublished papers. A final two-page list details errata and corrections to the original volume. Unfortunately, dozens of the periodicals listed in the bibliography are small-press publications not generally available to the average researcher. Library collections specializing in twentieth century American horror fiction will need this definitive Lovecraft bibliographical supplement as well as the original bibliography. For other Lovecraft-related material see items 84, 127 and 215.

185. Larson, Randall D. *The Complete Robert Bloch: An Illustrated Comprehensive Bibliography.* Sunnyvale, CA: Tandom Unlimited Enterprises, 1986. 126p.

The Complete Robert Bloch is one of the best, most complete and most detailed bibliographies ever compiled for a living SF/fantasy author. The volume also is a continuation of bibliographic research on Bloch which Larson has been doing for many years. Bloch provides a brief introduction, and separate listings provide information on short stories, novels, collections, nonfiction, introductions and forewords, verse, radio/film/TV scripts, bibliographic and biographic materials, and miscellaneous. There is even a bibliography of fanzine materials, and supplemental listings for short stories by magazine, a chronology of first appearances, unanthologized stories, "Lefty Freep" stories, collaborative stories, and pseudononymous stories. Remarkably complete, the separate bibliographies list hundreds of foreign publications—generally a weak area in bibliographies of living SF/fantasy authors. There are even special codes to denote stories which have been adapted for TV and film. Hundreds of cover photos of books and magazines, some interior magazine illustrations, and numerous film/TV stills greatly enhance the bibliography. The cover photos of foreign editions of books provide an interesting glimpse into Bloch's work as an internationally-known writer of horror fiction. This book is highly recommended for collections specializing in bibliographies of contemporary SF/fantasy/horror authors. For other Bloch-related material see item 24.

186. Laughlin, Charlotte and Daniel J.H. Levack. *De Camp—An L. Sprague De Camp Bibliography.* Columbia, PA: Underwood-Miller, 1983. 328p.

The de Camp bibliography begins with an introduction which explains how the bibliography was compiled. Listings include books written by de Camp, edited books, non-book appearances (includes verse, radio scripts, book reviews, etc.). Supplementary material includes indices to the fiction, verse, book reviews, radio scripts and other non-fiction, as well as a chronology, a list of pseudononymous works, a guide to "connected works, continuing characters and series," a list of the books de Camp has written which may be categorized as belonging to non-fantasy and non-SF genres, a list of collaborations, a checklist of magazines to which he contributed (title, volume, number and date), a checklist of works by Catherine Crook de Camp (she collaborated with her husband on several projects) and an index. This book contains more primary bibliographical information on de Camp than any other existing work, though it has two weaknesses—one of which is a lack of coverage of secondary material. The other is the catch-all listing of "non-book appearances," although the effects of that are somewhat moderated by the separate indices. Still, it is possible that a researcher might want all the titles of radio scripts, or all the listings for verse, in one list for ease of use or for photocopying. The book is highly recommended for collections emphasizing SF author bibliography. See Appendix I for an evaluation of the Underwood-Miller author bibliographies.

187. Levack, Daniel J.H. *Amber Dreams: A Roger Zelazny Bibliography.* San Francisco and Columbia, PA: Underwood-Miller, 1983. 151p.

Levack's Zelazny bibliography has listings for books, edited books, stories (a mixed category including verse, nonfiction articles, short fiction, etc.), a checklist of magazines in which Zelazny's work has appeared, a checklist of works about Zelazny, a list of miscellaneous items, a cross-reference of connected stories and continuing characters, and lists for pseudonyms and collaborations. Indices provide access to verse and nonfiction titles, and the book includes a chronology. Although book reviews probably constitute the bulk of critical material on most SF authors, reviews of Zelazny's books are not listed. Critics, researchers, collectors and others interested in Zelazny will find much useful information on Zelazny in this book, including numerous entries for foreign editions of his books. The annotations are occasionally rendered in a silly pseudo-rustic style ("...that the enemies besetting his land may be conquered") and unprofessionally colloquial ("...and remains a basket case until his mid-teens), but the bibliography is thorough and would make a fine addition to an author bibliography collection. For other Zelazny-related material see item 148; see Appendix I for an evaluation of the Underwood-Miller author bibliographies.

188. Levack, J.H. and Tim Underwood. *Fantasms: A Bibliography of the Literature of Jack Vance.* San Francisco, CA: Underwood-Miller, 1978. 91p.

This Levack and Underwood bibliography lists the English language appearances of Jack Vance, under his real name (John Holbrook Vance) and his pseudonyms. There are separate listings for novels and short fiction, as well as indices for series, connected stories and pseudonyms; a publishing chronology; and a list of television screenplays by Vance and screen adaptations of Vance's work. The bibliography is liberally illustrated with reproductions of book and magazine covers, and even though the compilers claim in their introduction that the listings are thorough only for English-language publications, the book contains a substantial amount of information on foreign language appearances of Vance's books and short fiction. As with all U-M bibliographies, this work is recommended for any collection emphasizing SF or fantasy author bibliography. For other Vance-related material see item 141; see Appendix I for an evaluation of the Underwood-Miller author bibliographies.

189. Lord, Glenn, ed. *The Last Celt: A Bio-Bibliography of Robert Ervin Howard.* West Kingston, RI: Donald M. Grant, 1976. 416p. RSF.

Rather than forming a unified interpretive Robert E. Howard biography, *The Last Celt* is a collection of reminiscences, biographical sketches and memorial tributes by E. Hoffmann Price, Alvin Earl Perry, H.P. Lovecraft, Harold Preece and Glenn Lord. A letter and autobiographical fragments by Howard complete the biographical section. The bulk of the volume is taken up by an extensive bibliography which lists books, short fiction by Howard (including cross references for variant titles), short fiction co-written by Howard and others (some were "posthumous collaborations," usually a story fragment left by Howard that was later finished by someone else), stories of "uncertain authorship" which are suspected of being written by Howard, verse (with title, first-line and heading indexes), articles, letters, an index of stories by the periodicals in which they were published, foreign book publications, short fiction translated into foreign languages, verse translations, article translations, letter translations, unpublished fiction, unfinished fiction, unpublished verse, and numerous other miscellaneous items. Material about Howard also is included in separate listings. Some miscellaneous inclusions are offset reproductions of handwritten Howard material, typewritten manuscripts, letters from Farnsworth Wright to Howard, and other items. *The Last Celt* is not a comprehensive biography, but it contains a useful accumulation of biographical information, and the bibliography is the best Howard bibliography in existence. The book is an important addition to any library collection emphasizing twentieth century popular fantasy writers, pulp fiction studies and research or modern epic/barbaric fantasy. For other Howard-related material see items 126 and 144.

190. Owings, Mark. *James H. Schmitz: A Bibliography.* Baltimore, MD: Croatan House, 1973. Unpaginated (31). TYS.

The introduction to this bibliography (the introduction was written by Janet Kagan) takes up more than half the book. Kagan suffers from at least as many unreasonable assumptions as she points out in male readers, male writers and male characters, and in fact most of what she rails against is composed of paper tigers she has erected for quick and easy demolition. The tone is argumentative rather than explanatory or exploratory, and at one point her word choice gets so colloquial as to be offensive. She also uses exclamation marks to denote instances of amazement which she apparently assumes will amaze the reader also. The bibliography is the single-entry type, arranged alphabetically and all works chronologically. Schmitz began writing in the 1940s and was part of the "Campbell Cadre," contributing stories occasionally to *Astounding/Analog*. Though he is not one of the best-known or most widely recognized SF writers, his Telzey stories are generally accepted as a ground-breaking series featuring a female protagonist and extensive use of ESP powers. This bibliography seems to be the most complete and current Schmitz bibliography, notwithstanding the fact that it is now more than 15 years out of date.

191. Rathbun, Mark and Graeme Flanagan. *Richard Matheson: He Is Legend*. Chico, CA: Mark Rathbun, 1984. 55p.

The Rathbun/Flanagan bio-bibliography of Richard Matheson is everything a fan-generated bibliography should be but often is not. It contains short articles, letters, reminiscences and appreciations by several writers, including Rathbun, Robert Bloch, William Campbell Gault, Jerry Sohl and Matheson himself, with additional one-paragraph comments by William F. Nolan and Jack Finney. The bibliography lists, in separate sections, novels, short story collections, short stories, published television scripts, interviews, foreign translations, miscellanea (articles, afterwords, introductions), novels adapted by other writers from Matheson's film and TV scripts, films, television programs, other television work, unproduced motion picture and television scripts, and teleplays. The booklet is profusely illustrated. An introduction by Ray Bradbury was printed on a separate sheet, folded, and tipped into the booklet between the cover and the first page. One rather serious shortcoming is the lack of a listing for reviews or criticism, rather an important category of information for a writer such as Matheson who has scripted literally dozens of films and television programs. The booklet format notwithstanding, any library attempting to provide basic bibliographic research materials for the SF/fantasy/horror genres will want to consider locating a copy of this Matheson bibliography.

192. Robinson, Roger. *Ken Bulmer*. Essex, England: Beccon Publications, 1983. 51p.

Current bibliographical information for contemporary writers can be difficult to find. The SF field been fortunate because fans always have been willing to undertake the difficult and time-consuming task of gathering information about favorite authors. This bibliography, done as a tribute to Ken Bulmer on the occasion of his appearance as the guest of honor at an SF convention, is not as complete as it could be, probably due to time limitations. Because so much information was left out, a 1984 update was issued on two 8½ x11 sheets which were stapled, folded and inserted as an addendum to the booklet. The 50-page booklet includes an introduction by Ken Bulmer, an appreciation by John Clute, a list of pseudonyms, an alphabetical listing of fiction, a listing of nonfiction, a list of professional and amateur edited works, a "career schematic," a list of book series, a list of short story series, and a chronological publication list. The booklet and addenda sheets contain a great deal of information about Bulmer—probably more than is available on the prolific author anywhere else—and that makes the booklet a valuable contribution to SF bibliography, but the booklet format makes it awkward for library use.

193. Sidney-Fryer, Donald. *Emperor of Dreams: A Clark Ashton Smith Bibliography*. West Kingston, RI: Donald M. Grant, 1978. 303p.

As with many of the best bibliographies of genre writers, *Emperor of Dreams* was compiled as a labor of love and yet turned out to be perhaps more detailed and more useful than a "standard" scholarly bibliography might have been. The first chapter, "Principal Facts of Biography," presents the basic information on Smith's life in the form of an extensively annotated chronology, and the numerous bibliographical listings detail such subject areas as Smith's poems in French, poems in Spanish, uncollected poems, uncollected tales, juvenilia, contributions to periodicals, published letters, and pseudonyms. There are eight photos and 14 letters of appreciation by such SF/fantasy notables as Fritz Leiber, Ray Bradbury, August Derleth, Stanton Coblentz, Avram Davidson, H. Warner Munn, Harlan Ellison, E. Hoffman Price and Sam Moskowitz. The volume includes an index to the first lines of poems, a list of materials about Smith, and a description of library holdings of Smith manuscripts. *Emperor of Dreams* is an excellent bio-bibliography of a genre writer, and the standard bibliographic reference for research on Clark Ashton Smith.

194. Wilson, Richard, and Chris Drumm. *Adventures in the Space Trade and A Richard Wilson Checklist*. Polk City, IA: Chris Drumm, 1986. 36p.

Like many other mid-range SF authors—that is, writers who have authored a sizeable body of excellent fiction but are somehow overlooked and neglected critically—Richard Wilson is undervalued. The Drumm booklets fulfill a definite need in SF—the need for continuously revised and expanded bibliographic coverage of living authors who are still writing. Wilson is best known for his 1960 novel *30-Day Wonder*, but he has written a great deal of fiction over a period of 45 years. The Drumm bibliography of Wilson's work is chronological with the separate entries identified as short stories, novels, etc. Because the bibliography was published with Wilson's assistance, unpublished items are included, as are some translated items. The individual items are numbered and the title index refers to the items by the numbers. Bound in with this booklet is a 20-page memoir by Wilson titled "Adventures in the Space Trade." Full-length autobiographies or memoirs still are relatively rare in the SF field, and with Wilson's recent death, this too-brief autobiographical essay may be one of the only major sources for biographical material on Wilson available to fans and researchers. The inclusion of the autobiographical essay in this checklist makes the booklet an essential source for the study of Wilson and his writing. See Appendix I for an evaluation of the Drumm booklet series.

Section 5
Biography, Autobiography, Letters & Interviews

195. Aldiss, Brian W. and Harry Harrison, eds. *Hell's Cartographers.* New York: Harper & Row, 1975; London: Orbit, 1976. 246p. RSF, SRB, TYS.

When *Hell's Cartographers* was first published in 1975, the publication of SF author biographies was a fledgling field. Aldiss and Harrison paved the way for the numerous SF author biographies and autobiographies that would make sporadic appearances beginning in the late 1970s by editing and publishing this collection of autobiographical essays by Aldiss, Harrison, Robert Silverberg, Alfred Bester, Damon Knight and Frederik Pohl. The essays are an excellent source of biographical material about these important SF authors, though most of the essays have been published before (Aldiss' own essay, "Magic and Bare Boards," appeared in *Foundation*). The six authors selected for inclusion all are major creative talents in the SF field, and their essays are interesting and entertaining as well as biographically informative. The most obvious complaint about the book is that it should have included more than six subject authors—or that the book logically should have become the first of a series of such volumes. An appendix provides selected bibliographical listings for the authors represented. The only major flaw in the book is the lack of an index. *Hell's Cartographers* is

highly recommended as a worthwhile addition to any collection emphasizing SF biography and autobiography. For other Aldiss-related materials see
items 1, 2, 3 and 282; for other Harrison-related material see item 287.

196. Asherman, Allan. *The Star Trek Interview Book.* New York: Pocket
Books, 1988. 278p.

If any interview subject has been "done to death," that subject is *Star
Trek.* Yet Asherman's volume of interviews is far better than the ordinary
run of fan-generated interviews. The usual major figures are interviewed—
Roddenberry, Shatner, Nimoy, Kelley, Takei, Nichols, Koenig and Whitney,
but Asherman goes several steps further and includes people connected with
the pilot programs (Butler, Goldstone and Peeples); writers involved with
the series (Sohl, Kandel, Johnson, Spinrad, Dixon); producers (Dobkin,
Senensky, Daniels, Pevney); plus two guest stars, ten members of the technical crew, and three people connected with the ST feature films. There are
38 interviews; the questions were not "fill in the blank" formula inquiries,
but appear to have been researched and formulated separately for each interview. Asherman obviously researched the interviewees as well as the questions, and the book does not inundate the serious reader with in-group fan
talk and inside jokes. The one major flaw is the lack of an index, regrettable
in light of the fact that in the text of the interviews a plethora of names and
titles are mentioned in passing, and easy access to this information would
have been helpful. No doubt uncritical ST fans will be happy with the book
just because it contains interviews with the people of *Star Trek,* but the volume also is suitable for inclusion in collections with SF literature and film
interview source materials.

197. Born, Franz. *Jules Verne: The Man Who Invented the Future.* New
York: Prentice-Hall, 1963. [hardcover]. New York: Scholastic Book Services, n.d. 143p. [paperback]. Translated from the original German edition
by Juliana Biro.

Shelley, Wells and Verne are the only pre-1900 SF authors known to the
average reader (with the possible exception of Poe, depending upon how the
descriptor "SF author" is used), so accurate and interesting studies of these
authors are important for all age levels. *The Man Who Invented the Future*
is a clear and readable translation from a German-language biography. It is
not a detailed and comprehensive biography, but a "broad outline" account
that sketches in the general contours of Verne's life and then fleshes out
the sketch with some anecdotes and other personal information about Verne.
Verne's major novels are examined chronologically as the events in the
subject author's life caused or allowed him to write them. This Scholastic
Book Services paperback has been issued in numerous printings, is readily

available, and represents a more than adequate introduction to Verne for students at the the junior high school level. For other Verne-related material see item 301.

198. Campbell, John W., Jr. *The John W. Campbell Letters, Volume I.* Franklin, TN: AC Projects, Inc., 1985. 610p. Edited by Perry A. Chapdelaine Sr., Tony Chapdelaine, George Hay.

As SF grows in respectability, more and more literary paraphernalia, such as letter collections, will become available. This volume is perhaps the single most important collection of SF-related letters that will be published, simply because Campbell was one of the pre-eminent twentieth century forces that shaped modern science fiction. Although hardly a complete collection—Campbell was widely known as an inveterate and tireless letter-writer, and the final count, if anyone ever tallies the number of individual letters, could run to the tens of thousands—this book, apparently the first in a projected series, brings together a generous sampling of the thoughtful, witty, intelligent, and provocative letters which Campbell produced in such profusion. A complete catalog of topics covered in the letters would be almost impossible, but the collection contains dozens of letters sent to such well-known figures as L. Ron Hubbard, A.E. van Vogt, William Rotsler, L. Sprague de Camp, Jack Williamson, Will Jenkins, Eric Frank Russell, Poul Anderson, Harry Stine, Fred Pohl, Jim Blish, Chad Oliver, Mark Clifton, Cliff Simak, Don Wollheim, Jerry Pournelle, and Alfred Bester, among others. The first letter is dated April 5, 1938, and the last is dated July 1, 1971. Campbell's brilliance, and his familiarity with many different fields of study and inquiry, is amply displayed by this volume of letters, but the letters were selected specifically for their discussions of the merits (or lack of merit) of specific SF short stories or novels. Because of Campbell's unquestioned—and perhaps unparalleled—influence in the SF field as editor and, to a lesser extent, as writer, his letters are certain to become a major research source for future literary analysis and biography. Collections emphasizing associational SF research materials, such as letters and biographical information, will need this book.

199. Carpenter, Humphrey. *Tolkien: A Biography.* Boston: Houghton-Mifflin, 1977. New York: Ballantine, 1978. 327p. RSF, SRB.

Carpenter's biography, the "authorized" biography researched with the benefit of access to letters, diaries and other Tolkien papers, is thorough, readable, and of inestimable value to those who want to know more about Tolkien. Professor Tolkien himself disapproved of biography as a tool for prying into an author's fiction, and in deference to that point of view, Carpenter has avoided direct evaluation or critical reference to Tolkien's fiction in light of events in Tolkien's life. *Tolkien: A Biography* is widely accepted as being very nearly a definitive biography, yet Carpenter does use some writing strategies that are of questionable value in a biography. The most serious problem is the use of a journalistic technique which foreshadows, and in so doing heightens the reader's expectations. In the introductory section "The Visit," for example, Tolkien is described as having a "strange voice," with a quality that cannot be defined, "...as if he had come from another age or civilization." This type of description obviously is intended to sensitize the reader to the idea that Tolkien lived in "another world," so to speak, and simply wrote down events he had witnessed in unimaginable realms, but a biographer should know better than to set up a self-fulfilling prophecy which already has come true. This kind of writing technique is used by journalists especially in feature material because it creates an air of inevitability; it is a form of "shorthand" to establish atmosphere and direction without honest labor. The biographical excesses, though serious, are not debilitating. The book contains 32 pages of black and white photos, a genealogical table of Tolkien's family, a list of published works, an explanation of sources and acknowledgements, and an index. Because it is an authorized biography prepared with the cooperation of the subject and, later, his family, it should remain an indispensible element in the biographical study of one of the greatest authors of modern fantasy. For other Tolkien-related material see items 35, 85, 95, 104, 105, 123 and 140.

200. Carr, John L. *Leigh Brackett: American Writer.* Polk City, IA: Chris Drumm, 1987. 67p.

Few SF writers—excepting Heinlein and Asimov, the two most visible monoliths in the field—have been the subject of unified book-length biographies and critical analyses. Leigh Brackett is one of the unsung heroes of the genre, a master storyteller and scriptwriter both in and out of the SF environs who was overshadowed by the big names and left behind during the recent mass confusion in the "scholarly evaluation" arena. John L. Carr has come along quietly, picking up the pieces and sorting out the facts of Brackett's life, and is in the process of assembing one of the best and most interesting SF author biographies written to date. This booklet seems to be a condensation of a much larger body of material, perhaps because Carr was working on a dissertation (with Brackett as the subject) at the time he was preparing this booklet. Collector-completists will want to acquire the Brackett booklet, but it is to be hoped Carr will render Brackett, SF fans and SF researchers an invaluable service by editing his own dissertation into a publishable book on Brackett. For libraries, a bound copy of the dissertation would be better than this booklet, but if Carr will split the difference between the booklet and the dissertation and present the SF world with the first book-length Brackett biography and critical evaluation, the biographical and critical information in this Drumm booklet suggest that the expanded version would become the standard reference for Brackett and her work. See Appendix I for an evaluation of the Drumm booklet series.

201. Clarke, Arthur C. *The View From Serendip.* New York: Random House, 1977. 273p. MIN.

Arthur C. Clarke has not only witnessed the development of all the major space programs, from Sputnik to Apollo and Voyager, he has accurately predicted some aspects them. He co-wrote the novel and screenplay of the single most influential science fiction film in history (*Space Odyssey*) and is a renowned scientist and science fiction author. This "fragmentary biography" is important for these reasons alone, but it is regrettable that the book could not have been structured more in the form of a true autobiography. Separate chapters and sub-sections deal with various experiences—scuba diving near Ceylon, working on the book/film *2001* with Kubrick, acting as a TV commentator during the Apollo launches—but the book, though interesting, entertaining and valuable, is unorganized. It is unindexed as well, and will be a very difficult-to-use source text for biographical research. Notwithstanding the structural shortcomings, the book does contain a high concentration of biographical information on Clarke, and will have to serve in the stead of a true autobiography unless and until Clarke decides to write one. It is a suggested acquisition particularly for collections specializing in SF autobiographies or SF biographical materials. For other Clarke-related material see items 102, 116, 137, 252 and 253.

202. Cowart, David, and Thomas L. Wymer, eds. *Dictionary of Literary Biography, Vol. 8: American Science Fiction Writers.* (Two vols. Part I: A-L, 306p. Part 2: M-Z, 346p.) Detroit, MI: Gale Research, 1981.

Biographical treatment in this two-volume set ranges from three pages for Katherine Maclean to 15 pages for Isaac Asimov, averaging perhaps 7-10 pages per author. Each entry includes some preliminary biographical information (birth date, parents' names, education, spouse's name, awards, etc.), a list of selected books, the biographical essay itself, and a list of other books, periodical publications and references (the periodical publications and references, presumably, are quite selective, at least in some cases). Most entries include a photo, and some feature cover or interior illustrations from books or magazines. There is an occasional "special" inclusion—for example, in the case of Robert Silverberg, the illustrations include a reproduction of a page of the typescript from "Schwartz Between the Galaxies." The "selected books" and "other" categories are in chronological rather than alphabetical order, which makes it difficult to find a specific title. There seems to be no apparent justification for dividing an author's publications arbitrarily into two lists; the lists of publications, for the sake of convenience (especially in the case of the extremely prolific authors), should have been reduced to one single alphabetical listing. The essays are lengthy and detailed, offering more information about a writer in one place than may be found in almost any other single source (with the exception of the authors who have been treated in book-length studies). Of special note are the essays on SF writers who have been deceased for many years; authoritative biographical information on these authors is extremely difficult to locate, and the essays on such authors as Stanley Weinbaum, H. Beam Piper, C.M. Kornbluth, Cordwainer Smith (Paul Linebarger), Henry Kuttner and Ray Cummings help to "humanize" writers who are virtually unknown, except through their fiction, to the contemporary reader. Appendices include Trends in Science Fiction; The Media of Science Fiction; Fandom and SFWA; A World Chronology of Important Science-Fiction Works (1818-1979); Selected Science Fiction Magazines and Anthologies; and Books for Further Reading. There is also a cumulative index to the first eight volumes of the Gale *Dictionary of Literary Biography*. Highly recommended as an acquisition for collections rerquiring basic biographical research sources for SF writers.

203. Elliot, Jeffrey M. *Science Fiction Voices #2*. San Bernardino, CA: Borgo Press, 1979. 62p. MIN.

The first Borgo Press volume of SF author interviews was compiled by Darrell Schweitzer (item 216). This second volume of *SF Voices* still has no table of contents and no index. An introduction by Richard A. Lupoff opens the book, and in this volume the interviews at least are visibly separated by interview titles and the name of the author interviewed. Each interview is introduced with a brief foreword by Elliot, though these forewords tend to be overly enthusiastic and more like advertisements than introductions. The interviewer's questions are reasonable, answerable, and lead the authors into lengthy explanations of their lives, their opinions, and their works. *SF Voices* as a series-within-a-series tends to feature well-known writers who have been over-interviewed already rather than newer or more obscure authors for whom biographical information is scarce, but the interviews are well-conducted and interesting. The authors interviewed in this book include Larry Niven, Ray Bradbury, A.E. van Vogt, Poul Anderson and Robert Silverberg. Recommended for collections with a strong emphasis in contemporary author interviews.

204. Elliot, Jeffrey M. *Science Fiction Voices #3.* San Bernardino, CA: Borgo Press, 1980. 64p. MIN.

The third volume in the interview series continues the tendency to interview "name" writers rather than lesser-known authors for whom interviews and biographical data can be difficult to find. A.E. van Vogt provides the introduction; authors interviewed are Harlan Ellison, David Gerrold, Richard Lupoff, Gregory Benford and Jerry Pournelle. This volume includes a black and white photo of each author interviewed. Elliot has an annoying habit of asking two questions almost simultaneously, without giving the subject time to answer the first question, but in general Elliot's questions are well-planned and directed toward getting good responses from the subjects rather than injecting himself into the interview as "interpreter" of the authors' comments and explanations. The volume is recommended for collections emphasizing author interviews and related material.

205. Greenberg, Martin H., ed. *Fantastic Lives: Autobiographical Essays by Notable Science Fiction Writers.* Carbondale, IL: Southern Illinois University Press, 1981. 215p.

Biographical information has been in short supply in the SF field for most of the time the field has been a recognized literary subdivision. *Fantastic Lives* helps fill the void, especially in regards to several SF authors for whom there is very little biographical material available. Authors represented by the autobiographical essays collected into this volume include Harlan Ellison, Philip Jose Farmer, R.A. Lafferty, Katherine MacLean, Barry N. Malzberg, Mack Reynolds, Margaret St. Clair, Norman Spinrad and A.E. van Vogt. In some respects, many of the essays included here are not traditional autobiographical essays—that is, essays concerned with the complete scope of an author's life and experiences. Ellison's essay focuses on one of his most popular and controversial stories, "I Have No Mouth, and I Must Scream"; Lafferty's essay is an unconventional view of the development and value of the SF field, but contains very little actual autobiography; Malzberg's contribution is a mosaic of previously published ppieces brought tohether to explain the ten-year period when he was most active as an SF writer and his subsequent "burnout"; and so on. However, several of the essays are the more traditional "life summaries"—for example, the Mac-Lean and the Reynolds essays. None of the essays is quite long enough to provide as much information as might be desirable for major contributors to the SF genre, and in some cases, the essays in this collection may turn out to be the single most important source of autobiographical information on certain authors, so this volume (and those to come, if the concept evolves into a continuing series) must be considered a key addition to any collection which features any degree of concentration in SF biography/autobiography.

206. Lane, Daryl, William Vernon and David Carson. *The Sound of Wonder: Interviews From "The Science Fiction Radio Show," Volume 1.* Phoenix, AZ: Oryx Press, 1985. 203p.

"The Science Fiction Radio Show" was an SF interview program broadcast from 1980 to 1983. The program began as a local broadcast and ended as a nationally syndicated production. In the beginning, "theme" or "author" programs were the norm, though occasionally the subjects interviewed included "...movie and television people, scientists, artists, editors, agents, critics, fans, translators and collectors." A photo and introduction are provided for each person interviewed. The interviews range from a half-dozen pages to 25 pages, averaging perhaps 15-20 per subject. Authors interviewed in this volume include Stephen R. Donaldson, C.J. Cherryh, Hal Clement, Charles Harness, Theodore Sturgeon, Howard Waldrop, Jack Williamson, Rudy Rucker and Michael Whelan. The questions asked are handled more professionally than in many interview volumes, but the book reads as if only the most interesting questions and answers were retained from a transcript with other material, perhaps less well explained or less interesting, being edited out. The interviews don't end so much as they just go on for a time and then are stopped at a certain point—a sure sign of extensive editing. The mixture of older and younger authors, genre masters and less-well-known writers, also is better than average. *The Sound of Wonder* is a recommended addition to collections specializing in SF author interviews and supplementary biographical sources.

207. Lane, Daryl, William Vernon and David Carson. *The Sound of Wonder: Interviews From "The Science Fiction Radio Show," Volume 2.* Phoenix, AZ: Oryx Press, 1985. 201p.

Most of the comments pertaining to volume one of this series can be applied to volume two as well. The introduction to this volume does explain a bit more about the abrupt and "fractured" nature of the interviews—the interviews were "cut and pasted" to fit a five-minute format. The producers taped up to two hours of interview with a single subject, sometimes visiting the interviewee in his or her home and sometimes taping the conversations over the telephone, and then editing out everything except the "most interesting" segments. The format of volume two is the same as the first book—a photo and one to two pages of introduction for each subject, followed by 10 to 30 pages of interview excerpts. Authors interviewed include Piers Anthony, Edward Bryant, Philip Jose Farmer, Donald A. Wollheim, James P. Hogan, Marion Zimmer Bradley, Roger Ebert, Gene Wolfe, Gordon Dickson and George R.R. Martin. The second volume also is recommended for collections with concentrations of biographical, autobiographical, or interview material representing SF authors.

208.   Platt, Charles. *Dream Makers* New York: Berkeley Books, 1980. 284p. MIN, SRB.

Charles Platt excels at a form of slick article/interview that might be called "interpretive interview." In this volume, the first of two collections of SF author interviews, Platt interviews 28 of the best-known and most important authors who have contributed to the SF genre. Biographical information can be difficult to find on many SF authors, despite the SF-related nonfiction publishing expansion in recent years, so the Platt volumes will be a good source of information for many years to come. One unusual chapter concerns Cyril Kornbluth, who died in 1958. Platt interlaces his own critical assessments and an interview with Kornbluth's widow for a useful fusion of information and viewpoint. At least two of the authors represented in the collection have died since the book was first published, so their interviews will become one additional source of biographical information in the patchwork quilt of such sources which often serves as biographical source material for SF authors. Platt has a tendency to let his own ideas and observations get in the way of the interviews upon occasion, but he is extremely knowledgeable about science fiction and is able to avoid the common fan-interview problem of asking the same questions over and over in slightly different terms. Each interview is followed by a bibliographical note which provides, in most cases, an admirably concise overview of each author's work. The one serious problem is the lack of an index. Authors represented in this collection of interviews: Isaac Asimov, Thomas M. Disch, Robert Sheckley, Kurt Vonnegut, Hank Stine, Norman Spinrad, Frederik Pohl, Samuel Delany, Barry Malzberg, Edward Bryant, Alfred Bester, C.M. Kornbluth, Algis Budrys, Philip Jose Farmer, A.E. van Vogt, Philip K. Dick, Harlan Ellison, Ray Bradbury, Frank Herbert, Damon Knight, Kate Wilhelm, Michael Moorcock, J.G. Ballard, E.C. Tubb, Ian Watson, John Brunner, Gregory Benford, Robert Silverberg and Brian Aldiss. A "self-profile" of Platt, himself an occasional writer who has contributed several minor novels to the genre, also is included. The book is recommended for collections with an emphasis in SF author interviews or for collections needing interesting and useful biographical materials on contemporary SF authors.

209.   Platt, Charles. *Dream Makers Volume II: The Uncommon Men & Women Who Write Science Fiction.* New York: Berkley, 1983. 300p.

It was perhaps too much to expect that the second volume of interviews would maintain the same level of quality as the first. In this second collection, Platt injects too much of himself into the interviews—they become, in effect, biographical essays with quotes rather than interviews. The spectrum of writers represented is broad, and includes non-SF authors (Alvin Toffler), horror writers (Stephen King), and all types of SF authors from venerable "first names in SF" (Clarke, Vance, Leiber, Sturgeon) to relative newcomers. The last interview in the book is an interview of Platt done by Douglas E. Winter. There is no index, though an index would have been quite useful for access to the extensive information presented in the interviews. Not all of the authors in this collection have been "over interviewed" in other publications (Christopher Priest, Joanna Russ, Kit Reed, etc.) and some of the authors are now deceased (Wollheim, Sturgeon), so the book represents a useful and valuable collection of information about many SF or SF-associational authors. Authors represented include Jerry Pournelle, Larry Niven, Christopher Priest, William S. Burroughs, Arthur C. Clarke, Alvin Toffler, John Sladek, D.M. Thomas, Keith Roberts, Andre Norton, Piers Anthony, Keith Laumer, Joe Haldeman, Fritz Leiber, Robert Anton Wilson, Poul Anderson, Jack Vance, Theodore Sturgeon, L. Ron Hubbard, Joanna Russ, Janet Morris, Joan D. Vinge, Harry Harrison, Donald A. Wollheim, Edward L. Ferman, Kit Reed, James Tiptree (Alice Sheldon) and Stephen King. Each interview is followed by a "bibliographical note," and the book includes a reference bibliography, a list of the interview dates, and an interview of Charles Platt done by Douglas E. Winter. The two Platt interview volumes would make excellent acquisitions for a collection needing representative biographical materials on a large number of well-known and popular SF/fantasy authors.

210. Pohl, Frederik. *The Way the Future Was: A Memoir.* New York: Ballantine Books, 1978. 312p. New York: Ballantine Books, 1979. 293p. MIN.

Pohl has been a major SF writer since his first novel was published in 1953 (a collaboration with C.M. Kornbluth), and he also has been a major contributor to the field as an editor and anthologist. His memoirs are an important SF historical document because he has spent virtually his entire career contributing to the SF field. Pohl fans and readers will be interested in his memoirs, as will libraries specializing in biography and autobiography of SF/fantasy authors, but beyond the obvious interests, SF author memoirs—a relatively new phenomenon in the SF field—represent untapped reserves of biographical material for future literary historians who will one day attempt to piece together a more or less accurate historical view of the major twentieth century SF writers and their contributions to the field. Sixteen pages of black and white photos are included, but a serious flaw in the book is the lack of an index. Most important SF authors and many minor SF authors and personalities are mentioned in some context in the book, and an index would have made access to the mass of information much more convenient. For other Pohl-related material see item 272.

211. Pollock, Dale. *Skywalking: The Life and Films of George Lucas, the Creator of Star Wars.* New York: Harmony Books, 1983; New York: Ballantine Books, 1984. 332p.

Lucas, the creator of the continuing *Star Wars* saga, is a major SF/fantasy film figure, so a biography was both inevitable and necessary. The problem of a biography of Lucas is his age—he isn't very old just yet, and if he lives the average threescore-and-ten years or more, and barring any severe physical debilitation that could occur, his filmmaking career is perhaps not yet half completed. With only a handful of films to survey (admittedly, among that handful are some of the most successful screen fantasies ever filmed) it is to be expected that Pollock would dwell on each film at great length. The first hundred pages constitute a general biography of Lucas' life and the early influences. Later chapters undertake to explain the genesis, incubation, and maturation of the Lucas films, including details about personal relationships (much wordage is devoted to the relationship between Lucas and Francis Ford Coppola) and anecdotes about filming, editing, test screening and other phases in the life of a film project. The account is valuable for the amount of material gathered together, including numerous quotes from friends, relatives, associates and others who have (or once had) close personal contact with Lucas. But the author of the biography sometimes takes liberties with the portrayal of some of the people mentioned in the book, especially Lucas' father. There is, perhaps, an unsubtle overdependence on hindsight of the "Lucas foresaw, correctly..." variety, which tends to impart mythic abilities to a person who is described as if he were an oracle rather than a talented filmmaker. This may be a small point in itself, because the author likely had no way to find out about the things Lucas might have foreseen incorrectly, but it is part of a larger pattern that is too often evident in popular biography—a biographer should set out to tell the truth, whatever the truth turns out to be, but a "popular biography" usually is directed by a pre-supposition about how the subject should be viewed by the reader. The resulting book is an attempt to get the reader to see and believe the "right" view. This biography, therefore, is an interim effort, and will have to do until someone decides to do the job a bit better. The book includes 16 pages of black and white photos, a filmography, source notes and an index.

212. Porges, Irwin. *Edgar Rice Burroughs: The Man Who Created Tarzan.* Provo, UT: Brigham Young University Press, 1975. 820p. AOW, RSF, SRB, TYS.

Prepared with the complete cooperation of Edgar Rice Burroughs' company and his family, including unrestricted access to all files, records and correspondence, Porges' biography of ERB is, and probably will remain, the definitive biography and the universal starting point for all research into the life and work of ERB. Burroughs was a prolific author, producing vast quantities of published fiction as well as a large volume of unpublished material. Many of the unpublished works are described in Porges' book, which makes the volume a valuable bibliographical source as well as a thorough biography. Because of ERB's position as one of the originators of the barbaric fantasy genre, and because of his prodigious output, descriptions and synopses of his stories could not be avoided. Porges integrates these descriptions into the text and, in so doing, provides sharp and insightful criticism across the entire spectrum of ERB's work. Family relationships are detailed, and excerpts from letters and published sources paint a complete portrait of the strengths and weaknesses of an author who has come to be regarded as a major force in the development of commercial fantasy fiction in the twentieth century. The introduction was written by Ray Bradbury. Statements in the text of Porges' biography are well documented with notes, but the notes are separated into an appendix. More than 270 photos were selected for inclusion in the book, many never before published. Numerous book jackets and magazine cover illustrations are included. ERB's relationship with book and magazine publishers is particularly well-documented, and film researchers will find in the book valuable details about the transfer (or attempted transfer) of ERB's works to film. Appendices provide detailed information about ERB's parents and genealogy; a short, humorous fictional autobiographical sketch by ERB; a list of ERB's works taken from information supplied by the Burroughs family; a list of Tarzan films; reminiscences by Hubert Burroughs and Forrest J Ackerman; and an index. Any collection which addresses modern epic or barbaric fantasy, or any collection intended to provide complete biographical or bibliographical information on twentieth century fantasy authors, should include a copy of this invaluable book. For other Burroughs-related material see items 107 and 125.

213. Price, Vincent. *Vincent Price: His Movies, His Plays, His Life.* Garden City, NY: Doubleday, 1978. 117p

Vincent Price is an "All I Want to Know" Book, a juvenile that should be of interest to students through high school. The book is profusely illustrated with film stills and other photos. The text is short, many of the photos are full-page, and pages facing the first page of some chapters are blank, all of which mean the autobiography has the look and feel of an article puffed up and stretched out to book size. Price is one of the best-recognized and most popular horror film actors, and an autobiography should be of great interest to SF/fantasy/horror film devotees, but the writing style employed in this book is so obviously directed toward a juvenile audience that the tone is almost condescending. Price has worked with most major screen and stage actors over the years (he was himself a "mainstream" screen/stage actor for many years before making the decision to "specialize" in horror films), so he has many amusing anecdotes and "behind the scenes" stories to tell, but the total effect is a foreshortened and watered-down autobiography with none of the depth or detail required to make it a useful research volume on any level above high school. Recommended only for high school or junior high libraries with collections emphasizing horror film biographies/autobiographies or books on widely-known and popular actors.

214. Rickman, Gregg. *Philip K. Dick: The Last Testament.* Long Beach, CA: Fragments West/The Valentine Press, 1985. 241p.

Rickman's extensive interviews and conversations with Philip K. Dick, gathered into several books, form the core of what may come to be regarded as the single most important collection of biographical and interview material on a twentieth century SF author. Dick is considered one of the best authors ever to work in the SF field, and his stature as a major author means there will be many books and articles about him and his work in the years to come. Rickman's interview volumes will provide for future researchers a source of inestimable value; what the researchers will make of Dick's often confusing views on mysticism, religion, and philosophy undoubtedly will be tempered by the lengthy and freewheeling discourses in this book, apparently the last major series of interviews Dick granted before his death. That the material overall has great value is unquestioned, yet the format in which it is presented is awkward. Interviewer intrusions are almost constant, and often are unnecessary. An 11-page interview with one of Dick's ex-wives is inserted into the middle of the book with promises to include other Tessa Dick interview material in other volumes. Careless (or nonexistent) proofreading has produced awkward and embarrassing typos such as, "The book will also include an interview with Doris Sauter, a cancer who lived with Phil briefly in the mid-1970s." Rickman's prose could have profited from the attentions of an editor, copy editor or proofreader, and the book has somewhat less value than it might have had because of the decision to exclude an index. *The Last Testament* is destined to become a major source work for research on a major SF author, and it must be recommended on those grounds, but librarians and potential readers and researchers should be aware of the book's considerable flaws and weaknesses. For other material related to Philip K. Dick see item 143.

215. Schultz, David E., ed. *H.P. Lovecraft: Commonplace Book* (2 vols). West Warwick, RI: Necronomicon Press, 1987. i-xxvi, 1-81p.

Though likely to be of interest only to a very limited readership, this version of Lovecraft's commonplace book (several other versions are identified in the introduction, including the handwritten original, a typed copy with significant variances from the handwritten original, etc.) addresses most of the serious problems with publication of a "definitive" version of the book (e.g., Lovecraft's tendency to erase "used" entries). In the first volume, the introduction explains the approach used for assembling this version of the Lovecraft commonplace book and the problems encountered. There are tables showing the disposition of leaves in manuscript A; the disposition of entries in manuscript A; the disposition of entries in manuscript B; entries omitted from manuscript B; and a list of the items in the three separate published versions of the book. Volume one also contains the Schultz-edited version of the book. Volume two, keyed to the commonplace by entry number, explains each entry (indications of which items have been used by Lovecraft or others in their fiction, etc.). There is a bibliography and index. Lovecraft is one of the seminal horror/supernatural authors of the twentieth century, and any well-done Lovecraft study—such as this definitive study of the Lovecraft commonplace book—will be useful for searching out influences in the horror fiction genre in general or for Lovecraft studies in particular. For other Lovecraft-related material see items 84, 127 and 184.

216. Schweitzer, Darrell. *Science Fiction Voices 1.* San Bernardino, CA: Borgo Press, 1979. 63p. MIN, RSF.

Interviews in *SF Voices 1* are well-conducted and directed, with the interviewer keeping his intrusion to a minimum and his questions reasonable and answerable, but the book itself is not very attractive. There is no table of contents and no index, and the interviews are separated so rudimentarily it is difficult to tell, just by leafing through the book, where one interview ends and the next begins. Authors interviewed include Theodore Sturgeon, Alfred Bester, Frederik Pohl, James Gunn, Fritz Leiber, Hal Clement and L. Sprague de Camp. Most of these authors have been interviewed many times before in SF books and publications, so this volume may be considered an accessory publication intended primarily for fans of the authors interviewed, but the book also could be useful as a supplemental acquisition for collections with an emphasis in author interviews and related materials.

Section 6
Encyclopedias, Dictionaries, Indexes & Checklists

217. Ash, Brian. *Who's Who in Science Fiction*. London: Elm Tree Books, 1976; New York: Taplinger, 1976. 219p. RSF, SRB.

Ash's *Who's Who* is a volume of basic biographical information about SF authors. The book contains approximately 400 briefly-sketched biographies arranged in alphabetical order. Biographical coverage is very much a "surface" coverage—authors and other personalities are characterized in a minimum of space, and in most cases there is some mention of the major works by each author. Some of the entries, however, are so brief as to tell virtually nothing about the subject, while others are primarily a list of major works with little basic biographical data. The sketchy and ill-defined coverage occasionally includes artists, editors, and foreign writers, as well as English-language writers. Some minor figures (Samalman, Low, Hall, Schachner) are included. Although the book is titled *Who's Who in Science Fiction*, many purely fantasy authors are included—Kline, Burroughs and Cabell among them, though Tolkien, for whatever reason, was excluded. Erich von Daniken is included, the rationalization for which is known only to Ash. The book includes a select bibliography of books on SF. The volume has been superseded (and, in some cases, preceded) by better researched, better organized, better written and more comprehensive efforts: Reginald (item

160), Tuck (item 240), Nicholls (item 232), Cowart (item 202), etc., so Ash's biographical dictionary is not recommended.

218.   Ash, Brian, ed. *The Visual Encyclopedia of Science Fiction.* New York: Harmony Books, 1977. 352p.

The Visual Encyclopedia represents a departure from the normal "encyclopedia" because it is not an alphabetical listing of authors, books or films. Instead, it concentrates on grouping themes and ideas commonly explored in SF literature and film. An extensive chronology (1805-1976) lists writers, books, films, television, radio, and fandom milestones in the progression of SF. Thematic explorations in the main body of the book are briefly introduced by such SF luminaries as Poul Anderson, Jack Williamson, Harry Harrison, Lester del Rey, Brian Aldiss, John Brunner, J.G. Ballard, Robert Sheckley, Fritz Leiber, Fred Pohl, Isaac Asimov, Arthur C. Clarke, etc. A "deep probes" section presents lengthy opinionated essays by Brian Ash, Edmund Cooper, George Turner, Damon Knight and L. Sprague de Camp, and several short chapters deal with such topics as fandom and media, SF art, SF film, SF television, SF magazines, books and anthologies, juvenile material, comics and comic strips, and fringe cults. The volume is indexed, but a weakness of the index is page number citations for pages where a particular author is mentioned or discussed but no citations for written contributions to the book by the same author. The Poul Anderson entry, for example, has 19 page references, but no reference for the introduction he contributed on page 68. Treatment of themes is broad yet detailed, and the sections are followed by bibliographies listing novels and stories that expand upon the ideas discussed in each section. There is extensive use of graphics and photographs, and many of the photos are in color. This encyclopedia would make a good thematic supplement to a more conventional SF encyclopedia, but when acquisition is limited to one volume, the Nicholls compilation (item 232) is the preferred SF encyclopedia.

219.   Ashley, Michael, comp. *Fantasy Readers Guide: A Complete Index and Annotated Commentary ,to the John Spencer Fantasy Publications (1950-1966).* Tyne and Wear, England: Cosmos Literary Agency, 1979. 54p.

Ashley, noted SF indexer and bibliographer, has produced in this volume a detailed index of the British John Spencer fantasy publications. Besides a brief history of the Spencer magazines, the volume has a checklist of publications with approximate publication date, number of pages, number of stories and cover artist; issue by issue listing of contents; a list of magazine novels later reprinted as separate novels (along with alternate titles for book publication); and an author index extensively cross-referenced for pseudonyms. Contributors to the magazines included such writers as Chetwynd-Hayes, E.C. Tubb and Murry Leinster, as well as multiple-pseudonym high-volume writers like Glasby and Fanthorpe. The 6x8½ softbound stapled booklet, apparently printed offset from cloth-ribbon-typed originals, is likely to present some use and storage problems for libraries.

220. Barron, Neil. *Anatomy of Wonder: Science Fiction.* New York: R.R. Bowker Co., 1976. 471p. MIN, RSF, SRB.

To date, *Anatomy of Wonder* is the best organized treasure trove of information for the librarian charged with the task of beginning or upgrading a library collection in the science fiction field. The book is well-organized. SF literature is divided into five categories: "proto" SF from the beginnings to 1870; SF romance 1870-1926; the Gernsback era 1926-1937; the modern period 1838-1975; and juvenile material. The second part of the book deals specifically with research materials and general interest information. The various indices include history/criticism/biography, bibliography/index/teaching aids, magazine and book review indexes, periodicals, literary awards, a core collection checklist, and library collections. There is a directory of publishers, and an author-title index. All the contributors (Neil Barron, Robert Philmus, Thomas Clareson, Ivor Rogers, Joe DeBolt, John Pfeiffer, Francis Molson, H.W. Hall) are extremely knowledgeable about the SF field. Although not without errors, the mistakes are not as glaringly apparent as in many nonfiction/reference volumes. For example, the synopsis for Heinlein's *Have Space Suit—Will Travel* states that Kip wants to go to the moon but never makes it; in fact, pages 64-116 of the novel chronicle Kip's adventures on the moon. Another problem crops up occasionally in the annotations for nonfiction and reference books. Alva Rogers' *A Requiem for Astounding* is said to be "gravely impaired" because it deals with a single magazine. Rogers' book may have limited research uses, and critical judgments may be softened somewhat by nostalgia and sentimentality, but criticizing a one-topic book because it does not deal with other topics makes no more sense than belittling a Shakespeare biography because it contains no information about Faulkner or Hemingway. Two or three index entries have a name reference but lack page numbers. Yet the mistakes and omissions are few and far between and very difficult to find, and overall the mistakes do very little to reduce the volume's utility for a librarian needing maps to the "here be dragons" areas in SF.

221. Contento, William. *Index to Science Fiction Anthologies and Collections.* Boston: G.K. Hall, 1978. 608p. MIN, SRB.

Index to Science Fiction Anthologies and Collections is a major research source for those interested in SF book collecting and SF bibliography, though its usefulness to the general reader or undergraduate student is limited. The index covers over 2,000 books with full contents listings for 1,900 books containing 12,000 stories by 2,500 authors. There is a list of abbreviations, a checklist of books indexed, an author index, a story index, and the contents listing. The computer used to sort the index and print out camera-ready copy apparently did not have a printer with lower case letter capability. All text in the index is set in all caps, though that fact and the reduction percentage used for reproducing the printed material detract only slightly from the volume's utility. It is possible to find small errors (for example, on p. 233 the name "Tincrowdor" is spelled "Tincrowder"), but the errors are few and of little consequence. Because SF books in general and anthologies in particular go in and out of print so quickly, this anthology/collection index is likely to be of more use to collectors and bibliographers. Few libraries maintain an extensive collection of SF anthologies and SF short story collections, so even if a general reader were to look up his favorite author and find 20 anthology entries under that name, he would be unlikely to find those 20 anthologies in the library's holdings. Still, adequate indexing and bibliography are the basis for literary research in any genre, and the Contento index is recommended as one of the very basic acquisitions for any SF holdings that include the most important research tools.

222. Fletcher, Marilyn. *Science Fiction Story Index*, second edition. Chicago: American Library Association, 1981. 610p.

Fletcher's anthology index is an expansion of the earlier Siemon index (item 237). The listings are similar: a list of anthologies with identifying code numbers; a title index, listing story title, author, and anthology code numbers; and an author index, listing story titles and anthology codes. The book apparently was sorted by computer and the printouts used for camera-ready copy. Ironically, the Fletcher index is less comprehensive and less useful than the Contento index (item 221), yet the Contento index is listed in the Fletcher book as one of the sources used to identify anthologies. Why a compiler would use a comprehensive standard reference to compile a less comprehensive and less useful volume dealing with exactly the same subject matter is unclear. Fletcher's compilation indexes about 1,000 anthologies and collections, perhaps less; the Contento book not only indexes 1,200 volumes, but provides more information, including a contents listing for each anthology and collection indexed. The Fletcher index represents unnecessary duplication of information better arranged and presented elsewhere. When an SF collection/anthology index is required for a reference collection, the Contento volume is the recommended acquisition.

223.   Franson, Donald, and Howard DeVore. *A History of the Hugo, Nebula and International Fantasy Awards.* Dearborn Heights, MI: Howard DeVore, 1975. 129p. AOW, RSF, SRB, TYS.

Numerous SF reference and "source books" list award-winning stories, novels, films, etc. in the genre, but the Franson-DeVore history of the Hugo, Nebula and International Fantasy awards is the standard reference. Histories of the three awards are provided, as well as lists of nominations for each category (the winning entry in each category is printed in boldface type). Starting with 1966, both the preliminary list of nominees for the Nebula and the "second" or "final" ballot are given. The volume is indexed, and coverage is complete through 1979. The book is now dated, and an updated edition would be very useful. Even more useful would be an updated edition that includes some of the newer awards, such as the annual Jupiter Award for fiction and the Pilgrim Award for scholarly work done in the SF/fantasy field. Despite the fact that the information on award-winning stories, novels, films and so on is not current, the book still offers excellent summary histories of the awards themselves and complete balloting information from 1966 to 1979 that is not to be found in other "title checklist" awards summaries.

224.   Hagemann, E.R. *A Comprehensive Index to Black Mask 1920-1951 with Brief Annotations, Preface and Editorial Apparatus.* Bowling Green, OH: Bowling Green University Popular Press, 1982. 236p.

Black Mask was one of the longest-running "hardboiled detective" magazines in early magazine publishing history. The fiction published in the magazine probably holds little interest for the average SF reader/researcher today, but this index will be important to SF bibliographers because the list of *Black Mask* contributors includes such well-known SF, fantasy, horror and supernatural writing talents as Leinster, Boucher, Brown, England, Cummings, Dent, Siodmak, Pangborn, Starrett, Wandrei, Hyne, Cave, Woolrich, Bedford-Jones and others. Research apparatus includes a register of the BM issues published, including volume numbers and a code list indicating where the copies indexed were located; an issuance listing which records the frequency of publication and the changes in frequency; the names of the editors and the dates of their tenure; title changes; price changes; a combination list of editors and writers arranged by debut and including the total number of appearances in the magazine; a select bibliography; and a main listing which is alphabetical by author with detailed information including page numbers. Libraries with strong detective fiction research holdings, SF "associational" research titles, magazine index collections or pulp magazine research materials will want to give serious consideration to acquiring this extremely well-researched index to a popular and influential early detective magazine.

225. Hall, H.W. *Science Fiction Book Review Index 1923-1973.* Detroit, MI: Gale Research, 1975. 438p. AOW, RSF, SRB, TYS.

One of the very basic SF reference books, Hall's index lists book reviews of SF books for the 50-year period 1923 to 1973. The majority of the reviews are to be found in the SF magazines themselves, although listings for numerous other journals and periodicals are included—*Saturday Review, Best Sellers, Center for Childrens' Books—Bulletin, College English, English Journal,* etc. The main listing is alphabetical by author; under the author's name the books are listed by title, and under each title the reviews are arranged alphabetically by the code indicating where the reviews may be found. Information includes a code for the periodical title; volume, number, page and year date information; and reviewer's name (if the review was bylined). There is a directory of magazines indexed, an editor index (editors of books included in the listings), and a bibliography of SF magazine indexes. Hall's index, the annual cumulations, and subsequent bound volumes for later periods are an indispensible SF reference which supplement the "standard" book review sources (until recently, the "standard" sources usually did not index book reviews found in popular or genre fiction magazines). Hall's index is recommended as one of the most primary acquisitions for a basic SF reference and research collection.

226. Holdstock, Robert, ed. *The Encyclopedia of Science Fiction.* London: Octopus Books, 1978. 219p.

Few SF encyclopedias are truly encyclopedic, and *The Encyclopedia of Science Fiction* is no exception. Information in the book is presented on a random hit-or-miss basis in round-up essays divided into sub-sections such as "Labelling" or "SF Art." Brian Stableford provides an introduction to the Victorian genesis of the scientific romance, and Douglas Hill contributed to the volume an essay on such SF themes as dystopia, the resistance, machines, invasion, earth's future, and so on. Additional chapters and contributors include Mike Ashley on pulps and magazines, Alan Frank on films, Harry Harrison on machines, Chris Morgan on aliens, David Hardy on art, Patrick Moore on the closure of the gap between speculative fiction and reality, and Christopher Priest on the "new wave." Appendices and miscellaneous matter include brief discussions of collecting, fandom, awards, pseudonyms, magazines, film, and conventions, plus an index. None of the sections is truly comprehensive, and many of the items reduced to abbreviated appendices (pseudonyms, SF film, awards, etc.) are themselves the subjects of full-length books which more adequately explore each topic. The volume is profusely illustrated, in color, and that remains one of its strongest features. The book is now dated and serves little purpose except as supplement to more comprehensive efforts. Where an excellent general SF encyclopedia is needed, the Nicholls volume (item 232) is the preferred acquisition.

227.   Jakubowski, Maxim and Malcolm Edwards. *The SF Book of Lists.* New York: Berkley Books, 1983. 384p.

Partly a collection of meaningless SF-related information and partly an SF-trivia maniac's treasure trove, *The SF Book of Lists* is a marvellously useless volume with such ephemeral and ultimately unusable "factoids" as lists of "highly overrated" SF novels, items of "SF terminology," and "Spider Robinson's All-Time-Favorite Larry Niven Titles." Most of the book is pointless fan-generated nonsense, apparently intended to be extremely lightweight entertainment for SF fanatics who would rather hypnotize themselves with boring facts and opinions of questionable value than read a book containing real information. There are two useful features in this otherwise meaningless compendium: some of the year-by-year fiction listings contain titles of Hugo and Nebula award winners (the major SF awards are covered in more detail in *A History of the Hugo, Nebula and International Fantasy Awards* by Franson and Devore, item 223), and some of the listings serve as a rudimentary theme or motif index, e.g. lists of novels and/or short stories dealing with computers, fictional worlds inhabited only by women, prehistoric eras, dinosaurs, clones, crucifixion, Atlantis, etc. Otherwise, the book has little or no research value and is not recommended for acquisition.

228.   Justice, Keith. *Science Fiction Master Index of Names.* Jefferson, NC: McFarland, 1986. 394p.

In spite of the somewhat awkward title, the *Master Index* was intended to make secondary materials in the SF field more accessible. The major index to secondary information about SF—and a landmark volume—is the Hall book review index, but the Hall volume is by definition a book review index and provides no direct access to any secondary material other than reviews. The *Master Index* is a compilation of index references for 132 reference and nonfiction books in the SF and fantasy fields. Of the works indexed, 22 do not have integral indexes and are not indexed in any other way. A list of indexed books by the abbreviations used to identify them, a listing by author of the books indexed, and a listing by title are included as supplementary indices. The main listing includes page numbers, and the index can be used not only to generate a working list of books which will contain information about a specific author, but also can act as an aid to interlibrary loan by indicating page numbers for ordering photocopies from books not otherwise available through the interlibrary loan process. Although not intended as a thorough index of pseudonyms, because of the necessary cross-referencing the index provides a good working list of pseudonyms used by the authors represented. Some references were not indexed in the original sources, and in some cases they were indexed improperly, which makes them difficult to research in the originals; the *Master Index* corrects many indexing errors in the integral listings of the volumes indexed.

229. Lester, Colin, ed. *The International Science Fiction Yearbook 1979.* United Kingdom: Pierrot Publishing, Ltd., 1978. 394p.

Information collected in *The International Science Fiction Yearbook* is similar to data gathered into other general reference volumes such as *The Science Fiction Reference Book* (item 241), but Lester's volume is international in scope. A vast amount of information is included—and that contributes to the major problem, which is a glut of information that will date very quickly in a "yearbook" type publication. There are 29 sections offering data on obituaries, book publishing, magazines, organizations, fanzines, agents, anthologies, criticism/commentary/bibliography, translators, libraries, book clubs, conventions, artists, films, and more. The volume contains much that is of value, but the use of a clumsy and confusing code system and the lack of an index are serious faults. Apparently the 1979 edition was the only edition of the yearbook published.

230. McGhan, Barry. *Science Fiction and Fantasy Pseudonyms.* Dearborn, MI: Howard DeVore, 1973. 77p. AOW, RSG.

The importance of McGhan's compilation of pseudonyms, originally published in 1976, was overshadowed in 1979 with the publication of the James Rock dictionary of pseudonyms. The Rock book (item 235) is more ambitious, with a wider scope, but the McGhan book is more reliable. (Rock also includes book titles and publishing information in his book; the McGhan book is strictly a pseudonym listing.) Rock does not provide notes to indicate where his information on pseudonyms originates; McGhan provides notes. McGhan's listing has an author's real name in bold print and pseudonyms in normal print. Several extra pages of names were added to the listing for the 1979 edition of the McGhan pseudonym directory. A random sampling of the two books shows more pseudonyms listed for Jack Vance in the McGhan book, but more pseudonyms listed for William Rotsler in the Rock volume. Because the books have complementary strengths and weaknesses, collections with an emphasis in research into SF pseudonyms and pseudononymous SF literature and will need both books.

231. Metcalf, Norm, comp. *The Index of Science Fiction Magazines 1951-1965.* El Cerrito, CA: J. Ben Stark, 1968. 249p. AOW, RSF.

The Metcalf index is one of two SF magazine indexes for the period

1951-1965. It has features which are lacking in the Strauss index (item 238) and the Strauss index has features not included in the Metcalf index. The Metcalf volume has author and title indexes, an artist/illustrator index, an editor index, a magazine checklist, and an errata/addenda listing for the 1926-1950 Day index. The story index has some minor inconsistencies—for example, in the Damon Knight listing, "An Eye for What?" is alphabetized under "A" rather than "E". However, the Metcalf index includes information on Knight as a translator for several stories by French writers, and this information is not included in the Strauss volume. Metcalf also includes miscellaneous material, such as book review columns, photos, and nonfiction articles not listed in Strauss. Another strength of the Metcalf volume is the cross-referencing of co-authored material; the Strauss index is not cross-referenced. If a library or individual planned to acquire a magazine index and for budgetary or other reasons were limited to one book, the Metcalf index is generally the more useful in every aspect except for one: in the Strauss volume, the contents of each issue of each magazine is listed. The ideal situation is to acquire both indexes so information can be cross-checked for accuracy and completeness.

232. Nicholls, Peter, ed. *The Science Fiction Encyclopedia.* Garden City, NY: Doubleday, 1979. 672p. MIN, SRB.

The past decade has seen the publication of a number of volumes purporting to be encyclopedias of the science fiction field, but the Nicholls compilation comes closest to fulfilling the promise of the word "encyclopedia." Coverage is extremely broad but is also in-depth where the subject requires. Listing is alphabetical, and subjects include fantasy and SF authors, films, awards, SF fandom, television, comics, art and magazines. Even items of terminology are included, such as "gas giant," a planetary descriptor originated by James Blish, and "waldo," a term coined by Robert Heinlein for a mechanical materials-handling device; both terms came to be accepted and used by the scientific community. House names and major pseudonyms also receive entries, as do major social, philosophical, scientific and science fictional concepts such as utopia, time travel, terraforming, disaster, nuclear power, clones, genetic engineering, perception and others. To make the volume even easier to use, it is extensively cross-referenced; within each article key words or phrases which are explained in detail in separate entries are indicated in all caps. Each author entry is given an amount of space more or less coincidental with his or her relative importance to the field, and a title listing (not always exhaustive) completes the entry. Phenomenally successful or important books and films are given separate listings. The Nicholls volume is the nearest thing to a "compleat" SF encyclopedia yet published, and is the preferred acquisition when purchase is limited to one SF encyclopedia.

233. Robinson, Roger. *Science Fiction and Fantasy Magazine Collector's Checklist 1926-1980.* Essex, England: Beccon Publications, 1984. Unpaginated (97).

The compiler of this booklet states in a brief introduction that he intended to produce a handy checklist of all issues of all SF magazines published from 1926 to 1980, and he has done exactly that. This booklet should be of value to anyone who collects magazines and needs a compact and portable file for keeping track of titles already acquired. The book's small size (4x7) and plastic "comb" binding make it ideal for serving its intended purpose. Some irregularities do exist in the checklist—for example, in the *Astounding/Analog* entry, volume 40 shows six issues, and is followed by volume 50 with one issue and volume 41 with issues two through six. This apparently was a simple error not corrected during proofreading, and it does not seriously damage the utility of the checklist. However, the volume and issue numbers are a bit too compressed, leaving nearly one-inch margins on both sides of the printed listing—and that leaves but little space to mark issues of magazines a collector has acquired. Publications listed include English-language SF and SF-related magazines (American, Canadian, British and Australian) and some "paperback" magazines such as *Destinies.* Robinson's booklet is recommended for use as a handy checklist and record-keeping booklet for magazine collections.

234. Robinson, Roger, comp. *Who's Hugh? An SF Reader's Guide to Pseudonyms.* Essex, England: Beccon Publications, 1987. 173p.

Pseudonyms are a problem in the serious study of any literary field, and particularly so in SF. There are several pseudonym dictionaries compiled specifically for the SF genre; the McGhan volume (item 230) is the best, though now out of date, and James Rock's pseudonym index (item 235) contains a vast amount of information mixed with a dismaying amount of misinformation. Robinson's index probably contains more information about each name in each entry than any earlier indexes, but the format is extremely awkward. The book actually is two indexes in one—an index by pseudonym and one by "usual name," but rather than being arranged consecutively they are interlaced page by page, creating one of the most needlessly confusing SF reference volumes ever published. An update of existing research sources for SF/fantasy pseudonyms was a good idea, and Robinson's book gathers together some information not previously compiled into a pseudonym index, but the uselessly confusing format was a serious error. The discovery (and, in some cases, the use) of pseudonyms is an ongoing process, and periodic updates of pseudonym indexes are necessary. The Robinson index, however, should be used primarily as a supplement. Libraries with the McGhan and Rock indexes do not need the Robinson book, though for larger collections the extra cross-referencing and and additional names provided by an additional index could prove useful. Where the acquisitions budget presents no problem, obviously it would be best to have all three books; but McGhan is the primary acquisition, and Rock and Robinson are supplements which must be used with care and cross-checked for accuracy.

235. Rock, James A. *Who Goes There: A Bibliographic Dictionary of Pseudononymous Literature in the Fields of Fantasy and Science Fiction.* Bloomington, IN: James A. Rock & Co., 1979. 201p. MIN, SRB.

Intended as a comprehensive bibliography of pseudononymous literature in the science fiction and fantasy fields, *Who Goes There* has a substantial number of useful entries as well as a dismaying number of mistakes. The number and magnitude of the mistakes should cast some doubt on the overall usefulness and accuracy of any entry not easily double-checked in a more authoritative source. The work comes highly recommended by some scholars and critics—for example, in *The Science Fiction Reference Book* Tymn says of Rock's bibliography that it is "now the standard work," but those who intend to use the book should be wary of its weaknesses. The bibliography is arranged alphabetically by author's name, and a supplementary index and cross reference lists pseudonyms in bold print and actual authors' names in regular typeface. Some book titles are garbled, pseudonyms for which accurate identification has been available for years are listed as questionable or unknown, some well-known pseudonyms are excluded completely, and mistakes which occurred in other reference sources (e.g., an entry in a *Book Review Index* listing for Robert Silverberg under the mistaken pseudonym Walter Chapman rather than the correct Walker Chapman) are repeated here. Once a bibliographic detail has appeared in two reference sources it takes on a life of its own and may never be completely corrected, and while Rock's bibliography can serve as an excellent preliminary checklist of pseudonyms and titles, it also manages to contribute a lamentable number of bibliographic mistakes to a field already overburdened with such problems. The coffee-table size also makes it a difficult volume for libraries to handle efficiently. The book is recommended only for acquisition by larger collections for use as a cross-reference with other pseudononym dictionaries such as McGhan (item 230) and Robinson (item 234).

236. The Science Fiction Foundation. *Foundation: The Review of Science Fiction; Index, Numbers 1 Through 8, March 1972 to March 1975.* London: The Science Fiction Foundation, n.d. 14p.

Originally, this booklet was sent to subscribers to *Foundation—The Review of Science Fiction* because it indexes the first eight numbers of the British journal. The booklet has three listings; the first listing is by the author of each review or article, the second by the titles of articles published in the journal, and the third by the names of the authors of the books reviewed. The index was republished as part of the Gregg Press "omnibus" *Foundation* volume, a photo-offset reproduction of the first eight numbers of *Foundation* in a single hardcover book.

237. Siemon, Frederick. *Science Fiction Story Index.* Chicago: American Library Association, 1971. 274p. AOW, MIN, RSF.

Siemon's anthology index was an early effort to provide index access to the growing number of science fiction anthologies. The index served its purpose until it was superseded by the Contento index (item 221), which is far more comprehensive. Siemon's index has an author listing, a bibliography of anthologies indexed, and a title index. Only 200 anthologies are indexed. Siemon's introduction is elitist, condescending and self-congratulatory; in his discussion of alternate sources for information covered in his index, he states, "...they (other sources) reflect the approach used by nonlibrarians, being almost too specific and giving too much information. They are also less comprehensive." Exactly what "too much information" means is not explained. *Science Fiction Story Index* does not provide enough information, and its comprehensiveness is suspect. Anthology indexing, because of the more-often-out-of-print-than-in-print nature of paperback SF anthologies, is a secondary research concern, probably of interest to bibliographers more than anyone else. When a reliable and comprehensive anthology index is deemed a necessary addition to a basic SF reference and research collection, the Contento volume is the preferred work.

238. Strauss, Erwin S. *The MIT Science Fiction Society's Index to the SF Magazines 1951-1965.* Cambridge, MA: MIT SF Society, 1965. 207p. AOW, RSF, SRB.

A complete discussion of the relative merits of the Strauss and Metcalf science fiction magazine indexes may be found under the Metcalf entry (item 231). Both obviously contain very similar information, but Metcalf is far more complete, indexing even miscellaneous data such as photos, articles, and book review columns. However, the Strauss index has one major feature that is of great potential value to the researcher—a contents listing for each issue of each magazine indexed. This feature is useful for finding out what other stories appeared in the same issue of a magazine with a given story, and also provides access to contents information for hundreds of issues of magazines when the actual magazines themselves may not be available to a researcher. Useful though this feature may be, it represents a very specialized type of research, and a special book just to provide this extra dimension of information access is not a high priority acquisition. Because major features differ between the Metcalf and the Strauss indexes, it is best to acquire both when the budget or the scope of the SF reference collection permits. If a choice must be made between the two, the Metcalf book is the preferred index.

239. Sullivan, Jack, ed. *The Penguin Encyclopedia of Horror and the Supernatural.* New York: Viking-Penguin Books, 1986. 482p.

The Penguin Encyclopedia is a landmark compilation containing between its covers a wealth of basic information about the horror genre. Entries are alphabetical and include major authors, illustrators, films, and selected subject areas such as small press magazines, ghosts in Shakespeare's plays, Romanticism, poltergeists, and so on. Major authors are treated at length while lesser writers receive proportionately less coverage. The book is an extraordinary achievement and should go a long way toward providing a universally available and reasonably priced one-volume horror reference, but the volume possesses some idiosyncrasies of which the prospective user should be aware. The book is well-illustrated, but many of the illustrations lack any credits or acknowledgments whatsoever. For example, of the five illustrations accompanying the Edgar Allan Poe entry, three are identified by the artist and the story each was used to illustrate, one is identified only by the story it was once used to illustrate, and one is not identified in any way. The 55 essays include some unusual titles and subject areas—such as "The Pits of Terror," an idea which is unlikely to be researched as a topic unless a browser notices the title in the list of essays in the front matter. Because there is a list of the essays, locating a given essay or determining subject matter for a particular essay is more a minor inconvenience than a major problem, but the essays could have been titled more effectively for subject matter emphasis. An extensive amount of material is covered by the essays, but the information is inaccessible except through complete readings; the book's most regrettable failure is its lack of an index. The second most serious shortcoming evidenced by the book is an understandable tendency by the contributors to cast every writer even vaguely associated with horror fiction in an extremely favorable light. James Herbert, for example, is given lavish praise and is compared to John Wyndham when, in fact, Herbert's first several novels are pedestrian, inconsistent, and very much lacking in ability to suspend disbelief. But despite the limitations, this encyclopedia is an extremely useful and valuable reference, and is highly recommended for moderate to large collections needing good reference materials on the horror/supernatural genres.

240. Tuck, Donald H. *The Encyclopedia of Science Fiction and Fantasy (3 vols.).* Chicago: Advent, 1974-1982. 286p., 530p. AOW, MIN, RSF, SRB, TYS.

Tuck's three-volume SF encyclopedia was the first of the comprehensive science fiction "bio-biblio-enclylopedias." The books contain massive amounts of accurate information on American writers even though Tuck lives in Australia. Volumes 1 and 2 are arranged alphabetically, A-L and M-Z respectively. Listings are alphabetical by last name and include full name, birth date, death date (where applicable), a general background on the author or artist, and bibliographical entries which include brief descriptions of novels and lists of short stories in collections. The Tuck encyclopedia, though in part superseded by the Nicholls encyclopedia (item 232), is of particular interest for two reasons—it includes information, virtually unobtainable in any other English language publication, on foreign editions; and it is broadly representative of the SF/fantasy fields, with entries for artists, prominent fans, "marginal" Sf/fantasy writers, and others who are not recognized members of the hardcore mainstream of SF/fantasy writers. Volume 3 is a general "round-up" volume with information on series, pseudonyms, paperbacks, and magazines. Though the Nicholls encyclopedia is the most comprehensive in terms of broad scope and detailed coverage of mainstream SF, the Tuck volumes have substantial depth and detail and are far more useful than Nicholls for bibliographic purposes. Where budgets allow, it is recommended that the Nicholls encyclopedia be acquired first as the primary reference, and the Tuck volumes then added to extend biographic and bibliographic coverage for any general SF collection.

241. Tymn, Marshall B., ed. *The Science Fiction Reference Book.* Mercer Island, WA: Starmont House, 1981. 536p. MIN.

The Science Fiction Reference Book is a scattershot attempt to provide a wide range of information about many different aspects of science fiction and fantasy. A preliminary "Backgrounds" section has short essays on the history of SF, children's fantasy and SF, science fiction art and SF film. A chapter on critical studies and reference works provides too-brief annotations which do little more than identify works; there is not enough evaluation or critical commentary to familiarize a potential buyer or user with the strengths and weaknesses of a book. Fandom is the subject of the second major section, with subchapters on the history of fandom, writing awards, literary awards, and SF and fantasy periodicals. Section three is devoted to academe. Subjects include another historical overview and an annotated checklist of primary SF and fantasy works. A list of SF collections in U.S. and Canadian libraries and a bibliography of teaching resources (articles, handbooks and teaching guides) for the implementation of SF/fantasy courses in schools and universities round out the academic section. The method of structuring the library collection entries in the academic section is somewhat awkward and difficult to use. Several appendices provide lists of doctoral dissertations on SF and fantasy, names of SF organizations and societies, a list of specialty publishers, and a list of definitions of SF and fantasy. The volume is indexed, but the index includes misspellings (such as George Allen England), fictional characters (such as Tom Edison, Jr.) whose names are alphabetized by last name rather than by surname, and SF writers whose names are indexed twice, once under first name and once under last name, usually with different page references. The bulk of the information in this volume is of little use to the "average" Sf fan and reader. Small press and specialty publisher information in particular tends to date very quickly, and the "definitions" section is little more than an interesting frill. The book contains much information, but little of it will be of direct use to the average undergraduate student. Essays placing SF history, fan history and other SF-related subjects in perspective remain the book's most useful feature, but even these subjects have been handled better elsewhere. A library with no budget restrictions may want to get the book for the sake of completion, but any library with copies of the Barron survey (item 220), the Aldiss/Wingrove SF literary history (item 3) and the Nicholls encyclopedia (item 232)—three of the most important and basic library references on SF/fantasy—have no need for *The Science Fiction Reference Book*.

242.   Tymn, Marshall B., Martin H. Greenberg, L.W. Currey and Joseph D. Olander. *Index to Stories in Thematic Anthologies of Science Fiction.* Boston: G.K. Hall, 1978. 193p.

In the preface to this volume, the compilers state that the book is designed specifically for teachers "constructing thematic units for SF classes," for acquisitions librarians who want to add core titles to developing collections, and for scholars in the field. However, SF books go in and out of print so quickly it is doubtful that by the time the book was published any of the anthologies represented were available. There is no cross-referencing, which is difficult to understand in light of the compilers' intention that the book should be of use to teachers and others who may be assigned the task of teaching an SF course but who may not be thoroughly familiar with the field. There are, for example, separate reference citations for Lyle Monroe and Robert Heinlein, Murray Leinster and Will Jenkins, Henry Kuttner and Lewis Padgett, Raccoona Sheldon and James Tiptree, Jr., etc., without a word to indicate that each of these pairs of names represents a single author. The name index is not only deficient in cross referencing, but was carelessly typed, carelessly proofread, or both. Misspellings and erroneous rearrangements of authors' names are rife: F. Arlin Tremaine, K.M. O'Donnel, P.G. Wyal, H.B. Pyfe, Mildred Downey Broxor, Stephen Golden, L. Sprague Decamp, Doris Leesing, H. Beampiper, Ron L. Hubbard and Katherine Maclean are examples that leap from the pages. Even fictional characters are given authorial life, e.g. Helen O'Loy. Three confusing entries are given as Martin Greenberg, Martin Harry Greenberg and Martin Greenburg, with no word of explanation as to who is who. (There have been two Martin Greenbergs active in the SF field, but never a Martin Greenburg.) The mistakes are too many and too serious in this volume, and that should not have happened considering the professional stature of the compilers. As it stands, the book is all but useless, and a reference collection probably is better off without a copy of it.

243. Wingrove, David, ed. *The Science Fiction Source Book.* Essex, England: Longmans, 1984. 320p.

Like most of the numerous SF source books (general references that attempt to bring together something about everything), this Wingrove-edited volume presents a wide range of information—much of which is not overly helpful. The book opens with a concise history of the genre by Brian Aldiss. A section on "the SF sub-genres," by Brian Stableford, gives rather selective and spotty coverage of such themes, ideas and devices as man and machine, time travel, aliens, space travel, galactic empires, ESP, disasters, religion and mythology, parallel worlds and alternate histories, sex, alien ecology, and others. Frederik Pohl introduces a chapter on "the SF writer and his work," a slight section devoted to two-page descriptions by 11 writers who tell how they develop ideas, write outlines, and so forth. A list of authors and their first year of magazine publication, an essay on magazine publishing, a magazine checklist, author and title index, and other miscellanea complete the preliminary material. The main body of the book is a listing of SF authors, brief descriptions of the authors and their work, and a four-tiered coding system using a scale of none to five stars to rate readability, characterization, idea content and literary merit. The 880 bioliterary entries, ranging from a paragraph to a page in length and including some of the more obscure writers for whom information can be difficult to locate, is the most useful feature. Major problems are the inclusion of listings that should have been left out to make room for more appropriate items; the choice of the one-to-four novels or short stories selected for rating; and the near-useless rating system, which is predicated on the puzzling assumption that elements of a novel or story are entirely separate and unrelated, i.e. that "characterization" could be excellent in a book with extremely poor "readability," or that a book could have mediocre "idea content" but high "literary merit." Another weakness is the faulty criteria used to decide what would go in and what would stay out. A novel by Nat Schachner is flatly panned, for example, yet a novel like *Central Passage*, which is a solid contribution to the human superintelligence subgenre, is not even listed. There is no point in listing forgotten books by forgotten authors if the books have little reading value today; better to leave them out and include more references for books that *are* worth reading. There is some useful information in this volume, but it fails at its central purpose and cannot be recommended for use as a general SF reference or "source book."

244. Wysocki, R.J. *The Science Fiction, Fantasy, Weird, Hero Magazine Index.* Westlake, OH: Raymond J. Wysocki, 1985. 90p.

Magazine checklists are of use primarily to magazine collectors, although a librarian responsible for an SF magazine collection (either a static collection to which nothing is likely to be added or an active collection to which missing issues or new issues are constantly added) probably could put a checklist to good use. The Wysocki checklist, according to the foreword, "...lists those magazines that contain the printed word rather than illustrations" and assumes "...that the word is literature of the speculative type and fantastic in meaning. Closely allied would be the fantasy and weird/mystery stories." The compiler may be slightly muddled about terminology and phraseology in explanations of his checklist, but he has produced a compact (6x9) folded and stapled booklet which will serve the intended purpose adequately. While the form seems a bit awkward, the form of most checklists seems awkward—apparently this awkwardness is a structural hazard of collector checklists. The information is complete enough to require an extremely knowledgeable collector with a bibliographic memory and a vast magazine collection to find errors, and Wysocki provides a great deal of incidental and supplementary information about magazine sizes, title changes, paper stock, titles and author names for magazine-novels, "missing" (mistakenly numbered) magazines issues, and so on.

Section 7
Television,
Film &
Radio

245. Agel, Jerome, ed. *The Making of Kubrick's 2001.* New York: Signet, 1970. 367p. AOW.

2001 has been hailed as the single most significant SF film ever made. Whether or not such an evaluation is accurate, the film is important enough that a book about the making of the film is an important SF-filmmaking document. Agel's book should be important—and it is, in a limited sense— but it fails more often than it succeeds. There is a pleasant variety of material included in the volume, yet much of it has nothing to do with the film. There are cartoon satires of *2001,* pages of assorted quotes about everything from movie studios to Bob Dylan, and interviews with prominent scientists (many of the interviews do not even mention *2001*). These devices are, perhaps, an avant garde attempt to establish an atmosphere, and in that they are successful. The book easily could have been cut by 100 pages, and such editing would have made it a stronger, more focused and more useful book about film. A 96-page photo section provides generous (in some cases, over-generous) illustration with informative explanations of many special effects used in the film. Clarke's short story "The Sentinel," from which the *2001* screenplay was adapted and expanded, is reprinted in Agel's book, along with profiles of Kubrick, manuscript pages from the screenplay, excerpts from letters sent to Kubrick praising or damning the film, and other bits and pieces of fact, speculation and opinion. A few of the essays/

reviews are brilliant and stimulating, but the book is more a potpourri of wide-ranging *2001* film trivia and vaguely-related or unrelated tidbits of information than an organized effort to explain the evolution of a film from conception to finished product.

246. Anderson, Craig W. *Science Fiction Films of the Seventies.* Jefferson, NC: McFarland, 1985. 261p.

Science fiction films probably are more widely scrutinized and criticized than any other form of SF. Films are catalogued and surveyed from various viewpoints, but the classification by decade seems to be gaining the greatest acceptance as a method for identifying films types, trends, and "eras." Anderson surveys a representative sampling of good, bad and ugly SF films from the 1970s (a total of 50 films) by providing, for each film, release information; a synopsis; lengthy commentary; and complete cast/credit information. Occasionally he makes the critical error of using his impressions to infer a director's or producer's state of mind, e.g. "The film suffers from a lack of interest on the part of director Wilde," (p. 21). This is sometimes done by book reviewers and is patently unfair. A critic may determine that not enough attention was given to detail, that a film lacks polished production values, or that the director was not sufficiently skilled to meet the challenges presented by a particular film project, but the critic cannot deduce a director's state of mind at the time of filming just by viewing a film. Otherwise, Anderson provides generally solid evaluation, though he takes some unusual critical stands (which he acknowledges in his introduction). For example, he extols the virtues of the *Star Wars* films as mindless but exciting and pyrotechnic juvenile entertainment (most critics pan the films for the same reasons), and he has nothing but vitriolic distaste for SF/horror schlockmeister Roger Corman ("...after Corman and the others had completed their rape of the genre..." p. 7), whose films are idolized by millions as cult favorites. Anderson pays particular attention to film scores, an aspect of filmmaking which is often overlooked, and he offers a knowledgeable and interesting tour of a decade that produced some of the most popular box office successes of all time. A 32-page section of black and white photos and film stills is included, and the book is indexed. The book is a valuable supplement to collections with a strong SF film emphasis.

247. Bahrenburg, Bruce. *The Creation of Dino De Laurentiis' King Kong.* New York: Pocket Books, 1976. 273p.

Apparently this chronicle of the remaking of *King Kong* was written from the point of view of someone who witnessed the entire process, although there is no introductory material to explain whether or not this conjecture is correct. A great deal of information about the film is contained in this book, but most of the information is likely to be only of marginal research value. There is no index to simplify access to what information the book does contain, and the only appendix is a complete listing of the cast and credits. Fifty stills from the film are scattered through the book. The writing style employed by the author is closely related to the "magazine style"—slick, cynical and sarcastic, making everything about the film and its production seem dark and vaguely suspicious. Occasionally the author slips into long, circuituous asides, such as the lengthy segment on the death of Sal Mineo, which have little or nothing to do with the making of the most recent version of *King Kong* except to plump up the wordage and make the book bigger. Libraries with comprehensive popular holdings on SF films may need a copy of this paperback, but most SF collections will do just as well without it.

248. Benson, Michael. *Vintage Science Fiction Films, 1896-1949.* Jefferson, NC: McFarland & Co., 1985. 219p.

The earliest SF films often are "surface surveyed" in film books, discussed briefly if at all, partly because the SF film did not mature until mid-century and did not reach "staple blockbuster" status until the 1970s. Benson rectifies the problem of finding research materials on older SF films by discussing at length the SF and SF-related films produced from the beginnings of film to mid-century. Films are discussed in three divisions: the silent films, the sound films, and the serials. A representative sampling of films discussed includes *A Trip to the Moon, The ? Motorist, The Motor Valet, Tunneling the English Channel, Dr. Jeckyll and Mr. Hyde, The Picture of Dorian Gray, Metropolis, The Diamond Maker, Life Without Soul, The Inventor, The Conquest of the Pole, The End of the World, The Green Terror, The Death Ray, Mysterious Island, The Invisible Man, The Lost World, King Kong,* etc. The filmography section includes complete cast and production credits for all the films discussed. A bibliography and index are provided and approximately 20 black and white frame stills and rare publicity photos are reproduced. The book might have profited from an extra proofreading, but the minor mistakes do nothing to offset the value of the extensive information about early SF films.

249. Brosnan, John. *The Horror People.* New York: St. Martin's Press, 1976; New York: Plume/New American Library, 1977. 306p. RSF.

Brosnan's survey of horror films, and the people who make them, approaches its subject by way of detailed but readable biographical essays on major film figures. The survey begins with the Lon Chaneys (both Jr. and Sr.) and proceeds through such horror film legends as Lugosi, Karloff, Price, Lee and Cushing. Several chapters examine other aspects of horror cinema—a chapter on the writing of horror cinema (Matheson and Bloch), one on directing (Francis and Baker), and one on producing (Subotsky and Francis). There is even a chapter devoted to Hammer Films, one to American International Productions and Roger Corman, and one to horror fans. An epilogue discusses some recent developments in horror film, such as the release of *The Exorcist*. Of necessity, the book is somewhat dated because, as Brosnan observes in his epilogue, horror films underwent a major revitalization in the 1970s, apparently as part of a regular cycle of waxing and waning popularity which first began in the 1930s. While not exhaustive, Brosnan's survey is representative, and a valuable general overview of "pre-Stephen King" horror film. Liberally illustrated with black and white stills, the volume also has an appendix with capsule biographies of 49 additional horror film actors and other personalities, a name index, and a title index.

250. Brosnan, John. *Movie Magic: The Story of Special Effects in the Cinema.* New York: St. Martin's Press, 1974. 285p.

In *Movie Magic*, Brosnan presents a readable and interesting account of the development and use of special effects in filmmaking. Because most science fiction and fantasy films involve a large number of special effects of varying types and complexity, Brosnan's book is of more than passing interest to SF film research. Of particular interest to SF film researchers are a separate chapter on science fiction films and a chapter on *2001: A Space Odyssey* titled "The Ultimate (Special Effects) Trip." First published in 1974, Brosnan's book predates the boom in SF/fantasy film production that began in the late 1970s (*Star Wars, Star Trek, Raiders of the Lost Ark*, etc.), and the volume includes nothing on the extensive use of computer-generated visuals in films such as *Tron*, factors which reduce the value of the book considerably even as a general overview of the development and use of special effects. Recommended for collections specializing in SF film but not for general SF collections where a single volume may be needed as the sole representation for an important sub-topic.

251. Butler, Ivan. *Horror in the Cinema.* New York: Paperback Library, 1971 (second revised edition). 221p.

The strength—and weakness—of this horror in film (as opposed to "horror film") survey is its publication just before the advent of the modern era of graphic horror/atrocity portrayal. *Rosemary's Baby, Frankenstein Must Be Destroyed* and *Eye of the Cat* are the last three entries in the annotated chronology of selected horror films. Butler discusses, in the first three chapters, the general concept of horror in film, beginning with silent cinema; later chapters are devoted to more specific subject areas. There is a chapter on Dracula and Frankenstein, one on Hitchcock and *Psycho*, one on Roger

Corman and his Poe adaptations, one on Polanski and *Repulsion*, and some general chapters, such as "British Horror" (mainly a Hammer Films survey), which expand the scope of the survey. Critical evaluations are sound, especially judgments of earlier film efforts which are considered in the context of cultural milieu rather than dissected under the imprecise and misleading glare of comparison to contemporary methods, standards and production capabilities. The text presupposes a wide familiarity with most aspects of horror film and the reading level is suitable for the undergraduate college level. Includes approximately 60 black and white film stills, bibliography and index. Though dated, the book is recommended for collections with a strong emphasis on SF and horror film.

252. Clarke, Arthur C. *The Lost Worlds of 2001.* New York: Signet/New American Library, 1972. 240p.

The Lost Worlds of 2001 is only partly nonfiction. Clarke has gathered together into this volume bits and pieces of prose, alternate chapters, unused sequences and other leftovers from the *2001* book/film. As a piece of fiction, *Lost Worlds* is interesting but incomplete, and probably is of more use and interest to someone studying the simultaneous development of a novel and screenplay than to a general reader. Also provided are notes and explanations of the genesis and metamorphosis of *2001*, as well as the complete text of "The Sentinel", the Clarke short story which was the starting point for the film *2001*. This book is a literary oddity which shows how the novel and the film are similar yet different and how one must be changed to accommodate the modes of expression of the other, especially while a parallel novel/film project is underway. The most obvious research value of the book is its chronicle of the development of a novel and film that are considered to be classics in their respective SF fields. Collections specializing in SF film will need a copy of this paperback; for other collections, acquisition is completely optional. For other Clarke-related material see items 102, 116, 137, 201 and 253.

253. Clarke, Arthur C. and Peter Hyams. *The Odyssey File.* New York: Del Rey/Ballantine, 1984. 132p.

The Odyssey File is a glimpse into the friendship of two talented men. It is not really a glimpse into the making of a major SF film, despite the 16 pages of color plates from the movie *2010*. When Clarke and Hyams decided to make the film *2010*, they acquired computers and communicated electronically from Hollywood to Sri Lanka in spite of the time difference and the distance. This book is a collection of their electronic "letters." Some of it concerns the film, at least peripherally, but most of it does not. Interesting in its own right as an exchange of ideas, anecdotes, explanations, etc.

between intelligent, talented and creative people, it nevertheless fails to do the one thing a reader—who sees cover copy such as "An exclusive look at the making of 2010"—might expect it to do: provide information and technical background on the filming of *2010*. The book is much more likely to be enjoyed by computer hackers who can appreciate, and find humor and entertainment, in the trials and tribulations of two men who started from scratch and learned to use computers to solve complex recreational and creative problems. Clarke is an important SF figure, and the book may be recommended for that reason, but it is not a necessary acquisition for collections specializing in SF film. For other Clarke-related material see items 102, 116, 137, 201 and 252.

254. Cohen, Daniel. *Horror Movies.* New York: Gallery Books, 1984. 80p.
  The lack of attention to detail evident in this book may be exemplified by a statement from the introduction: "Other types of films—westerns, musicals, gangster films—rise and fall in popularity. Horror goes on forever." Horror films *do* rise and fall in popularity in regular cycles that have been well-documented and widely discussed for many years. The author of this survey makes it clear, also in the introduction, that he will be dealing not with SF, fantasy, suspense, thriller, or supernatural films, but with what he calls "hardcore horror." He begins the survey with the "roots" of screen horror (*Nosferatu, Caligari*, etc.) and moves forward through the various cycles of Dracula, Wolfman, Mummy, Frankenstein, Black Lagoon, and other monster motifs. There is some discussion/description of other film types (*Rhodan, Godzilla, Night of the Living Dead*, etc.) and the last chapter, "The Return of Big Time Horror," surveys such films as *The Birds, The Omen, Carrie, The Howling* and *The Shining*. A "stars" listing has brief biographies of 33 horror film stars, and a filmography presents extremely abbreviated cast/credit information for 139 films. The book is indexed, and many of its photos are in color. The author apparently got bogged down in semantics in the introduction and ended up doing exactly what he said he would *not* do, i.e., including discussions of SF, supernatural or fantasy films, but this is more a problem with saying one thing in the introduction and doing another in the book than making any serious errors in the book—there is no doubt all the films selected for inclusion can be classified, in some form, as "horror" films, though whether or not they are all "hardcore horror" may be a matter open for some speculation. The book is recommended only for junior high or high school libraries that do not already have any general illustrated horror film surveys for readers in the 13-18 age range.

255. Edelson, Edward. *Great Monsters of the Movies.* New York: Pocket Books, 1974. 119p.

Horror or "monster" films have increased dramatically in popularity over the past decades, and interest in the monsters that populate the films continues to expand. Edelson's monster survey is divided into five chapters. Legendary monsters are the subject of the first chapter and it introduces the reader to vampires, werewolves, zombies, the mad scientist or Frankenstein, and mummies; "The Pioneers" explores early film efforts such as *The Cabinet of Dr. Caligari* and *Nosferatu;* "Three Frightening Men" is a brief overview of the careers of Bela Lugosi, Boris Karloff and Lon Chaney, Jr.; "The Big Beasts" introduces such specific films or monsters as *King Kong,* dinosaurs and giant octopi; and "A Miscellany of Monsters" considers a range of topics, from remade versions of *Phantom of the Opera* to Roger Corman's films. The book has numerous black and white stills, it is indexed, and is suitable for use by students up to the junior high level.

256. Edelson, Edward. *Great Science Fiction from the Movies.* New York: Pocket Books, 1976. 149p.

Great Science Fiction from the Movies is a "surface" survey of SF films, done in a familiar, conversational style suitable for junior high or high school students. Edelson hits only the high points of SF film, beginning with Melies' *A Trip to the Moon* and ending with the *Star Trek* films. Coverage excludes horror films, and critical judgments on the value of particular films—which films should be considered "classics," which are relatively minor, and so on—generally are the standard and widely accepted judgments. Because of the shallow coverage, much of each film's discussion is devoted to plot synopsis. There seem to be few errors of fact, although the author occasionally uses one word when he apparently means another (for example, on p. 116 he says "molecules" when he actually means "anti-bodies"). Numerous still photos are reproduced in the book, and it includes an index. This paperback was originally published in hardcover as *Visions of Tomorrow: Great Science Fiction from the Movies.* Recommended for use in secondary education libraries with SF film holdings; the hardcover, of course, would be preferred for library use.

257. Everson, William K. *Classics of the Horror Film.* Secaucus, NJ: Citadel Press, 1974. 247p.

Horror film classics are examined both individually and in groups of films with related themes in Everson's horror film survey. He begins in the 1930s with the Frankenstein films and the successors and inheritors of that filmic tradition; later chapters are devoted to such individual films as *Vampyr, Murder by the Clock, Dr. Jeckyll and Mr. Hyde, Freaks, The Old Dark*

House, White Zombie, The Mummy, Dr. X, King Kong, The Mystery of the Wax Museum, and dozens of others. Some chapters are devoted to two closely related films, such as "Two Ghost Classics: *The Uninvited* and *Dead of Night*," and still others trace the origin and development of a theme or idea through numerous films. Multi-film "theme/idea" chapters include "Old Houses," "Hauntings and Possession," "Madness," "Edgar Allan Poe" and "Werewolves." The book is profusely illustrated, though all the illustrations are black and white. There is no index. Everson's survey of horror films is well-done and well-organized, and is a useful general horror film history providing excellent coverage for what might be called the classic horror films. Obviously, because of its publication date, it does not cover any of the most recent cycle of high-budget "hardcore gore" horror films. Recommended for any library needing informed and authoritative discussion and description of horror films from the 1930s to the 1970s.

258. Frank, Alan. *The Science Fiction and Fantasy Film Handbook.* Totowa, NJ: Barnes & Noble, 1982. 187p.

Another of the numerous alphabetical-by-title listings of SF films, *The Science Fiction and Fantasy Film Handbook* has features which are slightly different than the average listing—features which could be considered strengths or weaknesses, depending on the intended audience for the book. Each film entry includes cast and production credits, a brief plot summary, an evaluative comment, and a short quote about the film from a secondary source. For example, in the entry for *The Brain from Planet Arous,* the complete text of the evaluative commentary is "Energetic hokum with poor special effects," while the quoted secondary material for *Brides of Blood* is "...an ingeniously contrived piece..." The space (and reading time) saved by the extremely telegraphic plot synopses and commentary is considerable, but the book is liberally illustrated with film stills, so the total number of films covered numbers perhaps 300. A "People" section provides biographies and genre filmographies for 67 film-related personalities. Most of the biographical sketches, too, are brief except for major figures (Bradbury, Lucas, Spielberg, Pal, Melies, etc.). A "Themes" section, potentially one of the most useful features, is instead a throwaway frill: a theme is explained in a couple of paragraphs, then the next page-and-a-half lists films which use or display the theme in some form. Properly organized, the theme listing could have made the book a unique and useful addition to film reference. The book, overall, apparently is intended for light browsing, and could serve as a supplementary acquisition if an SF film reference collection already has the necessary volumes for basic SF film research.

259. Friedman, Favius. *Great Horror Movies.* New York: Scholastic Book Services, 1974. 160p.

Grade school students are the target audience for this very simple and very shallow survey of 70 films ranging from *The Birds* to *Fantastic Voyage.* There is too much emphasis on being cute and not enough on providing information, although that probably is a concession to the age and reading level of the intended audience; one chapter title, for example, is "Early Horror and The Late Late Show: The First of the Real Cool Ghouls." The entries provide some basic information about each film, but some of the "explanations" are oversimplified or just plain wrong. In the *Dracula* entry, Friedman states that Count Dracula has to *bury* himself in his native soil during the day. The general film and novel consensus seems to be that Dracula's coffin must contain a thin layer of native soil to retain the supernatural properties which allow Dracula to survive. There are unattributed quotes in the book and the text exhibits a tendency to rely too heavily on rhetorical questions and exclamation marks. Includes 32 black and white photos, but there is no index. The book will serve if a book on horror film is needed and no other is available, but internal flaws in the volume prohibit its recommendation as a general-principle acquisition.

260. Grossman, Gary. *Superman: Serial to Cereal.* New York: Popular Library, 1976. 186p.

Superman is the pop-culture embodiment of the super hero, the man with special powers and abilities. That he is a native of another planet makes him at least of marginal interest to the SF world. Superman is known virtually to every American over the age of two or three, through his various appearances and incarnations in numerous media, including comics, books, serials, radio, cartoons, television, animated films and feature films over a period of more than 50 years. Grossman's examination of Superman is interesting and thorough, following the career of the caped crusader from the serials to the TV series. The actors involved in the various phases of American "supermania" are well represented, not just as they fit into the Superman film mythos but as "complete" actors, their biographical material often accompanied by stills showing them in films they worked in either before or after the Superman experience. Understandably, the bulk of the book is concerned with the George Reeves television episodes. Until the Christopher Reeves feature films (and in spite of the recent feature films, for most older Americans who remember the television series), George Reeves was the definitive Superman character. Several appendices provide production dates and other information for Superman cartoons, the Superman serials, the 1951 Superman feature film *Superman and the Mole Men*, the 104 episodes of the TV series, Superman features, Superpup, and the adventures of Superboy. Liberally illustrated with photos, the volume is almost encyclopedic on the Superman subject, though now somewhat dated because of its publication years in advance of the recent and hugely successful Superman feature films. Highly recommended for collections emphasizing science fiction television and film.

261. Haley, Michael. *The Alfred Hitchcock Album.* Englewood Cliffs, NJ: Prentice-Hall, 1981. 173p.

Alfred Hitchcock was not a science fiction film director and producer *per se*, but his psychological thriller *Psycho* (screenplay by internationally known SF/mystery/horror writer Robert Bloch), his one SF film *The Birds*, and his numerous anthologies (some of which include stories that are borderline SF if they are not SF outright) make him a personality of some interest in SF research. Haley's book is a compilation of film stills and photographs in a generally chronological progression through Hitchcock's life and filmmaking career. The text is explanatory rather than interpretive, and outlines basic biographical material as well as background information on the films. A glossary of the Hitchcock films includes full cast and production credits. Other books on Hitchcock are far more definitive, so this volume will be of interest primarily as yet another volume to add to holdings emphasizing film-photo books or books on Hitchcock.

262.   Hayes, R.M. *Trick Cinematography: The Oscar Special-Effects Movies.* Jefferson, NC: McFarland & Co., 1986. 370p.

Special effects cinematography is of particular interest to science fiction film studies because of all the various film genres, SF films probably require more special effects work per film than any other type of film. Hayes has researched the films from 1927 to 1984 that were special effects Oscar nominees and winners, and presents complete information about the special effects award, the changes in the award categories, and the controversies surrounding some of the changes. There is an alphabetical list of films included and a list of Oscar-nominated special effects personnel. The main body of the index is arranged by year date, presenting for each year a list of the nominees (winners for each year are indicated) followed by complete cast and production credit information for each film. Where appropriate, notes and commentary are provided to clarify or to furnish critical assessments. A glossary and index are included. The production credits are particularly thorough, and a large percentage of the information compiled in this book was never available in a reference book before the publication of this volume. There are some small mistakes—for example, a dubbing mixer, Arthur Piantadosi, is credited on p. 195 but does not appear in the index. But the mistakes and omissions are very few, very far between, and very difficult to find, and are not likely to affect substantially the utility of the book. It is an important addition to film reference, and should be included in any film reference collection with a subject sub-emphasis in special effects or cast and production credit indexing.

263. Hogan, David J. *Dark Romance: Sexuality in the Horror Film.* Jefferson, NC: McFarland & Co., 1986. 333p.

Sex in cinema is fairly well documented, but sexuality in particular film genres—the horror film, for example—has not been explored quite so well. *Dark Romance* is in some respects a ground-breaking survey of sexuality in the horror film, but its major weakness is the fact that it is a survey rather than an in-depth study. Chapters are used to delineate particular sexual subjects (the perils of sexuality, family interrelationships, split personality, the "beauty and the beast" mythos, etc.) and the author then lists, synopsizes, and briefly discusses various films with elements, themes, motifs, ideas or conventions which allow them to fit into the category. As a survey, the book is quite thorough; literally hundreds of films are mentioned in one context or another. However, some of the topic areas have at best a marginal connection to the idea of sexuality. The first chapter, for example, describes the various film Frankenstein incarnations, but the sexuality aspects of the creator-created polarity are never explained. Frankenstein is examined in psychological terms as a perverse father-son relationship, which is acceptable on some levels—but nowhere is it mentioned that the continuing popularity of Frankenstein probably owes little to a perverse father-son relationship, but much to the Frankenstein mythos as the preeminent modern archetype for the scientific failure of imperfect creation (man's often clumsy and sometimes pathetic or tragic efforts to learn or create); technological retribution (the creation turning on its creator); and the popular conception of the scientist who refuses to recognize that complex functions, such as creation of a human being, might not be reducible to recipe-like formulas—in other words, "there are some things man was not meant to know." Though somewhat unfocussed, the book manages to touch on a vast array of sexuality-related matters as they have been incorporated into horror films, and for that reason is of unquestionable value as part of any collection specializing in criticism and analysis of horror films.

264. Javna, John. *The Best From Science Fiction TV: The Critics' Choice from Captain Video to Star Trek, from The Jetsons to Robotech.* New York: Harmony Books, 1987. 144p.

Caught halfway between "book" and "magazine," *The Best of Science Fiction TV* isn't quite sure just exactly what it is supposed to be. The basic idea was good; survey some of the top TV critics in the country and use the results to put together a list of the best and worst SF television programs. After the text and photos were assembled the entire project was handed over to an art director who splattered the pages with little drawings of rockets and flying saucers and little photos that are either uncredited or which have captions that explain nothing. There are too many different "headlines," a graphic mistake which sometimes obscures the actual title of the program under discussion, and rather than presenting anything resembling a unified discussion or description of a program the writer/editor/compiler more or less machine-guns the reader with little fragments of statements made by contributing critics and writers. Sections and listings include the top 15 programs, the worst ten programs, and cult favorites. Minor space-wasting sections used to fluff up the book to a larger size include features on classic openings from the programs, robots, aliens, and "classic lines." There is some useful information and critical material buried in this unindexed conglomeration, but it is effectively lost in a format apparently intended to appeal only to mainline SF television junkies and adolescents with a morbid fear of reading any book-like object that doesn't appear to be at least 50 percent photos. Libraries maintaining a comprehensive collection of visual media SF references, both scholarly and popular, may want to consider acquisition, but other collections are not likely to have much use for the book.

265. Koch, Howard. *The Panic Broadcast.* Boston: Little, Brown & Co., 1970; New York: Avon, n.d. 163p.

H. G. Wells' *War of the Worlds* has the distinction of being the only SF novel ever to be the basis for a nationwide panic, so the famous Orson Wells broadcast holds an important position in the study of American acceptance of SF and its influence on popular culture. Howard Koch wrote the radio script, and the complete script is included in the book. There are maps and photos and several newspaper columns, including the famous Dorothy Thompson column, detailing contemporary reactions to the broadcast and ensuing panic. A chapter titled "The Aftermath" relates some experiences during the panic, as recounted by several of those who were caught up in the hysteria, and another too-short chapter presents the author's musings on his return to Grover's Mill 30 years after the broadcast to talk to local inhabitants who have lived with the long-term legacy of the panic. The most glaring deficiency is the "padding" used to fluff the book up to acceptable length (a chapter on Mars in "fact and legend," for example, has nothing at all to do with the broadcast or panic). Any book about the "panic broadcast" is likely to be an important research resource in some respects, because the Martian invasion is now a major component of American SF mythology and folklore. Koch's direct participation in the cause of the panic means the book is a basic research tool for understanding the panic and the after-effects, but the book would have been much more useful if it had been more a structured and researched effort than a collection of bits and pieces of information relating to the broadcast. Recommended for collections emphasizing SF film/TV/radio or SF as an increasingly important element of modern popular culture.

266. Lentz, Harris M., III. *Science Fiction, Horror & Fantasy Film and Television Credits (2 vols.)* Jefferson, NC: McFarland & Co., 1983. 1,374p.

The Lentz two-volume dictionary of SF, horror and fantasy film and television credits is the most comprehensive combined film/TV credit dictionary published to date for the combined SF, fantasy and horror film genres. Volume I has two sections. The first section is a performer index which provides birth and death dates, titles of films and year of release for each, and indications of each part or character played by the performer, as well as titles of television programs in which the performer appeared (both series name and specific episode name), date of first broadcast, and indication of character played. The second section of the first volume is an index of producers, directors, writers and artists, which provides information similar to that in the performer index. Volume II has a film index (information includes date of release, director, and actors, as well as alternate titles and, where appropriate, country of origin); and a television index with similarly complete information. Coverage is complete through the fall of 1982. The introduction is by Forrest J Ackerman, noted SF/fantasy/horror film expert, and a reference bibliography includes a long list of books and periodicals consulted to assemble the information presented in the two-volume reference work. For fantastic *films* only, the three-volume Walt Lee reference is still the standard work, but as a combined film/TV reference for SF/horror/ fantasy, the Lentz compilation is now the best and most complete reference source for cast and credit information. Libraries maintaining an extensive collection on SF, fantasy or horror film will need both the Lentz and the Lee sets.

267. Ormsby, Alan. *Movie Monsters: Monster Make-Up & Monster Shows to Put On.* New York: Scholastic Book Services, 1975. 80p.

Movie Monsters is a brief survey of the better-known movie monsters (the phantom, the wolfman, Frankenstein, the mummy, King Kong, Dracula, etc.). Each description, one to two pages in length, is accompanied by a film still. Section Two, "How to Make a Monster," tells youngsters how to use easily-obtainable materials to create monster make-up, and Section Three is a short play titled "The Monster of Frankenstein." An appendix, "Supplies and Sources," tells where the necessary materials for props and make-up may be found. The book is an excellent combination of simple background material on monster figures and horror film stars, and do-it-yourself suggestions for elementary school youngsters interested in creating and staging a skit or play on a monster theme. Recommended for elementary school use, though the make-up suggestions could be used effectively by older students for somewhat more sophisticated productions.

268.   Palumbo, Donald, ed. *Eros in the Mind's Eye: Sexuality and the Fantastic in Art and Film.* Westport, CT: Greenwood Press, 1986. 290p.

Though this essay collection is titled rather generally *Sexuality and the Fantastic in Art and Film*, the individual articles deal predominantly with sexual interpretations of fantasy, horror and science fiction films. Films considered and interpreted range from *Bride of Frankenstein* and *The Rocky Horror Picture Show* to the Star Trek films, the Star Wars films and the Star Trek television programs. The volume may be most useful for research done at the graduate level or higher because the constant references to Freudian interpretation, Oedipal complexes and other psychosexual concepts require a substantial background in psychology. Some of the essays seem to test the outer limits of interpretive credibility, and others apparently begin their film explorations from an overly defensive point of view, but as a group the articles present a broad spectrum of subject and viewpoint. There are 18 articles, of which 11 deal directly with SF, fantasy and horror film; 47 illustrations; an extensive bibliography of pertinent reference books and articles; a filmography/television listing; and an index. Candidly sexual interpretation of SF is relatively new, though undoubtedly will become a more important area of exploration; sexuality in fantasy and horror has a longer history (Dracula's preference for biting the necks of lovely young women, for example, has long been recognized as a plot device with thinly veiled sexual/erotic overtones). As the lack of adequate sexual interpretations of SF novels and film becomes more a perceived shortcoming, more such studies should appear—but until there is a more substantial established field for this specialized study, *Eros in the Mind's Eye* will remain a major research source of information and speculation.

269.   Parish, James Robert and Michael R. Pitts. *The Great Science Fiction Pictures.* Metuchen, NJ: Scarecrow Press, 1977. 382p.

Although this volume is titled the "great" SF pictures, the authors have included, in their own words, "some of the far lesser ones (the WORST by some critics' standards), in order to present a fair spectrum of the species." The main body of the book is an alphabetical listing of film titles; each title is followed by cast and production credits, and a variable amount of synopsis and evaluation. An appendix provides a list of science fiction programs on radio and television. In many cases, almost the entire "commentary" is simply plot synopsis. Approximately 350 films are included in the listing, and the films themselves, as per the authors' stated intentions, do represent a very broad spectrum of SF in the cinema. Serials (*Captain Marvel, Batman and Robin, Superman*, etc.), fantasy-comedy (Abbott and Costello, *The Absent-Minded Professor*) and true SF classics (*2001, The Day the Earth Stood Still*) all are represented in the listings, and the commentary often provides interesting historical information, especially on foreign films. There are better surveys of SF films, particularly limited-scope surveys (those which concern themselves with certain types of SF films or films from a particular decade), but the Parish-Pitts volume would make an excellent supplement to a reference collection already well-stocked with SF film reference titles.

270. Peary, Danny, ed. *Omni's Screen Flights/Screen Fantasies: The Future According to Science Fiction Cinema.* Garden City, NY: Doubleday, 1984. 310p. MIN.

SF film has been one of the most rapidly expanding of the SF subgenres. One of the best volumes of historical and critical overview of the SF film genre in the 1980s is *Screen Flights*, a mixture of the scholarly and the popular which not only describes past conventions but questions them as well, and develops interesting theories and opinions about the roles of accepted SF film conventions in the present and future. A mixture of articles and interviews, the book is composed of 42 essays written by SF authors and filmmakers and is divided into three categories: Perspectives, Journeys Into the Future, and The Creators. A lively and wide-ranging—if characteristically caustic—essay by Harlan Ellison serves as introduction, and other essays are provided by such SF luminaries as Isaac Asimov, Robert Bloch, Frederik Pohl, Robert Sheckley and Robert Silverberg. Subjects range the entire SF/fantasy spectrum from specific films (*Alien, Metropolis, 1984, Forbidden Planet, On The Beach, Fahrenheit 451, No Blade of Grass, Soylent Green*) to interviews (Buster Crabbe, Roger Corman, George Miller, Sigourney Weaver, Leonard Nimoy, Ridley Scott) to general topic overviews ("Welcoming the Future," "Thoughts on How Science Fiction Films Depict the Future," "Sex in Science Fiction Films," "The Fear of Intelligence in Futuristic Films"). *Screen Flights*, one of the most important SF film volumes to be published in the 1980s, is highly recommended for SF collections with a film emphasis. It also could serve well as a "stand alone" reference for an SF collection with no film representation if a one-volume general introduction to SF film is needed to expand category topic coverage.

271. Pitts, Michael R. *Horror Film Stars*. Jefferson, NC: McFarland & Co., 1981. 324p.

Horror Film Stars is a good basic reference volume for the horror film genre. Pitts selected 43 actors who were major stars or important character actors in horror film and provides for each a biography and filmography. Actors are divided into two sections: there are 15 in "The Stars" and 28 in "The Players." The section on the major stars includes Lionel Atwill, John Carradine, Lon Chaney, Sr., Lon Chaney, Jr., Peter Cushing, Boris Karloff, Christopher Lee, Peter Lorre, Bela Lugosi, Paul Naschy, Vincent Price, Claude Rains, Basil Rathbone, Barbara Steele and George Zucco. The filmography for each actor includes films that are not necessarily in the horror genre. Biographies are brief but thorough, averaging 5-7 pages for each of the stars and 1-4 pages for the character actors. Numerous photos are included. The book would be a useful addition to a collection emphasizing biography and filmography for the SF/fantasy/horror film genres.

272. Pohl, Frederik and Frederik Pohl IV. *Science Fiction Studies in Film*. New York: Ace Books, 1981; revised edition, 1982. 346p.

Few books on SF film can claim to be exhaustive, and *Science Fiction Studies in Film* is no exception to that general rule. Most of the films examined in the book are discussed at reasonable length, with each discussion averaging three or four pages. For obvious reasons, this severely limits the number of films that can be surveyed in one book. Little of the information offered is "new" in any real sense—film buffs will have read most of this information before, but in this case all the facts, figures and opinions have been gathered into a single volume rather than spread out through dozens of periodicals. Cast and production credits are supplied for each film discussed, and numerous writers, critics, and other SF-related personalities (Harlan Ellison, Isaac Asimov, Harry Harrison, Kurt Vonnegut, Jerome Bixby, etc.) are quoted at lengths ranging from a paragraph to a page. There are perhaps 35 black and white frame still reproductions, and the one appendix is a chapter on special effects. There is no index. The "expected" films are examined: *Metropolis, The Cabinet of Dr. Caligari, Frankenstein, King Kong, Things to Come, The Invisible Man,* and so on, up through *Close Encounters, Stars Wars,* etc. The text is unnecessarily colloquial at times, but the book offers sound perspectives and a respectable number of film discussions which are longer and more informative than those to be found in the average SF film survey/overview. Recommended for collections with a strong SF film emphasis. For other Pohl-related material see item 210.

273. Richards, Gregory B. *Science Fiction Movies.* New York: Gallery Books, 1984. 80p.

Science Fiction Movies is a short, heavily-illustrated book appropriate for readers through the high school level. It is extremely simplistic in approach, covering the history of SF cinema from Melies to Lucas in four sections: an introductory chapter, a chapter on silent films, one on sound films, and one on the "stars" of SF films. The survey moves quickly and predictably from the early days of film to the recent SF "blockbusters," mentioning dozens of film titles in a long "shopping list" of titles that had to be included—no matter how brief the mention of each—in a general survey. Most of the generally accepted significant films in SF film history are synopsized, and the critical comments (most are far too brief to be called evaluations) are the generally accepted verdicts. *Science Fiction Movies* is not an in-depth history or analysis, but a short pictorial survey with far more space devoted to film stills than to text. Many of the photos are in color. The "stars" section has short biographies of 12 actors and 11 directors, and the filmography has extremely telegraphic cast/credit information on 71 films. The book is indexed and is recommended for junior high or high school libraries that do not already have a pictorial survey of SF films on the shelf.

274. Schow, David J. and Jeffrey Frentzen. *The Outer Limits: The Official Companion.* New York: Ace Books, 1986. 406p.

The Outer Limits is considered to be one of the two or three best television SF series ever produced, and the Schow/Frentzen book is a definitive program-by-program companion to the series. The first section of the book has short articles on Leslie Stevens, Daystar Productions, the production crew that worked on the series anthology, Joe Stefano, and other topics. Included are numerous photos and program stills. The second section has, for each program, cast and credit information, date of first broadcast, a synopsis, and critical commentary. There are several appendices, one of which synopsizes unproduced *Outer Limits* filmscripts. Other appendices provide production and broadcast schedules and end credits. The book is indexed. Oddly enough, the programs are not presented in any recognizable order or pattern—they are not arranged alphabetically by individual program title, nor chronologically by broadcast date—but there is access by title through the index. This TV series companion is a basic reference for any collection with an emphasis in SF film and television.

275. Strick, Philip. *Science Fiction Movies.* London: Octopus Books, 1976. 160p.

General SF-associated film themes are treated at greater length in Strick's book than in most any other SF film survey. The categories are "Watching the Skies" (alien invasion); "Men Like Gods"; "The Mark of the Beast" (men turned into animals and vice versa); "Armageddon, and Later" (end of the world); "Out of Our Minds" (social paranoia, dystopia, etc.); "Taking Off" (space flight, interplanetary exploration, etc.); "Far Out" (myth, fantasy, psychological SF); and "Time Twisters" (time travel, disjoint/episodic SF). Strick is extremely knowledgeable about SF/fantasy films, though he makes occasional puzzling statements, e.g., "Science fiction is a vast subject rendered only more complex when translated into film," an obvious romantic overstatement when in fact SF is almost invariably simplified into escapist fantasy (often *silly* escapist fantasy) when a good novel is translated into film. At another point he describes the flying saucer of *The Day the Earth Stood Still* as "vast" when it is actually quite small in comparison with most film saucers. But these gaffes seem to be indicative more of rapid and somewhat careless writing than a lack of familiarity with the SF film genre. The writing style is lively and exhibits an entertainingly wry humor; there are film stills on every page, many of which are in color, and the surveys of each of the broadly-defined theme areas, while not absolutely exhaustive, are usefully thorough and detailed. The critical judgments are trustworthy, and the book has a film title index, though it lacks a general index. *Science Fiction Movies* is recommended for library collections supporting research in SF films at the undergraduate level, or for public libraries needing SF film volumes which should appeal to a wide range of fans and readers.

276. von Gunden, Kenneth and Stuart H. Stock. *Twenty All-Time Great Science Fiction Films.* New York: Arlington House, 1982. 250p.

Books on limited-category SF films—the best, the worst, those of a particular decade, etc.—are becoming an extremely popular publishing genre. The von Gunden-Stock volume concentrates on 20 SF films, and the information provided for each film includes production credits, cast, a plot synopsis, and a lengthy description and evaluation. Numerous stills, publicity photos and other illustrations are used throughout the volume, and the depth of detail concerning the genesis of filmscripts, social conditions at the time of a film's release, and other information make the book a valuable research source for the films included. Films represented in the compendium include: *Things to Come, Destination Moon, The Thing, The Day the Earth Stood Still, The Man in the White Suit, Donovan's Brain, The Magnetic Monster, Invaders From Mars, The War of the Worlds, Them!, This Island Earth, Forbidden Planet, Invasion of the Body Snatchers, Village of the Damned, Dr. Strangelove, Robinson Crusoe on Mars, 2001: A Space Odyssey, The Mind of Mr. Soames, Colossus—The Forbin Project, A Clockwork Orange.* The films' release dates range from 1936 to 1971 and the films are presented chronologically. Included are an appendix with additional information on the films, a bibliography and an index. The book is not a priority acquisition, but is recommended as a supplement to collections with strong holdings in SF film.

277. Warren, Bill. *Keep Watching the Skies! American Science Fiction Movies of the Fifties Vol. I 1950-1957.* Jefferson, NC: McFarland, 1982. 467p. MIN.

The practice of dividing post-World War II SF films into eras by decade seems to gain more popularity every year. The watershed decade for quantity (if not quality) of SF film production was the 1950s, and many film fans remember the SF/fantasy/horror films of that decade with particular fondness. Warren's survey of American SF films from 1950-1957 is an interesting and well-researched anecdotal account of film production, trends, and other matters related to the creation of SF films in that decade. The films are divided into sections by year of release, and each film is discussed at appropriate length—more wordage is spent on important films, less on the potboilers and the shabby exploitation flicks. 133 films are discussed, many at great length, including accepted classics such as *Destination Moon, The Day the Earth Stood Still, The War of the Worlds* and *20,000 Leagues Under the Sea.* Appendices include listings for cast and credits, the 133 films in order of their release, film titles announced for production in the 1950s that never were filmed, SF serials in the 1950s, and an index. Warren applies sound critical judgment and reasoning to his evaluations of the films, and it is clear his knowledge of film extends far beyond the bounds of the SF genre (lack of knowledge outside the genre, and the resultant lack of perspective, are severe handicaps to many who write about SF film). This panoramic survey of a film type and specific decade should appeal to most anyone with any interest in SF film, and the book should be in any collection with an emphasis on SF film.

278. Warren, Bill. *Keep Watching the Skies! American Science Fiction Movies of the Fifties Vol. II 1958-1962.* Jefferson, NC: McFarland, 1986. 837p.

Warren's thesis for a survey of 1950s SF films that extends to the year 1962 is the existence of the "1950s type" film until that year. The format of the book is the same as volume one—a division by year and a discussion of separate films within the chapter divisions, with supplementary material consisting of complete cast and production credits for the 148 films; a list of film titles announced for production from 1958 to 1962 but never filmed; and an index. Several dozen stills and line drawings are also scattered through the book. There are more films discussed in this second volume, and many are evaluated at somewhat greater length than the films in volume one. Commentary on each film is knowledgeable and precise, the critical evaluations informed and consistent. Warren's SF film surveys are well-researched and readable, and serve more than one purpose—the uncritical SF film buff may read them just for the fun of reading entertaining notes and behind-the-scenes trivia about favorite films, and SF film researchers and historians can use the books for their comprehensive synopses, useful historical information and accurate critical evaluation of SF-related films released from 1958 to 1962. Warren's two volumes of film surveys are important SF film historical and critical documents, useful both to the casual reader and the informed specialist, and their addition to an SF film collection allows the collection far greater flexibility in providing useful research materials for separate SF films rather than just general surveys which mention numerous films briefly.

279. Wingrove, David, ed. *Science Fiction Film Source Book*. Essex, England: Longmans Group Ltd., 1985. 312p.

A concise directory of science fiction films, *Science Fiction Film Source Book* provides plot synopses and evaluative commentary for hundreds of SF films. The foreword was contributed by Brian Aldiss and the brief introductory history of SF film—which is as good a capsule history of SF cinema as has been done in less than nine pages of wordage—is provided by Wingrove. There is a chronology of important films, from *Metropolis* (1926) to *Star Trek III* (1984); a listing of SF serials 1913-1956; a briefly annotated list of major SF film creators (actors, cinematographers, directors, producers, screenplay writers); a list of SF/fantasy writers whose books have been filmed (the book titles, film titles, publication dates and film release dates are included); a chapter on special effects in SF cinema (an essay by John Brosnan); a glossary of special effects terms; a list of all-time rental figures for SF film; and a select bibliography. The main body of the book is an alphabetical film listing which describes and offers critical commentary on the hundreds of films listed. There is little space wasted on truly bad films; minor entries are handled deftly in a short space, and more important films are given proportionately more wordage. Each film is rated in four categories—plot, technical skill, entertainment and artistic merit. The book is not definitive, but can make an extremely useful supplement to other sources of information on SF films, such as the three-volume Walt Lee fantastic film reference. Recommended for any collection with SF film holdings.

280. Wright, Gene. *Who's Who & What's What in Science Fiction Film, Television, Radio & Theater*. New York: Bonanza Books, 1983. 336p.

One of the many SF encyclopedias published in recent years, this compilation serves little purpose because coverage is very selective and thus very spotty. Arrangement is alphabetical and includes films, TV and radio programs, and major characters, directors and screenwriters, as well as a few odd bits of information which seem out of place. For example, "Alderaan" is an entry, because it is Princess Leia's home world (it was destroyed by the Death Star in the *Star Wars* saga); yet the best-known alien planet in all of SF film and literature, Krypton, Superman's home, has no entry (though there is an entry for Kryptonite, fragments of Krypton which are deadly to Superman). There are numerous SF film and TV reference books which are more complete and authoritative than this volume, though it does contain some information on SF radio programs not included in other books. The volume is not recommended except for collections emphasizing reference works in the extremely specialized area of SF radio.

281. Zicree, Marc Scott. *The Twilight Zone Companion.* New York: Bantam Books, 1982. 447p.

The Twilight Zone Companion is one of the best episode-by-episode program guides for a television series. *Twilight Zone*, which was broadcast for four years (1959-1963), has been in syndication almost constantly since original broadcast, and along with *Star Trek* and *Outer Limits*, is among the most popular SF/fantasy TV series in existence. Because of the magnitude of the program's popularity and success, a reliable guide to the series is an important acquisition for any collection with an emphasis in SF film and television. The book opens with an introductory chapter which places the series in perspective, then each program is synopsized. Broadcast dates are provided, along with complete writing, producing, directing and acting credits. An especially interesting feature is the inclusion of the complete text for the opening and closing monologues (which were narrated by Serling for broadcast) for each program. Numerous stills and other photos are included, and there are special chapters which deal with such topics as "Videotape Invades the Twilight Zone," "Serling as Narrator," "Richard Matheson" and "Charles Beaumont." The text is lively and entertaining and there is an index, but the index is very selective—e.g., there are index entries for Charles Beaumont but no references to p. 322 where he is given writing credit for the "Miniature" script. Robert Duvall, an actor in the "Miniature" broadcast, is given acting credits on p. 322 but there is no "Duvall" listing in the index. The mistakes and omissions in the index are an inconvenience, but do not negate the book's value as a thorough and concise compendium of information on one of the most important SF television series in broadcasting history.

Section 8
Comics,
Art &
Illustration

282. Aldiss, Brian W., comp. *Science Fiction Art: The Fantasies of SF.*
New York: Bounty Books, 1975. 128p. AOW, TYS.

A large format (10½ x15) book with 128 pages and literally hundreds of illustrations, *Science Fiction Art* is one of the most comprehensive of the SF art surveys. The arrangement is unique—the main body of the book is a "gallery" with groups of several illustrations by the same artist. Illustrators represented include 30 artists such as Bok, Bonestell, Cartier, Emsh, Finlay, Orban, Paul, Schneemann, Schomberg and Wesso, among others. Several pages of comics follow the gallery section, and the next section or chapter uses groups of illustrations to show the development of specific themes and ideas in SF literature and illustration (catastrophies, robots, spaceships, alien life, etc.). One short sections compares the emergence of two basic ideas in SF—the "city.spaceship" combination and various interpretations of H.G. Wells' famous tripodal invasion vehicles in *War of the Worlds*. The last few pages of the book are a collection of SF magazine cover reproductions. Aldiss provides a good overview of the history of SF illustration and several brief introductory sections scattered throughout the volume. The book is indexed by artist and magazine. At least half the artwork is in color, and many of the illustrations are full-page. *Science Fiction Art* is one of the best of the SF art books ever produced, and is highly recommended as an addition to any collection emphasizing SF art and artists. The book also would be an excellent addition to larger collections with no particular art emphasis if there is a need to select an occasional title to provide good general coverage for SF related topic areas that are not a primary concern. For other Aldiss-related material see items 1, 2, 3 and 195.

283. Beahm, George, ed. *Kirk's Works: An Index of the Art of Tim Kirk.* Newport News, VA: Heresy Press, 1980. 121p.

Indexing of an SF/fantasy artist's work obviously is an extremely specialized field, and such such an index has little interest or utility for the general researcher. But Kirk is one of the most popular contemporary SF and fantasy artists, so it is not inconceiveable that an index to his artwork could become a major research tool if someone eventually undertakes a biography. The book is large-format softcover, 9x12, with a wraparound full-color cover by Kirk. A color frontispiece, reproduced from a George Barr painting, includes Kirk's likeness along with seven fanciful non-human figures. The foreword is by William Rotsler and several introductions and appreciations were provided by Beahm, George Barr and Mike Glicksohn. Kirk wrote a short chapter titled "The Making of Monsters" and Beahm conducted an interview with Kirk, the text of which is included. The generous selection of artwork presented ranges from small "spot" illos to full-page covers, and from fan magazine work to professional magazine covers. Separate indexes list books, professional periodical appearances, fanzines, semi-professional periodicals, convention materials, APA materials, portfolios, calendars, greeting cards, flyers, games, and miscellaneous items. Recommended primarily for libraries with collections that specialize in SF, fantasy and fantastic art and the artists who produce such work.

284. del Rey, Lester. *Fantastic Science-Fiction Art 1926-1954.* New York: Ballantine, 1975. Unpaginated (89).

An unpaginated collection of color reproductions of magazine covers, *Science-Fiction Art* contains 40 color plates in a large-book format (8¾ x11¼). A short introduction summarizes the contributions of Frank R. Paul, Leo Morey and other early SF illustrators to the newly emergent genre fiction magazines of the first decades of this century. Del Rey also provides an overview of the genesis and development of the twentieth century magazines. The earliest magazine cover represented was published in 1924. Besides Paul and Morey, other artists with at least one magazine cover in this collection include Alex Schomberg, Kelly Freas, Alejandro, H.R Van Dongen, Hubert Rogers, Earle K. Bergey, Malcolm Smith, Robert Fuqua and Howard V. Brown. Recommended as an acquisition for collections emphasizing SF magazines or SF art/illustration. For other del Rey-related material see item 26.

285.   Durie, Alistair. *Weird Tales.* London: Jupiter Books, 1979. 128p.

Numerous SF magazines introduced "genre" science fiction to the public, but the similar introduction of fantasy, supernatural and fantastic fiction (lumped together as "weird" fiction) was accomplished almost exclusively by *Weird Tales.* This tribute to the cover art of WT magazine contains 24 color plates and 133 reproductions that are black and white or single-color reproductions (magneta, dark blue, etc.). Issue dates for the magazine covers reproduced here range from the first issue in 1923 to an issue in 1953, but the emphasis is on the "golden age" of WT from 1927 to 1940. An introduction provides a capsule history of the magazine and outlines major changes caused by economics, the publishing industry, the pulp fiction market, and changes of editorship (there were only three different editors from the magazine's beginnings in 1923 to its demise in 1954). Most of the illustrations/covers are reproduced one per page with a paragraph of commentary for each, but some of the covers are reduced and printed two or three per page. Weinberg's *The Weird Tales Story* (item 77) is the definitive history of WT, and that book plus this tribute to WT artwork provide an exceptionally clear and thorough understanding of a highly influential magazine. Durie's book is recommended for collections with emphasis in popular fiction magazines, SF/fantasy artwork, magazine history, or twentieth century "fantastic" fiction.

286.   Frewin, Anthony. *One Hundred Years of SF Illustration 1840-1940.* London: Jupiter Books, 1974. 128p. AOW.

After a six-page introduction—some of which is condescending and some of which represents an amusingly dry and satirical wit—Frewin's SF illustration survey begins in earnest with drawings and cover illustrations from a variety of sources. Illustrations which are easily identified—e.g., magazine covers, complete with title and month/year of publication printed directly on the cover—present no problem, but many illustrations are identified by only by artist. Each chapter of the book is "themed" and begins with some text, though the text is generally brief in each section and the book as a whole is dominated by the illustrations. Some chapters, such as the one on Albert Robida, may present a dozen or more pages of illustrations by the same artist; others, such as the chapter "By Pullman Car to Venus—Victorians...and Others!", present a basic idea illustrated by selected drawings by many different artists. The latter half of the book uses SF magazine covers almost exclusively for illustration and many of these are in color. Appendix One has illustrations from *Everyday Science and Mechanics* (edited by Hugo Gernsback) and *Modern Mechanics & Inventions Magazine,* and many of these magazine covers and internal illustrations have even more unusual "future technology" illustrations than the SF magazines of the time. Appendix Two gives a sampling of the advertisements to be found in the old pulp magazines—an unusual collage having very little to do with SF but a great deal to do with the social milieu from which twentieth century science fiction arose. Frewin's survey of SF illustration ends at a point where other surveys have barely begun; it goes more deeply into the past history of SF illustration than other such volumes, and has enough text to establish some context and perspective for the art form which eventually combined technical illustration with fantastic illustration to produce the pseudo-realistic form that would come to dominate SF illustration. Frewin's book is recommended as a "stand alone" volume for any collection needing a volume on SF illustration or as a useful supplement to collections with an estabished emphasis in SF art.

287. Harrison, Harry. *Mechanismo*. Los Angeles: Reed Books, 1978. 118p.

Harry Harrison's book of SF art is slightly larger and perhaps a bit more diverse than most such collections of illustrations, and may contain somewhat more textual material. The section divisions are Star Ships; Mechanical Man; Weapons and Space Gear; Space Cities; Fantastic Machines; and Movies. Within each section is an introduction and commentary averaging about two pages for each introduction, though there is additional "textual" material in the various charts and "printouts" from future manuals, files, specification sheets, etc. A wide variety of illustration types is presented; some of the illustrations are explicitly sexual. The illustrators are not identified on the pages with their work, but are identified only in an artist index. Artists represented include Fowke, Layzell, Chesterman, Burns, Achilleos, Hay, Wilkes, and 12 others. Film illustrations are taken from *Star Wars; 20,000 Leagues Under the Sea; Metropolis; 2001; Things to Come*; and others. Harrison's book is a well-produced volume of its type, but it is intended to serve not so much as an introduction to SF art as it is to appeal to those SF fans who like pseudotechnical manuals, pseudohistories of space wars, and charts/diagrams/etc. which are treated as if real rather than fictional. There is little or no research value attached to this type of book, although it is a volume of obvious interest to the segment of the SF audience caught up in technologically escalated war as the ultimate future fantasy. For other Harrison-related material see item 195.

288. Resnick, Michael. *Official Guide to the Fantastics*. Florence, AL: House of Collectibles, 1976. 212p.

Price guides, for experienced collectors, serve little purpose other than as handy checklists. The prices listed often are unrealistic (either too high or too low) and the volumes quickly go out of date. The Resnick guide contains eight pages of color plates and numerous black and white illustrations, and has separate listings for hero pulps, SF and fantasy magazines, fanzines, Edgar Rice Burroughs books, specialty publisher hardcovers, general publisher hardcovers, paperback books, Star Trek memorabilia, SF art, radio and TV premiums and miscellaneous collectibles. The guide is useful as a broad-spectrum checklist, but for collectors who specialize in paperback books the Hancer price guide is the recommended price guide and checklist. Price guides have little research value, other than for bibliographic details such as the series numbers of some paperback books, and they are not particularly useful in library reference collections.

289. Sadoul, Jacques. *2000 A.D.; Illustrations from the Golden Age of Science Fiction Pulps.* Chicago: Henry Regnery, 1975. 175p. AOW.

2000 A.D. brings together several hundred SF illustrations and paintings—many in color—and groups them into eight thematically-related chapters. Introductory material, both for the book in general and for each chapter, is simplistic, though some of the introductions contain useful material such as capsule biographies of major SF artists. The illustrations chosen for the book cover a broad spectrum of magazines and the groupings by theme allow comparisons of artistic approaches and elements that have changed since the early years of SF illustration. Some of the illustrations are accompanied by plot synopses of the stories involved to explain the context of the illustrations. Theme-group chapters include intelligent alien creatures, robots, space ships, women, weapons, monsters, machines and cities. The compiler's opinions and judgments are sometimes suspect—for example, after doing his research for the weapons chapter, he finds only two "genuinely original" weapons in the entire genre, possibly a case of deadline-induced shortsightedness when one considers the SF genre has produced an incredible array of weapons from "planet busting" bombs to rays that can cause a star to "go nova." Access to references in the text is hindered by the lack of an index. Collections specializing in SF art may need this book for the sake of thorough coverage of a topic, but other than for purposes of maintaining a complete research collection on SF art, the book is not a recommended acquisition.

290. Sheckley, Robert. *Futuropolis: Impossible Cities of Science Fiction and Fantasy.* New York: A&W Visual Library, 1978. Unpaginated (116). MIN.

Futuropolis is an art book with a small amount of accompanying text. It is unpaginated, but the illustrations are numbered from 1-154. Illustrations include line drawings, photos, film stills, comic book pages, color paintings, and reproductions of magazine covers. Some of the comics and magazine cover reproductions are foreign language publications. The city is an important concept and motif in science fiction and fantasy, and has been the subject of theme anthologies. The commentary in this book is fragmented because paragraphs to accompany some of the illustrations were taken from Mumford, Tennyson, Plato, O'Neill and others. Sheckley's own commentary is the unifying thread, and in his brief caption-like mini-essays he discusses cities in space, ideal cities, mobile and/or flying cities, and major SF works using the urban background, setting or motif. If the commentary had been more extensive the book would have been more useful; because of the production choices that were made concerning the publication of this book, it is more a coffee table volume of SF-related art than a serious and useful examination of the urban theme. Recommended only for collections emphasizing SF art.

291. Skeeters, Paul W. *Sidney H. Sime: Master of Fantasy.* Pasadena, CA: Ward Ritchie Press, 1978. 127p.

The names of Sidney H. Sime and Lord Dunsany are irrevocably connected through the fantastic fiction of the one and the fantastic art of the other. In this art anthology or portfolio, the first 11 pages provide some historical and biographical information about Sime, and the remainder is a collection of many black and white and 12 color reproductions of Sime's art. Many of the illustrations are accompanied by a few passages of Dunsany's text from the books illustrated by the Sime drawings. The plates vary in size from fairly small—less than a quarter of a page—to illustrations that nearly occupy an entire page (the book format size is 8¼ x11¾). Science fiction and fantasy art are gaining in respect as subjects worthy of study, and any individual or library with a collecting interest in fantasy, SF or fantastic art should find this Sime compilation of some interest. The book includes a brief introduction by Ray Bradbury. Typography, composition and production are very good, and because the volume is a "small press" item with a limited press run, it should accrue a definite collector's value over a period of time.

292. Summers, Ian. *The Art of the Brothers Hildebrandt.* New York: Ballantine, 1979. Unpaginated (101).

The Hildebrandt brothers are two of the most successful and widely-known fantasy illustrators of recent years. Their work is beautifully displayed in this volume, and ten pages of text by Ian Summers provide some biographical material about the artists. The first ten plates are black and white, and an additional 40 plates are in color. Illustrations are taken from the Hildebrandts' Tolkien paintings, cover illustrations for Ballantine Books, paintings from *The Sword of Shannara*, and the artists' private collections.

Section 9
Anthologies, Collections & Annotated Editions

293. Clifton, Mark. *The Science Fiction of Mark Clifton.* ed. Barry N. Malzberg and Martin H. Greenberg. Carbondale, IL: Southern Illinois University Press, 1980. 296p.

There are many SF writers who have done excellent work but who are, for one reason or another, largely forgotten. Mark Clifton wrote (or co-wrote) only three novels and 21 short stories. His reputation among critics and other writers is legendary; many critics consider him to have been a major catalytic force in the development of modern SF. Like Stanley G. Weinbaum, Clifton produced only a small body of fiction before his death, but his influence on other writers was far out of proportion to the quantity of fiction he contributed to the genre. As an example of the neglect suffered by many fine writers in the SF field, this Alternatives volume, collecting Clifton's 11 best SF stories, is the first collection of his fiction to see print. The introduction by Judith Merril, titled "A Memoir and Appreciation," includes a number of letters written by Clifton to Merril in the early 1950s, and the book is concluded by a short afterword by Barry N. Malzberg and a bibliography of Clifton's fiction. Each short story also has a brief introduction. Collections with a strong emphasis in primary materials by recognized masters of the genre will need a copy of this book.

294. Doyle, Arthur Conan. *The Best Science Fiction of Arthur Conan Doyle.* ed. Charles G. Waugh and Martin H. Greenberg. Carbondale, IL: Southern Illinois University Press, 1981. 190p.

Arthur Conan Doyle is better known for his Sherlock Holmes stories than for his science fiction, but he produced numerous pieces of fiction that hardly could be classified as anything other than SF. *The Best Science Fiction of Arthur Conan Doyle* is one of the short story collections in the Alternatives series, a series of volumes which presents generous selections of the short fiction of forgotten or neglected masters of the SF field. The introduction, by George E. Slusser, is detailed and extensive enough to qualify almost as an article rather than an introduction, and the 14 short stories included in the collection are well-selected to represent a solid cross-section of Doyle's SF. The stories are presented chronologically, from "The American's Tale" (1879) to "When the World Screamed" (1929). Two of the stories feature Professor Challenger, the ebullient scientist-protagonist of Doyle's SF-related novel *The Lost World*, and two stories were taken from the Sherlock Holmes file. All the Alternatives collections are recommended for libraries seeking suitable short story collections as core titles for primary SF holdings.

295. Franklin, H. Bruce, ed. *Future Perfect: American Science Fiction of the Nineteenth Century.* New York: Oxford University Press, 1966; 1978. 404p. AOW; RSF; SRB.

Too many younger SF enthusiasts seem to think that science fiction, as a concept and as a literary and film genre, was invented specifically as a vehicle for *Star Trek*. Little early SF, apart from some of the Verne and Wells novels, is popular enough to remain in print, so ignorance of the origins of SF is understandable. *Future Perfect* is an anthology of early SF—or, more accurately, an anthology of nineteenth century fiction displaying many of the conceits, themes, motifs and ideas now common in SF literature. The book is divided into eight sections. Six of the sections explore different ideas and two are devoted to several works by a single author. The theme sections deal with automata, marvelous inventions, medicine men, psychology, space travel and time travel, while the single-author sections present works by Poe and Hawthorne. Franklin provides a general introduction which places science fiction in a nineteenth century perspective as part of a developing tradition, plus separate introductions for the sub-sections. Only a few "historical anthologies" have been attempted in SF; Moskowitz is well known for his work in this field, but Moskowitz is primarily a collector and historian. Franklin is a critic, and *Future Perfect* is the best historical anthology assembled to date. The book works well as a collection of fiction and as a critical-historical analysis of nineteenth century SF, and so is highly recommended for collections with specifically historical rather than contemporary holdings, or collections with an emphasis in criticism of nineteenth century SF. Regrettably, there is no index to the critical and analytical material.

296. Hipple, Ted, and Robert Wright, eds. *The World of Science Fiction.* Boston: Allyn and Bacon, 1979. 248p.

The intent of *The World of Science Fiction* seems to have been to provide an introduction to SF at approximately the junior high school level. Many of the stories feature young protagonists, and all but one ("The Cask of Amontillado") were written in the twentieth century. In fact, with the exception of "Amontillado," all the stories were originally published after World War II. Story selection was excellent (though the one nineteenth-century Poe story seems out of place in the company of the more recent fiction); each story has an introduction of 100-150 words, each is illustrated, and each is followed by four to seven of the standard "questions" and paper-topic suggestions which are required in any book intended to be a textbook. The anthology is a good introduction to the SF short story for readers through the high school level.

297. Kelley, Leo P., ed. *Themes in Science Fiction: A Journey into Wonder.* New York: McGraw-Hill, 1972. 428p.

Themes in Science Fiction is a "no frills" SF textbook. There are seven chapters, each with a brief introdiction and four or five short stories. There is a total of 31 stories grouped into the seven "theme" chapters: Tomorrow; Outer Space; Human and Other Beings; Somewhere/Somewhen; Special Talents; Machineries and Mechanisms; The Day After Tomorrow. Separate story introductions are extremely telegraphic, averaging perhaps 100 words each. Story selection is generally quite good, and is representative both of "classics" ("X Marks the Pedwalk," "The Cold Equations," "EPICAC") and lesser-known stories by good writers, though one or two story choices were questionable trade-offs to get "modern" subject matter (rock music) into the anthology for better appeal to young adults (presumably at the high school or college freshman level). Kelley's compilation is one of the better attempts to provide a short story anthology style of SF textbook.

298. Neville, Kris. *The Science Fiction of Kris Neville.* Barry N. Malzberg and Martin H. Greenberg, eds. Carbondale, IL: Southern Illinois University Press, 1984. 241p.

In the late 1960s and early 1970s, Kris Neville was a moderately active though highly neglected SF author. Unwillng to accept the restrictions on the genre, Neville (after two attempts, separated by a number of years, to become a self-sufficient SF writer earning a living from freelance writing) stopped contributing to the SF field. He left behind a half-dozen novels and 70 short stories. This volume collects 11 of Neville's best short stories, including much-anthologized selections such as "Bettyann" and "New Apples in the Garden," and presents them along with an appreciation by Barry Malzberg and a bibliography. Neville is one of several SF authors (the most often evoked name is Stanley Weinbaum, but the number of excellent but forgotten master practitioners of the SF craft is surprisingly large) who deserve both popular and academic attention but rarely get it. Neville's short story collection is recommended for libraries maintaining holdings of selected primary materials by SF authors. For other Malzberg-related material see item 52.

299. Roselle, Daniel, ed. *Transformations II: Understanding American History Through Science Fiction.* Greenwich, CT: Fawcett Publications, 1974. 143p.

Numerous approaches have been attempted in the compilation of SF texts/anthologies for classroom use; none has proved capable of translating an essentially dynamic "leading edge" literary phenomenon into a static textbook format. *Transformations II* was an attempt to present "one of the few really new approaches to the teaching of social studies—the use of science fiction in social studies courses." Yet the use of fiction to teach a non-fiction course, except in the case of a literature course, has never worked well. Each of the stories selected for this anthology has a very brief introduction and a short list of questions. As an apparent afterthought, some of the questions direct the student to "justify your answers." It seems questionable that a student would understand American history any better by reading "alternate time track" stories or "holocaust/end of the world" stories. The most important thing accomplished by this anthology is the inclusion of good short stories often overlooked by other collections; good but neglected fiction by lesser-known authors Walter Van Tilburg Clark, Vance Aandahl and T.R. Fehrenback is included in the volume along with stories by established and recognized masters such as Clarke, Bradbury (the book has two stories by Bradbury), Silverberg and Dickson. *Transformations II* is a reasonably good anthology, but has little to recommend it as an SF textbook.

300. Silverberg, Robert, ed. *Robert Silverberg's Worlds of Wonder.* New York: Warner Books, 1987. 352p.

Robert Silverberg's Worlds of Wonder is one author's attempt to explain or define science fiction not just by pointing at it, but by selecting favorite stories and explaining or examining some of the technical aspects of the stories in separate afterwords. The book begins with a short foreword and lengthy introduction, then presents 13 classic, near-classic or at least extremely-well-known (and often widely anthologized) short stories by Damon Knight, Alfred Bester, C.L. Moore, Henry Kuttner, Robert Sheckley, James Blish, Cordwainer Smith, Brian W. Aldiss, Jack Vance, Philip K. Dick, C.M. Kornbluth, Bob Shaw and Frederik Pohl. Silverberg, a lifelong (and award-winning) SF writer and one of the most prolific SF anthologists, personally knows (or, in the case of deceased authors, knew) most of the writers represented in this collection; the afterwords, averaging five to ten pages each, represent a mixture of biography, autobiography, reminiscence, tribute, criticism, and explanation of the technical merits (or excesses) of the stories. There is a brief section on suggested further reading, but no index. Because the book is a mixture of so many different approaches to the explanation of what SF is, what it does, and how it does what it does, *Worlds of Wonder*, though it contains stories readily available elsewhere, makes an excellent addition to any collection relying on SF anthologies for selective representation of short fiction, and the 100 pages or so of afterwords allow the book to double as a volume of critical evaluation for several authors who have not received the attention they deserve. The book is highly recommended. For other Silverberg-related material see items 86, 163 and 173.

301. Verne, Jules. *The Annotated Jules Verne: From the Earth to the Moon.* Annotated by Walter James Miller. New York: Thomas Y. Crowell, 1978. 171p.

Translations always pose problems with linguistic accuracy, and foreign language books published over a century ago also pose problems with social contexts which may not be understood by a twentieth century English language audience. Miller's text of Verne's *From the Earth to the Moon* effectively solves most translational problems as they apply to this particular novel. Miller provides a text of the novel with explanatory notes in a narrow column alongside the text, and substantial accessory apparatus including a foreword that is also a capsule Verne biography; an afterword which re-evaluates the novel and Verne's successes and failures as a novelist, social satirist and scientific prophet; an appendix demonstrating how the initial velocity of the novel's space ship was calculated; notes on various previous translations of the novel; and an extensive bibliography. Mary Shelley may have "invented" the modern SF novel, but the prolific Verne was responsible for creating many of the archetypal modern SF story forms still in use today—and translations of his novels probably were largely responsible for the eventual acceptance of the SF form in English-speaking countries. Verne collectors and libraries specializing in annotated or critical editions of seminal SF novels should consider making an attempt to find this out-of-print volume through a book search service. For other Verne-related material see item 197.

302. Warrick, Patricia, Martin Harry Greenberg, Joseph Olander. *Science Fiction: Contemporary Mythology, The SFWA-SFRA Anthology.* New York: Harper & Row, 1978. 476p.

The mythological or "modern mythology" aspect of SF has come into recent prominence as an important function of the genre, and this anthology was assembled specifically to explore the mythic dimension of contemporary SF. The ten chapters of the anthology are devoted to major mythic patterns in SF: ambiguity, the remarkable adventure, beyond reality's barrier, aliens, the scientist, machines/robots, androids/cyborgs, the city, utopia/dystopia, and apocalypse. Each chapter begins with an essay written cooperatively by an SF writer and an SF critic, and each essay is followed by a bibliography of suggested novels which incorporate the mythic element examined in that chapter. Story selection is impeccable; short story contributions include fiction by Poul Anderson, Arthur C. Clarke, Cordwainer Smith, James Blish, Philip Jose Farmer, Philip K. Dick, Theodore Sturgeon, Larry Niven, Isaac Asimov, John W. Campbell, Jr., and others. Many of the short stories selected for inclusion are acknowledged classics. *Contemporary Mythology*, compiled with the cooperation of the Science Fiction Writers of America and the Science Fiction Research Association, is one of the most significant anthologies ever assembled, and the combined fiction and nonfiction approach makes it a useful study guide for an aspect of SF that has increased in importance since the publication of this book. The academic world has faced a number of difficulties in attempts to compile a reasonable and useful textbook for SF courses; this anthology, in a trade paperback format, could serve the textbook function better than many books published just for that purpose. The book is highly recommended for any library with a substantial primary or secondary SF collection.

303. Whaley, Stephen V. and Stanley J. Cook, eds. *Man Unwept: Visions From the Inner Eye.* New York: McGraw-Hill, 1974. 350p.

This Whaley-Cook edited SF textbook/anthology comes very close to a complete blending of SF/fantasy and the mainstream (in theory and physical juxtaposition if not in fact) by bringing together science fiction and fantasy stories, contemporary ("mainstream") short stories, and poetry. All the fiction and poetry, with few exceptions—such as an excerpt from *Gulliver's Travels*—were written in the twentieth century. Some parallels are obvious; Forster's "The Machine Stops" is followed by Campbell's "Twilight." Other contexts are not quite so easy to connect. Material by William Blake, D.H. Lawrence and William Butler Yeats appearing in the same text with fiction by Harlan Ellison, Roger Zelazny, Norman Spinrad and Ursula Le Guin is not aesthetically objectionable, but could be confusing to students who are likely to be familiar with Bradbury but not with Blake. Placing these different kinds of work together implies they are, in some form, of equal value, but few teachers (or, for that matter, students) will be deceived into believing that is true—and the "final determination" of what kinds of fiction have the most "value" are going to be determined by a number of variables, including relevancy, background, education and the personal tastes of each reader. The four sections are "Man and Technology: The Birth of Gods"; "Man Against Society: Rebellion and Escape"; Man Against Man: The Roots of Violence"; and "Man and His Children: Generations of Change." Each section has a five- to seven-page introduction, and each story is followed by several of the standard discussion questions. The book includes a list of suggested readings and several illustrations, and is an ideal textbook for SF courses which must be justified by mainstream association rather than the merits and strengths of the SF field itself.

304. Wilson, Robin Scott, ed. *Those Who Can: A Science Fiction Reader.* New York: New American Library, 1973. 333p.

Six technical writing devices were selected as the focus of this anthology: plot, character, setting, theme, point of view and style. For each section, each of two writers was asked to choose one of his or her own stories to display something about the chosen device, and each author also provided an afterword explaining the genesis or some other relevant aspect of the story. Wilson introduces each section. Contributors include Jack Williamson, Samuel Delany, Daniel Keyes, Harlan Ellison, Joanna Russ, Robert Silverberg, Ursula Le Guin and Damon Knight, among others. According to Scott's introduction, all the authors selected for inclusion have "distinguished themselves not only as writers but in a teaching capacity as well." Approximately 30 to 40 percent of the total wordage in the book is commentary on the fiction. The wide range of contributors, many recognized as some of the finest comtemporary English language SF writers, makes this book a valuable examination of standard elements of fiction and drama as their use relates specifically to SF and fantasy. The fact that the book is a paperback may make storage, retrieval and use a problem, but the book is a recommended addition to collections with an emphasis in good SF anthologies, general critical commentary on SF short stories, or the structural elements of fiction.

Appendix I

Evaluations of Critical and Bibliographical Book Series

Drumm Booklet Series (Chris Drumm)

The Drumm booklet checklists help solve the continuing problem of bibliography for contemporary science fiction authors, but they also create problems of storage and handling for libraries. For library use hardcover books are preferred because they are more durable and are easier to handle, but for contemporary writers who are still active in their craft a hardcover can be distressingly out of date by the time it is published. The Drumm booklets are well researched and accurate, often containing references to an author's non-SF material which is not mentioned in standard SF references, and can be useful supplements in those cases where the subject author has been treated at length in a previously published hardcover bibliography. In some cases, a Drumm booklet may be the only extant bibliography for a particular author, or the only recent update of an author's outdated bibliography. The Drumm booklets are 4x7 and stapled, and are offset printed from a typed original. Some of the booklets have a loose addenda sheet tipped in, and some feature letters or autobiographical essays by the subject authors. The main listings generally are chronological with each entry numbered, and the supplementary listing is an alphabetical index with books shown in all caps and short pieces in upper and lower case. Where storage and retrieval of the booklets does not pose too many problems, the booklets are recommended as supplements to existing bibliographical sources.

The Milford Series (Borgo Press)

There are two extensive series of critical "mini-books" on SF and fantasy authors—the Borgo Press series and the Starmont House series. The Borgo volumes lack such useful features as tables of contents, indexes, and other apparatus that gives reasonable access to the information contained in a single-author survey. Chapter titles often are not descriptive of the subjects discussed—for example, in the James Blish volume the first four chapters are titled "Foundation Stones," "Tectogenesis and Pantropy," "Cities in Flight" and "Experiments in Thought." Chapter three obviously discusses one of Blish's most popular creations, the "Cities in Flight" series, but the other chapter titles are not indicative or descriptive of their subject matter, and the lack of a table of contents or index makes it difficult to locate discussions of particular works. The entire supplementary apparatus of most volumes consists of a one-paragraph biography of the subject author and a bibliography of the author's published books. The Borgo books tend to offer in-depth and complex analyses which are more appropriate to graduate or post-graduate work, an obvious problem in view of the fact that relatively few SF authors have been the subject of book-length analysis and critical appraisal, and some of the volumes are so hopelessly pedantic, convoluted or esoteric as to offer the beginning reader—logically one of the primary "target" audiences for these books—very little of immediate use or interest. The structure of the books includes a Cliff's-Notes-like separate section at the end titled "Conclusion." In general, the Borgo books average 60 to 70 pages and are perfect-bound in the trade paperback format, a potential problem where the books are likely to be consulted often. Despite the serious problems with some volumes in this series, the series as a whole is recommended because so few SF authors have been represented by full-length studies. In cases where a subject author is represented in both the Borgo and Starmont series, the recommended procedure is to acquire both volumes. In this way, the weaknesses of one volume can be supplemented by the strengths of the other, and the reader may gain a better perspective on the author and his fiction through exposure to two critical approaches.

Starmont Readers' Guides (Starmont House)

The Starmont House Readers' Guide series is one of two extensive series of critical "mini-books" on SF and fantasy authors, the other being the Milford/Borgo Press series. Starmont House titles tend to be somewhat longer than the Borgo books, averaging 70-100 pages per book, and Starmont books have such useful apparatus as tables of contents and indexes, making the information they contain much more accessible than the Borgo Press volumes. Another useful feature of the Starmont books is a separate listing of secondary sources in the bibliography. Internal design of the Starmont books is better than the Borgo books because chapter divisions are clear, and chapters are titled to make it as easy as possible for a reader to locate discussion of a particular work. The quality of individual volumes, as with any open-ended series with many contributors, varies considerably; some volumes, such as the Frank Herbert volume, offer little of interest to fans, general readers, or undergraduate researchers in SF studies, while others, such as the Silverberg volume, are not only excellent examples of this series but serve as the only unified and comprehensive sources of criticism on their respective subject authors. As with the Borgo Press series, despite serious problems with some volumes, the series overall is recommended because of the lack of critical material on so many of the key figures in twentieth century science fiction. In cases where a subject author is represented in both series, the recommended procedure is to acquire both volumes; in this way, the weaknesses of one volume can be supplemented by the strengths of the other, and the reader may gain a better perspective on the author and his fiction through exposure to two critical approaches.

Stephen King Critical Series (Starmont House)

For better or worse, Starmont House has accepted the task of providing the SF/fantasy/horror nonfiction market with a steady stream of books about Stephen King. In general, the books are poorly produced—they are typeset with justified typewriting rather than phototypesetting, and single letters "lost" or "dropped" in the printing stage are not uncommon in the volumes. In at least one of the books, a page was left blank during the printing process. More importantly, the vast bulk of the "criticism" presented in these books is unabashedly, gushingly positive. Comments in the introductions, and statements in the text, make it abundantly clear that because the literary establishment has not accepted King with figurative hearty accolades, warm smiles, and open arms, these Starmont volumes will make up for real or imagined slights to King's art. Obviously a critic should believe an author's work has some importance—there would be no point in writing an entire book about a body of fiction so inherently bad that absolutely nothing good could be said about it. But by starting out with a critical approach designed to be overwhelmingly biased in a positive sense, rather than evaluative, many of the volumes in this series suffer tremendously from lack of perspective. Some individual articles or chapters often are useful contributions to King criticism, but as a whole these poorly planned and carelessly printed books are uncritical semi-professional appreciations rather than critical explorations. King, as a publishing and film phenomenon, is now so widely recognized as an important force in modern horror fiction that a number of excellent volumes on his work are available; the Starmont volumes are not recommended except for "completist" collections where the goal is to have a copy of every King-related book published.

Underwood/Miller Author Bibliographies

The single-author bibliographies published by Underwood-Miller are the best SF author bibliographies in existence. The U-M bibliographies have one serious weakness—they generally do not document secondary material. But aside from the lack of secondary documentation, the U-M bibliographies often contain a wealth of information not included in bibliographies compiled by academics for the scholarly press. In many cases the U-M bibliographies have lengthy descriptions of each book binding, plot synopses for each novel, and are profusely illustrated with cover photos of books and magazines. These bibliographies, because of their thorough information, are particularly useful to collectors who may need to be able to identify bindings and binding priorities for collecting purposes, but the plot synopses could be valuable to anyone researching an author without access to all the author's published works (in genre publishing, some of an author's works can be extremely obscure and difficult to find). The U-M bibliographies usually contain detailed information on foreign editions, a very difficult area to research. Though published in relatively small quantities (in both trade paper and hardcover editions), even the paperbound editions have sewn signatures and are printed on acid-free paper. The U-M bibliographies were one of the first bibliographic sources to offer reasonable explanations for the bibliographical problem of the Canadian editions of many SF authors' books. Underwood-Miller volumes are highly recommended for collections with a strong emphasis on bibliography and author studies.

Writers of the 21st Century (Taplinger)

Even by the late 1970s, very few organized and methodical book-length single-author studies had been published. Some pioneering work had been done, and the author study "booklets" now published by two companies were beginning to appear, but the Taplinger series was the first attempt to provide a continuing series of multi-faceted studies of major SF and fantasy authors. Shortly after the first volume was in print the plans for several more were announced, but after a half-dozen volumes were published the series apparently was discontinued. Announced volumes for Robert Silverberg, Stanislaw Lem and Theodore Sturgeon did not get into print. The books were published in simultaneous hardcover and trade paperback formats and featured introductions, eight to ten essays, a biographgical note, notes on contributors, a separate section with footnotes, a bibliography (many of these compiled by Marshall B. Tymn), and an index. Criticism is generally "access" criticism and analysis, not theoretical studies, and therefore is of immediate use to students and researchers across the broadest possible spectrum. Rather than reserving the books solely for contributions from academics, many of whom have a very limited perspective, the editors invited commentary from SF writers and other contributors, and in one case (the Jack Vance volume) allowed Tim Underwood and Chuck Miller, publishers of some of the finest collector's editions in the SF/fantasy field and noted experts on Vance, to compile the collection of Vance criticism. The books, when available, are highly recommended for collections with any degree of author-study emphasis.

Appendix II

Critical and Bibliographical Book Series Title Listings

Drumm Booklet Series (Chris Drumm)

Adventures in the Space Trade & A Richard Wilson Checklist (Item 194) Richard A. Wilson & Chris Drumm

An Algis Budrys Checklist (Item 176) Chris Drumm

A Hal Clement Checklist (Item 177) Chris Drumm

It's Down the Slippery Cellar Stairs (Item 44) R.A. Lafferty

J.T. McIntosh: Memoir & Bibliography (Item 174) J.T. McIntosh & Ian Covell

A James Gunn Checklist (Item 178) Chris Drumm

A John Sladek Checklist (Item 179) Chris Drumm

A Larry Niven Checklist (Item 180) Chris Drumm

Leigh Brackett: American Writer (Item 200) John L. Carr

A Mack Reynolds Checklist (Item 183) Chris Drumm & George Flynn

An R. A. Lafferty Checklist (Item 181) Chris Drumm

A Tom Disch Checklist (Item 182) Chris Drumm

The Milford Series (Borgo Press)

Against Time's Arrow: The High Crusade of Poul Anderson (Item 113)
    Sandra Miesel
The Bradbury Chronicles (Item 131) George Edgar Slusser
A Clash of Symbols: The Triumph of James Blish (Item 138) Brian M.
    Stableford
The Classic Years of Robert A. Heinlein (Item 132) George Edgar Slusser
The Clockwork Universe of Anthony Burgess (Item 110) Richard Mathews
Colin Wilson: The Outsider and Beyond (Item 81) Clifford P. Bendau
Conan's World and Robert E. Howard (Item 126) Darrell Schweitzer
The Delany Intersection: Samuel R. Delany Considered as a Writer of
    Semi-Precious Words (Item 133) George Edgar Slusser
The Dream Quest of H.P. Lovecraft (Item 127) Darrell Schweitzer
Earth is the Alien Planet: J.G. Ballard's Four-Dimensional Nightmare
    (Item 122) David Pringle
The Farthest Shores of Ursula K. Le Guin (Item 134) George Edgar Slusser
The Gospel from Outer Space: Or, Yes We Have No Nirvanas (Item 112)
    Clark Mayo
Harlan Ellison: Unrepentant Harlequin (Item 135) George Edgar Slusser
The Haunted Man: The Strange Genius of David Lindsay (Item 146)
    Colin Wilson
Robert A. Heinlein: Stranger in His Own Land (Item 136) George
    Edgar Slusser
Science Fiction Voives #1 (Item 216) Darrell Schweitzer
Science Fiction Voices #2 (Item 203) Jeffrey M. Elliot
Science Fiction Voices #3 (Item 204) Jeffrey M. Elliot
The Space Odysseys of Arthur C. Clarke (Item 137) George Edgar Slusser
Worlds Beyond the World: The Fantastic Vision of William Morris
    (Item 111) Richard Mathews

Starmont Readers' Guides (Starmont House)

Alfred Bester (Item 145) Carolyn Wendell)
Frank Herbert (Item 114) David M. Miller
Fritz Leiber (Item 96) Jeff Frane
James Tiptree, Jr. (Item 130) Mark Siegel
Joe Haldeman (Item 98) Joan Gordon
Philip Jose Farmer (Item 82) Mary T. Brizzi
Piers Anthony (Item 88) Michael R. Collings
Robert Silverberg (Item 86) Thomas D. Clareson
Roger Zelazny (Item 148) Carl B. Yoke
Theodore Sturgeon (Item 91) Lahna Diskin

Stephen King Critical Series (Starmont House)

Discovering Stephen King (Item 128) Darrell Schweitzer
The Many Facets of Stephen King (Item 87) Michael R. Collings
The Shorter Works of Stephen King (Item 90) Michael R. Collings & David
    Engebretson
Stephen King as Richard Bachman (Item 89) Michael R. Collings

Underwood/Miller Author Bibliographies

Amber Dreams: A Roger Zelazny Bibliography (Item 187) Daniel J.H.
    Levack
De Camp—An L. Sprague de Camp Bibliography (Item 186) Charlotte
    Laughlin & Daniel J.H. Levack
Fantasms: A Bibliography of the Literature of Jack Vance (Item 188) Daniel
    J.H. Levack and Tim Underwood

Writers of the 21st Century (Taplinger)

Arthur C. Clarke (Item 116) Joseph D. Olander & Martin Harry Greenberg
Ray Bradbury (Item 117) Joseph D. Olander & Martin Harry Greenberg
Robert A. Heinlein (Item 118) Joseph D. Olander & Martin Harry
    Greenberg
Jack Vance (Item 141) Tim Underwood & Chuck Miller
Ursula K. Le Guin (Item 119) Joseph D. Olander & Martin Harry
    Greenberg

Appendix III

Suggested Core
Collection Checklist

This core collection checklist is intended only as a guide to assembling a general collection of SF/fantasy/horror reference books; obviously, a library specializing in utopian literature, or some other specialty area, may need a very different set of reference books. The items suggested here are presented in three "levels" of priority. Levels one and two are primary and secondary acquisitions for a college or public library likely to serve SF readers and researchers with needs predominantly in the undergraduate range; the third level is a list of reference sources for the library that is contemplating an expansion of reference coverage at the graduate or post-graduate levels. Numerous factors were taken into consideration in the compilation of this list, from the kinds of research likely to be undertaken by students and the research materials that would be helpful to them to the cost and availability of the books themselves. The list is not intended to be definitive. It is a guide for librarians who recognize a need for a balanced, well-rounded collection of SF reference core titles, yet who are not themselves familiar enough with SF reference materials to be aware of the strengths and weaknesses of some SF reference materials. Only a few single-author study materials are included in this list, and these are included in the Level Three list because they represent specialized studies; the listing as a whole is intended to represent a solid, useful core of basic general reference materials.

Level I

Alternate Worlds (Item 32) Gunn
Anatomy of Wonder (Item 220) Barron
In Search of Wonder (Item 41) Knight
The Issue at Hand (Item 7) Atheling/Blish
More Issues at Hand (Item 8) Atheling/Blish
Keep Watching the Skies (Items 277 & 278) Warren
The Language of the Night (Item 45) Le Guin
Omni's Screen Flights/Screen Fantasies (Item 270) Peary
Pilgrims Through Space and Time (Item 9) Bailey
Science Fiction and Fantasy Authors: A Bibliography of First Printings of
     Their Fiction (Item 152) Currey
Science Fiction and Fantasy Literature (Item 160) Reginald
Science Fiction Criticism: An Annotated Checklist (Item 151) Clareson
The Science Fiction Encyclopedia (Item 232) Nicholls
Science Fiction Films of the Seventies (Item 246) Anderson
Science Fiction Writers (Item 12) Bleiler
Supernatural Fiction Writers (Item 13) Bleiler
Trillion Year Spree (Item 3) Aldiss & Wingrove
The World of Science Fiction (Item 26) del Rey

Level II

American Science Fiction Writers (Item 202) Cowart & Wymer
The Encyclopedia of Science Fiction and Fantasy (Item 240) Tuck
A History of the Hugo, Nebula and International Fantasy Awards (Item
     223) Franson & DeVore
The Index of Science Fiction Magazines 1951-1965 (Item 231) Metcalf
Index to Science Fiction Anthologies and Collections (Item 221) Contento
The Known and the Unknown (Item 79) Wolfe
The MIT Science Fiction Society's Index to the SF Magazines 1951-1965
     (Item 238) Strauss
Over My Shoulder (Item 31) Eshbach
The Penguin Encyclopedia of Horror and the Supernatural (Item 239)
     Sullivan
Science Fiction Book Review Index (Item 225) Hall
Science Fiction Film Source Book (Item 279) Wingrove
Science Fiction: History, Science, Vision (Item 69) Scholes & Rabkin
Science Fiction, Horror & Fantasy Film & Television Credits (Item 266)
     Lentz

Science Fiction Studies in Film (Item 272) Pohl & Pohl
Survey of Modern Fantasy Literature (Item 48) Magill
Survey of Science Fiction Literature (Item 49) Magill
Voices for the Future (Items 20, 21 & 22) Clareson & Wymer
The Year's Scholarship in Science Fiction and Fantasy (Item 166) Tymn &
    Schlobin

Level III

Against the Night, The Stars: The Science Fiction of Arthur C. Clarke (Item
    102) Hollow
British and American Utopian Literature (Item 161) Sargent
The Checklist of Science Fiction and Supernatural Fiction (Item 150)
    Bleiler
Edgar Rice Burroughs: The Man Who Created Tarzan (Item 212) Porges
The End of the World (Item 63) Rabkin, Greenberg & Olander
An H.G. Wells Companion (Item 100) Hammond
Heinlein in Dimension (Item 120) Panshin
Imprisoned in a Tesseract: The Life and Work of James Blish (Item 103)
    Ketterer
The Last Celt: A Bio-Bibliography of Robert Ervin Howard (Item 189)
    Lord
Metamorphoses of Science Fiction (Item 74) Suvin
Mind in Motion: The Fiction of Philip K. Dick (Item 143) Warrick
No Place Else (Item 62) Rabkin, Greenberg & Olander
The Pattern of Expectation (Item 23) Clarke
Ray Bradbury (Item 115) Mogen
Robert A. Heinlein (Item 97) Franklin
The Science Fiction of Isaac Asimov (Item 121) Patrouch
Some Kind of Paradise (Item 17) Clareson

Index I

Listing by Subject

Index II

Listing by Title

Master of Middle Earth: The Fiction of J.R.R. Tolkien (105) Kocher
The Mechanical God: Machines in Science Fiction (28) Dunn & Erlich
Mechanismo (287) Harrison
Metamorphoses of Science Fiction (74) Suvin
Mind in Motion: The Fiction of Philip K. Dick (143) Warrick
The MIT Science Fiction Society's Index to the Science Fiction Magazines
     1951-1965 (238) Strauss
Modern Science Fiction—Its Meaning and Its Future (14) Bretnor
More Issues at Hand: Critical Studies in Contemporary Science Fiction (8)
     Atheling (Blish)
Movie Magic: The Story of Special Effects in the Cinema (250) Brosnan
Movie Monsters: Monster Make-Up & Monster Shows to Put On
     (267) Ormsby
Moving Into Space: The Myths & Realities of Extra Terrestrial Life (57)
     New Dimensions Foundation
No Place Else: Explorations in Utopian and Dystopian Fiction (64) Rabkin,
     Greenberg & Olander
Non-Literary Influences on Science Fiction: An Essay (16) Budrys
The Odyssey File (253) Clarke & Hyams
Of Worlds Beyond (30) Eshbach
Official Guide to the Fantastics (288) Resnick
The Official Starlog Communications Handbook Vol. 1 (36) Hirsch
Omni's Screen Flights/Screen Fantasies: The Future According to Science
     Fiction Cinema (270) Peary
One Hundred Years of SF Illustration 1840-1940 (286) Frewin
The Origins of Dracula: The Background to Bram Stoker's Gothic
     Masterpiece (106) Leatherdale
The Outer Limits: The Official Companion (274) Schow & Frentzen
Over My Shoulder: Reflections on a Science Fiction Era (31) Eshbach
The Panic Broadcast (265) Koch
The Paperback Price Guide (156) Hancer
The Pattern of Expectation 1644-2001 (23) Clarke
The Penguin Encyclopedia of Horror and the Supernatural (239) Sullivan
Philip Jose Farmer (82) Brizzi
Philip K. Dick: The Last Testament (214) Rickman
Philosophers Look at Science Fiction (73) Smith
A Pictorial History of Science Fiction (43) Kyle
Piers Anthony (88) Collings
Pilgrims Through Space and Time: Trends and Patterns in Scientific and
     Utopian Fiction (9) Bailey
An R.A. Lafferty Checklist (181) Drumm
Ray Bradbury (115) Mogen

Science Fiction Movies (273) Richards

Science Fiction Movies (275) Strick

The Science Fiction Novel: Imagination and Social Criticism (24)
    Davenport, Heinlein, Kornbluth, Bester & Bloch

The Science Fiction of H.G. Wells (108) McConnell

The Science Fiction of Isaac Asimov (121) Patrouch

The Science Fiction of Kris Neville (298) Neville, Malzberg & Greenberg

The Science Fiction of Mark Clifton (293) Clifton, Malzberg & Greenberg

The Science Fiction Reference Book (241) Tymn

The Science Fiction Source Book (243) Wingrove

Science Fiction Story Index (237) Siemon

Science Fiction Story Index (222) Fletcher

Science Fiction Studies in Film (272) Pohl & Pohl

Science Fiction Studies: Selected Articles on Science Fiction 1973-1975
    (55) Mullen & Suvin

Science Fiction Studies, Second Series: Selected Articles on Science Fiction
    1976-1977 (56) Mullen & Suvin

Science Fiction: The 100 Best Novels (62) Pringle

Science Fiction—Today and Tomorrow (15) Bretnor

Science Fiction Voices #1 (216) Schweitzer

Science Fiction Voices #2 (203) Elliot

Science Fiction Voices #3 (204) Elliot

Science Fiction: What It's All About (47) Lundwall

Science Fiction Writers: Critical Studies of the Major Authors from the
    Early Nineteenth Century to the Present Day (12) Bleiler

The Science in Science Fiction (60) Nicholls, Langford & Stableford

Seekers of Tomorrow: Masters of Modern Science Fiction (54) Moskowitz

The SF Book of Lists (227) Jakubowski & Edwards

SF: The Other Side of Realism (19) Clareson

Shadows of Imagination: The Fantasies of C.S. Lewis, J.R.R. Tolkien
    and Charles Williams (35) Hillegas

The Shape of Further Things (2) Aldiss

The Shattered Ring: Science Fiction and the Quest for Meaning (67)
    Rose & Rose

The Shorter Works of Stephen King (90) Collings & Engebretson

The Shudder Pulps (38) Jones

Sidney H. Sime: Master of Fantasy (291) Skeeters

Skywalking: The Life and Films of George Lucas (211) Pollock

Sleepless Nights in the Procrustean Bed (29) Ellison & Clark

Some Kind of Paradise: The Emergence of American Science Fiction
    (17) Clareson

The Sound of Wonder: Interviews from "The Science Fiction Radio Show,"
    Vol. 1 (206) Lane, Vernon & Carson

Index III

Listing by Author, Editor, Compiler, or Major Contributor

Ashley, Michael
Barrington J. Bayley (170)
Fantasy Reader's Guide: A Complete Index and Annotated Commentary
to the John Spencer Fantasy Publications 1950-1966 (219)
Asimov, Isaac
Asimov on Science Fiction (6)
Atheling, William, Jr. (James Blish)
The Issue at Hand: Studies in Contemporary Magazine Science
Fiction (7)
More Issues at Hand: Critical Studies in Contemporary Science
Fiction (8)
Bahrenburg, Bruce
The Creation of Dino De Laurentis' King Kong (247)
Bailey, James Osler
Pilgrims Through Space and Time: Trends and Patterns in Scientific and
Utopian Fiction (9)
Barr, Marlene S.
Future Females: A Critical Anthology (10)
Barren, Charles
The Science Fiction Foundation—A Report; March 1976 (58)
Barron, Neil
Anatomy of Wonder: Science Fiction (220)
Beahm, George
Kirk's Works: An Index of the Art of Tim Kirk (283)
Bendau, Clifford P.
Colin Wilson: The Outsider and Beyond (81)
Benson, Michael
Vintage Science Fiction Films 1896-1949 (248)
Berger, Harold L.
Science Fiction and the New Dark Age (11)
Bester, Alfred
The Science Fiction Novel: Imagination and Social Criticism (24)
Bilyeu, Richard
The Tanelorn Archives: A Primary and Secondary Bibliography of the
Works of Michael Moorcock 1949-1979 (171)
Blackmore, L.D.
H.P. Lovecraft and Lovecraft Criticism: An Annotated Bibliography
Supplement 1980-1984 (184)
Blackmore, Leigh
Brian Lumley: A New Bibliography (172)

Bleiler, E.F.
The Checklist of Science Fiction and Supernatural Fiction (150)
Science Fiction Writers: Critical Studies of the Major Authors from the
    Early Nineteenth Century to the Present Day (12)
Bloch, Robert
The Science Fiction Novel: Imagination and Social Criticism (24)
Supernatural Fiction Writers: Fantasy and Horror (13)
Born, Franz
Jules Verne: The Man Who Invented the Future (197)
Bretnor, Reginald
Modern Science Fiction—Its Meaning and Its Future (14)
Science Fiction: Today and Tomorrow (15)
Brizzi, Mary T.
Philip Jose Farmer (82)
Brosnan, John
The Horror People (249)
Movie Magic: The Story of Special Effects in the Cinema (250)
Bucknall, Barbara J.
Ursula K. Le Guin (83)
Budrys, Algis
Non-Literary Influences on Science Fiction: An Essay (16)
Butler, Ivan
Horror in the Cinema (251)
Calderonello, Alice
Intersections: The Elements of Fiction in Science Fiction (80)
Campbell, John W., Jr.
The John W. Campbell Letters Vol. 1 (198)
Cannon, Peter
The Chronology Out of Time: Dates in the Fiction of H.P. Lovecraft (84)
Carpenter, Humphrey
Tolkien: A Biography (199)
Carr, John L.
Leigh Brackett: American Writer (200)
Carson, David
The Sound of Wonder: Interviews From "The Science Fiction Radio
    Show," Vol. 1 (206)
The Sound of Wonder: Interviews From "The Science Fiction Radio
    Show," Vol. 2 (207)
Carter, Lin
Tolkien: A Look Behind the Lord of the Rings (85)
Chapdelaine, Perry A.
The John W. Campbell Letters Vol. 1 (198)

Chapdelaine, Perry A., Sr.
  The John W. Campbell Letters Vol. 1 (198)
Clareson, Thomas D.
  Extrapolation: A Science Fiction Newsletter (18)
  Robert Silverberg (86)
  Robert Silverberg: A Primary and Secondary Bibliography (173)
  Science Fiction Criticism: An Annotated Checklist (151)
  SF: The Other Side of Realism (19)
  Some Kind of Paradise: The Emergence of American Science
    Fiction (17)
  Voices for the Future (20)
  Voices for the Future Vol. 3 (21)
  Voices for the Future Vol. 3: Essays on Major Science Fiction
    Writers (22)
Clark, Marty
  Sleepless Nights in the Procrustean Bed (29)
Clarke, Arthur C.
  The Lost Worlds of 2001 (252)
  The Odyssey File (253)
  The View From Serendip (201)
Clarke, I.F.
  The Pattern of Expectation 1644-2001 (23)
Clifton, Mark
  The Science Fiction of Mark Clifton (293)
Cohen, Daniel
  Horror Movies (254)
Collings, Michael R.
  The Many Facets of Stephen King (87)
  Piers Anthony (88)
  The Shorter Works of Stephen King (90)
  Stephen King as Richard Bachman (89)
Contento, William
  Index to Science Fiction Anthologies and Collections (221)
Cook, Stanley J.
  Man Unwept: Visions From the Inner Eye (303)
Covell, Ian
  J.T. McIntosh: Memoir & Bibliography (174)
Cowart, David
  Dictionary of Literary Biography, Vol. 8: American Science Fiction
    Writers (202)

Currey, L.W.
Index to Stories in Thematic Anthologies of Science Fiction (242)
A Research Guide to Science Fiction Studies: An Annotated Checklist of Primary and Secondary Sources for Fantasy and Science Fiction (167)
Science Fiction and Fantasy Authors: A Bibliography of First Printings of Their Fiction (152)
Dalby, Richard
Bram Stoker: A Bibliography of First Editions (175)
Davenport, Basil
The Science Fiction Novel: Imagination and Social Criticism (24)
Day, Bradford M.
The Checklist of Fantastic Literature in Paperbound Books (153)
de la Ree, Gerry
Fantasy Collector's Annual 1975 (25)
del Rey, Lester
Fantastic Science-Fiction Art 1926-1954 (284)
The World of Science Fiction 1926-1976: The History of a Subculture (26)
DeVore, Howard
A History of the Hugo, Nebula and International Fantasy Awards (223)
Dikty, Alan S.
The American Boys' Book Series Bibliography 1895-1935 (154)
Diskin, Lahna
Theodore Sturgeon (91)
Dizer, John T., Jr.
Tom Swift & Company: "Boys' Books" by Stratemeyer and Others (27)
Doyle, Arthur Conan
The Best Science Fiction of Arthur Conan Doyle (294)
Dozois, Gardner R.
The Fiction of James Tiptree, Jr. (92)
Drumm, Chris
Adventures in the Space Trade and A Richard Wilson Checklist (194)
An Algis Budrys Checklist (176)
A Hal Clement Checklist (177)
A James Gunn Checklist (178)
A John Sladek Checklist (179)
A Larry Niven Checklist (180)
An R.A. Lafferty Checklist (181)
A Tom Disch Checklist (182)
A Mack Reynolds Checklist: Notes Toward a Bibliography (183)
Dunn, Thomas P.
The Mechanical God: Machines in Science Fiction (28)

Durie, Alistair
  Weird Tales (285)
Edelson, Edward
  Great Monsters of the Movies (255)
  Great Science Fiction from the Movies (256)
Edwards, Malcolm
  The SF Book of Lists (227)
Ellik, Ronald
  The Universes of E.E. Smith (93)
Elliot, Jeffrey M.
  Science Fiction Voices #2 (203)
  Science Fiction Voices #3 (204)
Ellison, Harlan
  Sleepless Nights in the Procrustean Bed (29)
Engebretson, David
  The Shorter Works of Stephen King (90)
Erlich, Richard D.
  The Mechanical God: Machines in Science Fiction (28)
Eshbach, Lloyd Arthur
  Of Worlds Beyond: The Science of Science Fiction Writing (30)
  Over My Shoulder: Reflections on a Science Fiction Era (31)
Evans, William
  The Universes of E.E. Smith (93)
Evers, R. Michael
  Intersections: The Elements of Fiction in Science Fiction (80)
Everson, William K.
  Classics of the Horror Film (257)
Flanagan, Graeme
  Richard Matheson: He Is Legend (191)
Fletcher, Marilyn
  Science Fiction Story Index (222)
Flynn, George
  A Mack Reynolds Checklist: Notes Toward a Bibliography (183)
Fonstad, Karen Wynn
  The Atlas of Pern (94)
Foster, Robert
  The Complete Guide to Middle-Earth: From the Hobbits to the
    Silmarillion (95)
Frane, Jeff
  Fritz Leiber (96)
Frank, Alan
  The Science Fiction and Fantasy Film Handbook (258)

Hagemann, E.R.
A Comprehensive Index to Black Mask 1920-1951 with Brief Annotations, Preface and Editorial Apparatus (224)
Hahn, Ronald M.
Lexikon der Science Fiction Literatur (149)
Haining, Peter
The Dracula Centenary Book (99)
Haley, Michael
The Alfred Hitchcock Album (261)
Hall, H.W.
Science Fiction Book Review Index 1923-1973 (225)
Hammond, J.R.
An H.G. Wells Companion: A Guide to the Novels, Romances and Short Stories (100)
Hancer, Kevin
The Paperback Price Guide (156)
Harrison, Harry
Hell's Cartographers (195)
Mechanismo (287)
Hay, George
The John W. Campbell Letters Vol. 1 (198)
Hayes, R.M.
Trick Cinematography: The Oscar Special Effects Movies (262)
Heinlein, Robert A.
The Science Fiction Novel: Imagination and Social Criticism (24)
Herbert, Frank
The Maker of Dune: Insights of a Master of Science Fiction (33)
Hillegas, Mark R.
The Future as Nightmare: H.G. Wells and the Anti-Utopians (34)
The Shadows of Imagination: The Fantasies of C.S. Lewis, J.R.R. Tolkien and Charles Williams (35)
Hipple, Ted
The World of Science Fiction (296)
Hirsch, David
The Official Starlog Communications Handbook (36)
Hogan, David J.
Dark Romance: Sexuality in the Horror Film (263)
Hokenson, Jan
Forms of the Fantastic: Selected Essays from the Third International Conference on the Fantastic in Literature and Film (37)
Holdstock, Robert
The Encyclopedia of Science Fiction (226)

Kyle, David
A Pictorial History of Science Fiction (43)
Lafferty, R.A.
It's Down the Slippery Cellar Stairs (44)
Lane, Daryl
The Sound of Wonder: Interviews From "The Science Fiction Radio
Show," Vol. 1 (206)
The Sound of Wonder: Interviews From "The Science Fiction Radio
Show," Vol. 2 (207)
Larson, Randall D.
The Complete Robert Bloch: An Illustrated Comprehensive
Bibliography (185)
Last, Martin
A Reader's Guide to Science Fiction (162)
Laughlin, Charlotte
De Camp—An L. Sprague de Camp Bibliography (186)
Le Guin, Ursula K.
The Language of the Night (45)
Leatherdale, Clive
The Origins of Dracula: The Background to Bram Stoker's Gothic
Masterpiece (106)
Leland, Lowell P.
Intersections: The Elements of Fiction in Science Fiction (80)
Lentz, Harris M., III
Science Fiction, Horror & Fantasy Film and Television Credits (266)
Lester, Colin
The International Science Fiction Yearbook 1979 (229)
Levack, Daniel J.H.
Amber Dreams: A Roger Zelazny Bibliography (187)
De Camp—An L. Sprague de Camp Bibliography (186)
Fantasms: A Bibliography of the Literature of Jack Vance (188)
Lord, Glenn
The Last Celt: A Bio-Bibliography of Robert Ervin Howard (189)
Lundwall, Sam J.
Science Fiction—An Illustrated History (46)
Science Fiction: What It's All About (47)
Lupoff, Richard A.
Edgar Rice Burroughs: Master of Adventure (107)
McConnell, Frank
The Science Fiction of H.G. Wells (108)
McGhan, Barry
Science Fiction and Fantasy Pseudonyms (230)

Neville, Kris
  The Science Fiction of Kris Neville (298)
New Dimensions Foundation
  Moving Into Space: The Myths & Realities of Extra Terrestrial Life (57)
Nicholls, Peter
  Foundation—Numbers 1-8 March 1972-March 1975 (59)
  The Science Fiction Encyclopedia (232)
  The Science Fiction Foundation—A Report; March 1976 (58)
Olander, Joseph
  Arthur C. Clarke (116)
  The End of the World (63)
  Index to Stories in Thematic Anthologies of Science Fiction (242)
  No Place Else: Explorations in Utopian and Dystopian Fiction (64)
  Ray Bradbury (117)
  Robert A. Heinlein (118)
  Science Fiction: Contemporary Mythology, The SFWA-SFRA
    Anthology (302)
  Ursula K. Le Guin (119)
O'Reilly, Tim
  The Maker of Dune: Insights of a Master of Science Fiction (33)
Ormsby, Alan
  Movie Monsters: Monster Make-Up & Monster Shows to Put On (267)
Owings, Mark
  James H. Schmitz: A Bibliography (190)
Palumbo, Donald
  Eros in the Mind's Eye: Sexuality and the Fantastic in Art and Film (268)
  Erotic Universe: Sexuality and Fantastic Literature (61)
Panshin, Alexei
  Heinlein in Dimension: A Critical Analysis (120)
Parish, James Robert
  The Great Science Fiction Pictures (269)
Patrouch, Joseph F., Jr.
  The Science Fiction of Isaac Asimov (121)
Pearce, Howard
  Forms of the Fantastic: Selected Essays from the Third International
    Conference on the Fantastic in Literature and Film (37)
Peary, Danny
  Omni's Screen Flights/Screen Fantasies: The Future According to Science
    Fiction Cinema (270)
Philmus, Robert M.
  H.G. Wells and Modern Science Fiction (139)

Richards, Gregory B.
  Science Fiction Movies (273)
Rickman, Gregg
  Philip K. Dick: The Last Testament (214)
Riley, Dick
  Critical Encounters: Writers and Themes in Science Fiction (65)
Robinson, Roger
  Ken Bulmer (192)
  Science Fiction and Fantasy Magazine Collector's Checklist
    1926-1980 (233)
  Who's Hugh? An SF Reader's Guide to Pseudonyms (234)
Rock, James A.
  Who Goes There: A Bibliographic Dictionary of Pseudononymous
    Literature in the Fields of Fantasy and Science Fiction (235)
Rogers, Alva
  A Requiem for Astounding (66)
Rose, Lois
  The Shattered Ring: Science Fiction and the Quest for Meaning (67)
Rose, Mark
  Bridges to Science Fiction (72)
Rose, Stephen
  The Shattered Ring: Science Fiction and the Quest for Meaning (67)
Roselle, Daniel
  Transformations II: Understanding American HIstory Through Science
    Fiction (299)
Rottensteiner, Franz
  The Fantasy Book: An Illustrated History from Dracula to Tolkien (68)
Roy, John Flint
  A Guide to Barsoom: Eleven Sections of References in One
    Volume Dealing with the Martian Stories Written by Edgar Rice
    Burroughs (125)
Sadoul, Jacques
  2000 A.D.; Illustrations from the Golden Age of Science Fiction
    Pulps (289)
Sargent, Lyman Tower
  British and American Utopian Literature 1516-1975 (161)
Schlobin, Roger C.
  A Research Guide to Science Fiction Studies: An Annotated Checklist of
    Primary and Secondary Sources for Fantasy and Science Fiction (167)
  The Year's Scholarship in Science Fiction and Fantasy 1972-1975 (166)

The Space Odysseys of Arthur C. Clarke (137)
Smith, Nicholas D.
Philosophers Look at Science Fiction (73)
Spaink, A.
Fantasfeer: Bibliografie Van Science Fiction en Fantasy in het
Nederlands (164)
Stableford, Brian M.
A Clash of Symbols: The Triumph of James Blish (138)
Steen, Sara Jayne
Intersections: The Elements of Fiction in Science Fiction (80)
Stock, Stuart H.
Twenty All-Time Great Science Fiction Films (276)
Strauss, Erwin S.
The MIT Science Fiction Society's Index to the SF Magazines
1951-1965 (238)
Strick, Philip
Science Fiction Movies (275)
Sullivan, Jack
The Penguin Encyclopedia of Horror and the Supernatural (239)
Summers, Ian
The Art of the Brothers Hildebrandt (292)
Suvin, Darko
H.G. Wells and Modern Science Fiction (139)
Metamorphoses of Science Fiction (74)
Science Fiction Studies: Selected Articles on Science Fiction
1973-1975 (55)
Science Fiction Studies, Second Series: Selected Articles on Science
Fiction 1976-1977 (56)
Thiessen, J. Grant
The Science Fiction Collector (75)
Tuck, Donald H.
The Encyclopedia of Science Fiction and Fantasy (240)
Tyler, J.E.A.
The Tolkien Companion (140)
Tymn, Marshall B.
A Basic Reference Shelf for Science Fiction Teachers (165)
Index to Stories in Thematic Anthologies of Science Fiction (242)
A Research Guide to Science Fiction Studies: An Annotated Checklist of
Primary and Secondary Sources for Fantasy and Science
Fiction (167)
The Science Fiction Reference Book (241)
Survey of Science Fiction LIterature: Bibliographical Supplement (158)
The Year's Scholarship in Science Fiction and Fantasy 1972-1975 (166)

Wilson, Robin Scott
Those Who Can: A Science Fiction Reader (304)
Wingrove, David
The Science Fiction Film Source Book (279)
The Science Fiction Source Book (243)
Trillion Year Spree (3)
Winter, Douglas E.
Stephen King: The Art of Darkness (147)
Wolfe, Gary K.
The Known and the Unknown: The Iconography of Science Fiction (79)
Wood, Susan
The Language of the Night (45)
Wright, Gene
Who's Who & What's What in Science Fiction Film, Television,
    Radio & Theater (280)
Wright, Robert
The World of Science Fiction (296)
Wymer, Thomas
Dictionary of Literary Biography, Vol. 8: American Science Fiction
    Writers (202)
Intersections: The Elements of Fiction in Science Fiction (80)
Voices for the Future Vol. 3: Essays on Major Science Fiction
    Writers (22)
Wysocki, R.J.
The Science Fiction, Fantasy, Weird, Hero Magazine Index (244)
Yoke, Carl B.
Roger Zelazny (148)
Zicree, Marc Scott
The Twilight Zone Companion (281)